Digital Frontiers - Healthcare, Education, and Society in the Metaverse Era

Edited by Yu Chen and Erik Blasch

Published in London, United Kingdom

Digital Frontiers - Healthcare, Education, and Society in the Metaverse Era
http://dx.doi.org/10.5772/intechopen.1003424
Edited by Yu Chen and Erik Blasch

Contributors
Alex G. Lee, Emin Taner Elmas, Fevzi Daş, Ibtehal Nafea, İhsan Ömür Bucak, Jane Thomason, Jean Botev, Jiaqi Yan, Luke Heemsbergen, Ningyuan Sun, Pierre Boulanger, Victor Kuzmichev

First published in London, United Kingdom, 2024 by IntechOpen
IntechOpen is the global imprint of INTECHOPEN LIMITED, registered in England and Wales, registration number: 11086078, 167-169 Great Portland Street, London, W1W 5PF, United Kingdom

For EU product safety concerns: IN TECH d.o.o., Prolaz Marije Krucifikse Kozulić 3, 51000 Rijeka, Croatia, info@intechopen.com or visit our website at intechopen.com.

British Library Cataloguing-in-Publication Data
A catalogue record for this book is available from the British Library

Digital Frontiers - Healthcare, Education, and Society in the Metaverse Era
Edited by Yu Chen and Erik Blasch
p. cm.
Print ISBN 978-0-85466-521-1
Online ISBN 978-0-85466-520-4
eBook (PDF) ISBN 978-0-85466-522-8

Meet the editors

Dr. Yu Chen is an electrical and computer engineering professor at Binghamton University. He received a Ph.D. in electrical engineering from the University of Southern California (USC) in 2006. His research centers on Internet of Things (IoT) technologies and their applications in creating intelligent and interconnected environments. Dr. Chen's publications include over 300 papers published in scholarly journals, conference proceedings, and books. NSF, DoD, AFOSR, AFRL, New York State, and industrial partners have funded his research. He has served as a reviewer for NSF panels, the DoE Independent Review Panel, international journals, and the Technical Program Committee (TPC) of prestigious conferences. Dr. Chen is a fellow of SPIE, a senior member of ACM and IEEE, and a SIGMA XI member.

Dr. Erik Blasch is a research scientist at MOVEJ Analytics. He received a Ph.D. in electrical engineering from Wright State University, numerous master's degrees, and a BS from MIT. His research focuses on information fusion, human-machine teaming, and systems awareness. Dr. Blasch's publications include five books, 70 patents, 200+ journal articles, and 500+ peer-reviewed papers. Dr. Blasch is a Fellow of AIAA, IEEE, MSS, RAeS, and SPIE.

Contents

Preface

Welcome to *Digital Frontiers – Healthcare, Education, and Society in the Metaverse Era*. This book comes at a pivotal time when the boundaries between the physical and digital worlds are increasingly blurred. As a collective virtual shared space created by the convergence of virtually enhanced physical reality and physically persistent virtual reality, the metaverse is no longer a concept in imagination or confined to science fiction. Human society has been witnessing the wide spread of the metaverse as it is becoming an integral part of our daily lives, influencing how we interact, work, learn, and recreate. The proliferation of advanced technologies such as artificial intelligence (AI), augmented reality (AR), extended reality (XR), blockchain, Web3, and the Internet of Things (IoT) is accelerating the development and adoption of the metaverse. As we stand at the dawn of this new digital frontier, it is essential to comprehend both what the metaverse means and its promise, shortcomings, and trends.

This book is an effort of experts and scholars to understand the impact of the metaverse in healthcare, education, and society. Organized in three sections, its eight in-depth chapters explore new applications and case studies that showcase the ways metaverse technologies are redefining human experience and interaction across sectors, from digital therapeutics and surgical planning to virtual education and digital fashion.

Section 1: Foundations of the Metaverse

The book begins with the fundamental concepts and technologies that enable the metaverse. Chapter 1, "Data-Mediated Environments: Reality after the Metaverse", discusses the relational role of AR as media between computer and environment. Chapter 2, "Web3 – The Heartbeat of the Open Metaverse", explains a more decentralized world, an evolved data economy, and a metaverse privileged by potentially useful technologies like Web3 and blockchain to bring social utility in many areas.

Section 2: Healthcare Innovations in the Metaverse

The second section showcases how the metaverse can transform the healthcare industry. Chapter 3, "AI- and XR-Powered Digital Therapeutics (DTx) Innovations", discusses how AI-XR-powered digital therapeutics translate to better treatment options in a growing number of conditions noninvasively. Chapter 4, "An Immersive Collaborative Virtual Environment for Surgical Planning: Project VR-Surgical", presents a prototype that enables surgeons to interact with patient-specific structures in an immersive way, improving not only efficiency but also accuracy of surgical planning. Chapter 5, "Innovative Use of Machine Learning-Aided Virtual Reality and Natural Language Processing Technologies in Dyslexia Diagnosis and Treatment Phases", presents disVRtech, an early diagnostic and therapeutic system that combines virtual reality with natural language processing for a new approach to dyslexic diagnosis and treatment, representing an innovative use of VR technologies in the neurological healthcare domain.

Section 3: Culture and Education in the Metaverse

The final section explores the cultural and educational dimensions of the metaverse. In Chapter 6, “Contemporary Apparel and Historical Costume in Metaverse”, the authors examine the possibilities offered by digital twins and XR technology that directly impact numerous industry professionals as consumers are increasingly being reintroduced to cultural heritage through these creative unlocking experiences. Chapter 7, “Digital Partnerships: Understanding Delegation and Interaction with Virtual Agents”, focuses more on the relationships we have between humans and AI-assisted agents (even though they are not full-blown assists). Chapter 8, “Distance Learning Using Machine Learning in the Future of Digital Interaction”, discusses technologies such as e-learning platforms that leverage machine learning to transform educational models, mitigating geographic boundaries while creating new forms of learning.

The chapters in this book offer a broad overview of the ways in which the metaverse is changing human life. We hope to inspire readers to think critically about the opportunities and challenges ahead when it comes to using, working in, or enjoying the metaverse by bringing together a variety of perspectives and expertise.

Welcome to the metaverse era.

Yu Chen
Department of Electrical and Computer Engineering,
Binghamton University,
Binghamton, New York, USA

Erik Blasch
MOVEJ Analytics,
Fairborn, Ohio, USA

Section 1

Foundations of the Metaverse

Chapter 1

Data-Mediated Environments: Reality after the Metaverse

Luke Heemsbergen

Abstract

This chapter examines augmented reality (AR) not as a mere visual overlay of the virtual on the real but as fundamentally relational media between compute and environment. It does so to build toward a definition of the metaverse as media that perceive and persistently relate the physical world with computed data. Tracing mediation technologies (from print to metaverse) that continually shape our reality, this chapter critiques current electro-atomic divides tied to a continuum of virtuality and reality. This chapter explores how a relational understanding of compute and environment constructs and mediates perceivable reality by drawing from foundational concepts like Milgram and Kishino's continuum, modern works of art and product-science that Extend Reality, and the philosophy of Karen Barad. Understanding the augmentation of reality through this relational, integrative perspective is crucial for not only developing precision of what the metaverse is but also accurate understanding for experiencing and regulating the futures of connection that the metaverse offers.

Keywords: augmented reality, metaverse, spatial computing, intra-actions, reality

1. Introduction

This chapter shows how Augmented Reality (AR) is real. It offers a different way of thinking about AR media and other forms of Extended Reality (XR)—that speak to the future of the metaverse in ways that differ from having to bridge the virtuality-reality divide. To summarise common assumptions in XR research, a divide persists between reality-based media and virtuality-based media [1] that signal atoms on the one hand and electrons on the other. Relatedly, I argue it is not enough to say AR *overlays* the 'virtual' onto real life, we must understand that AR *relates* the 'digital' *into* real life. To provoke the point with a simplistic example, the printing press flicks ink on paper, and this is real. The newspaper or a billboard exists as a *real* thing. But, if pixels flick as a liquid crystal substrate, we say a *virtual* experience sits apart from our physical life. Pixels are transient and speak to the non-material virtuality jointly imagined by individuals and computers. Virtuality and reality spectra offer a clear *atomic-electronic* divide when we conceptualise technology that mediates reality for us. But does this divide remain useful as a way to describe and explain modern life? If the giant billboards that adorn the buildings in our environment with advertisements are crafted in pantones or pixels, which is more real? What are the consequences in pretending one has more reality than the other as we navigate a world saturated in media, and data? As spatial computing maps, reacts to, and mediates our personal and shared environments, will we continue to insist these experiences are virtual?

To answer some of those concerns, and explain where an accurate definition of the metaverse needs to come from and why it matters, the remainder of the chapter is structured to first map the history of some common definitions of how computers have extended Reality. Then the chapter works through some concrete examples of prior art and science that uproots the virtual-real and electronic-atomic versions of reality that are baked into display science and have come to define the industry. By questioning both the science and experience of 'virtuality' I can then apply a new relational logic to how AR mediates life. To do this I discuss two products not usually associated with AR or the Metaverse, the Apple Watch and Humane's AR-AI Pin. Discussing these products as available in 2024 allows a final section of the chapter to consider social and regulatory consequences of my proposed virtuality-reality reconfiguration, and fleshes out a philosophy attuned to the radically relational physical environment where the digital and physical mediate our real-time shared environments.

2. Defining VR, AR, and what may come of them in a metaverse

1994 saw Milgram and Kishino publish their taxonomy that classified mixed reality displays across a continuum strung between virtuality and reality. The majority of AR and VR scholarship cites this work in ways that have contributed to the boundary work of the field itself, offering useful ways to decide what is and is not AR [2]. This includes a visuality bias to AR-VR work—the continuum was about display technologies. Milgram and Kishiono [1] begin by defining objects at either end of their spectrum as either real: 'any objects that have an actual objective existence' or, virtual: 'objects exist in essence or effect, but not formally or actually'. The work then goes on to consider whether the perception of these objects are synthesised or directly observed (think pass through video vs. translucent lenses), and finally whether images are real or virtual based on whether there is 'luminosity at the location at which it appears to be located'. Luminosity here refers to the ability of the image to reflect or emanate photons (i.e. radiate light), or being see through—like a hologram or other optical trickery that does not occlude photons. It is important to note the virtuality-reality continuum is not just two dimensional, as usually communicated when citing Milgram and Kishino (see **Figure 1**). Mixing realities according to Milgram and Kishino requires considering how much 'world knowledge' technologies can model, the fidelity of the 'virtual' additions, and the overall 'presence' of the experience usually equated with screen immersion. At each of the high end of these

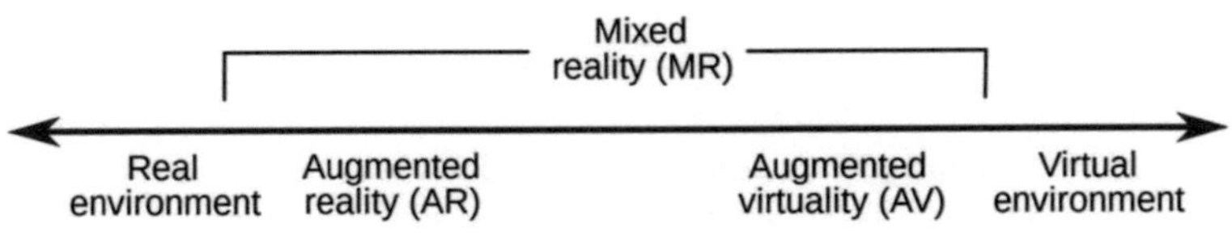

Figure 1.
Virtuality Continuum by Russel Freeman, as first crafted in [1].

three continuum are references to Naimark's [3] idea of real-space imaging, where 'the observer's sensations are ideally no different from those of unmediated reality' [1]. An unmediated reality is seemingly based on the biological perceptions of the physical environment.

Previously, Mann and Wyckoff [4] had defined eXtended Reality [XR] technologies that expanded visual perception spectrally to mediate infrared, ultraviolet, and other waveforms like radio or sound in novel ways. XR here took 'real' things that were imperceptible, and remediated them for human visual perception. In this way, Mann and Wyckoff defined XR as 'any kind of sensing [technology] + sensory [human] interaction with reality'. Notably, this depends on the idea that reality exists outside of the human sensory limits. Reality can include 'natural' phenomenon like infrared or man-made phenomenon like radiowaves that existed out of sight. Mann originated his techniques in the 1970s by building devices to create video sensing feedback loops for human perception. His 'displays' made of LEDs or other technologies would sense what cameras could see or radios emitted and show that spectra of sensing back to humans, who otherwise could not see them [5].

As we will see, while the building blocks of the virtuality continuum have held up well for a typology of display science and in turn approaches to building AR, MR, VR, and XR products, the continuum itself holds less well for explaining mediated reality. This is not surprising as the continuum was to help hardware researchers consider the ways that technical designs were 'juxtaposing "real" entities together with "virtual" ones' in order guide a path to 'distinguish among the various technological requirements necessary for realising, and researching, mixed reality *displays*' [6].

However, words matter. As Haraway [7] writes, 'Technologies and scientific discourses can be partially understood as formalizations... but they should also be viewed as instruments for enforcing meanings'. The meaning of virtual and real, and the potential of consequences for each in 'real life' have become entrenched. This dyad does not serve what Haraway reflected on through a metaphor of cyborg relations, obfuscating potentials and consequences of life for human with machine, and the resulting implications for identity, society, and politics. For clarity, a helpful technical taxonomy for display science might not set out to create an epistemological rift between electronic and atomic life. Yet, it manifests one nonetheless, in ways that often discredit electronic realness. In this vein, I am trying to reboot definitions of AR and the metaverse that refrain from a dichotomy, divide, or even continuum between virtuality and the reality. To consider the data-mediated environments that are reality, we need new ways of thinking about the metaverse.

I define the metaverse here as forms of connective digital media that perceive and mediate persistent relations between our biospatial world and digital data. This mediation Augments Reality. Biospatial surveillance is capture of data from or inferred from humans, as well as their spatial surrounds [8], and is required to augment perceptions of reality. However, unlike most technical definitions of AR, XR or the metaverse, I would not stress this mediation *happens* in 'real time', as while the temporal aspect of computed data might be relayed to humans in biological 'real time', the temporal provenance of the data relation can speak to past events or compute, present feedback loops, or generative future predictions, showing the 4-dimensional generative affordances of spatial computing [9]. Without acknowledging physical-digital relations, the 'metaverse' becomes merely a marketing term. At the most basic level, biospatial surveillance is required for the immersion that many corporate understandings of the metaverse promise. You cannot create perceptions of immersion without monitoring and leveraging environmental signals from the body and physical objects. AR media are then better described as relations between computing-data and environment-data made *perceptibly* real. That's AR—where divides across physical media and non-physical media are subsumed with radically relational accounts of what is perceptible. Here, it is the physical-digital relation of perception that is novel, and speaks past new platforms, content, or UI expectations. AR engenders a data-mediated environment to be reality.

To define terms like the metaverse, and those associated with it such as AR, XR, spatial computing, or consider the economic or social 'worlds' tied to persistent computing, is as much a political task as it is a technical one [10, 11]. Who is making the definitions and why is an important question while these technologies remain malleable and are socialised in evolving ways. Yet despite evolutions in technology and society, some definitional themes remain pertinent. Consider that during the first wave of VR hype, Nicola Green defined to 'become virtual' as not merely having 'access [to] a wholly "other" space and becom[ing] digital' but rather, the processes of 'making connections between programmed and nonprogrammed spaces in specific locales, and power-laden social, cultural, and economic relationships' [12]. A metaverse shows how those relations can be made perceivable not in the lab, or on a window to the WWW, or even on screen, but out and about in the lived world. This chapter offers an pathway to reconsider how we come to definitions of AR and the metaverse by considering the consequences of data-mediated reality as defining the metaverse. One consequence that loops back to the virtuality continuum is acknowledging how misconstrued technical assumptions about perceiving reality and displaying digital mediations of that reality limit our toolkits for defining and controlling reality. Yet the evolving definitions of AR and how these tie into grander plans of the metaverse are also instructive.

Comparing our working definition of the metaverse and AR to the majority of AR literature, we see that while the virtual and real signifiers persist in the latter, a relational realisation is starting to become more visible and performative in academia and common usage. The 'overlay' of not real is fading into the acceptance of real life. Azuma's [13] well known survey of AR techniques define the field as being those technologies in 'which 3D *virtual* objects are *integrated* into a 3D *real* environment in real time' [emphasis added]. The integration, as opposed to layering or superimposed speak to more potential for relations between digital and physical. Billinghurst et al. [14] considered making these relations seamless the goal, as in a 'larger context, Augmented Reality is the latest effort by scientists and engineers to make computer interfaces invisible and enhance user interaction with the real world'. The invisibility speaks to an occlusion of the 'virtual' itself and a nascent rebuttal to dualisms of cyberspace and real-space. Yet makers of these interactions still contested specific future visions of AR, with headworn and mobile systems charting unique material design and policies surrounding the technology, and stakeholder perceptions of the technology [15]. Finally, Apple's 2024 foray into a headworn product they define as 'spatial computing', was explained by The Verge.com's Nilay Patel as AR: '*virtual* projections that are directly *related* to objects in the *physical* world' [Patel 2024, emphasis added]. Here, while the virtual still serves to differentiate from a physical environment, there is explicit recognition that their relations make 'reality'.

In this way we can start to see understanding AR that it is not based on layering the unreal to the real, or superimposing virtuality over reality. Instead what defines the experience and interactions possible are relating the digital to physical, with less bias toward what is 'real'. Defining it this way also arrests visual biases, opening other senses and perceptions to augment, like auditory and haptic feedback loops.

Regardless of fidelity or levels of immersion, the metaverse will be defined through this pattern of breaking down the boundaries—or squeezing the continuum—of 'virtuality' and 'reality'. This definitional move would disassociate the underlying notions of electronic-atomic divides to recognise a more cyborgian existence of how augmenting the physical world with digital data defines real life in and of the metaverse. This is not meant as a science-fiction inspired take on digital life—where atoms are sucked into the machine (see Tron) or cyber-worlds exist outside our own (see early William Gibson novels) or even the digital-physiological relations present in the novel Snow Crash. Instead, it starts with what is, how we perceive that, and how digital mediation augments this. To show the path to these claims, we now turn to pencils, lasers, and quantum energy making art.

3. Some prior art in extending reality (before the metaverse)

This chapter was in part inspired by two pieces of art that seem to falsify the distinction between electron-based and atom-based reality—or at least media. This falsification serves to question the construction of categories of displaying, perceiving, and acting in atom-based reality and electron-based reality. That discussion helps shake the assumptions that designers, users, and policy makers might leverage for the metaverse, as AR shifts from technological niche into a more complex sociocultural regime [16, 17] that comes to define the metaverse. I explicitly picked two pieces of art that do not directly reference a metaverse. They are not connected to the internet. They are not particularly interactive for users. Instead, they show in isolation how distinctions between the virtual and real can fail even in the *physical* sense via digital mediation, before more subtle arguments around interactivity and the socialisation of our digital selves [18] or the changing nature of the internet [19] are explored in relation to the metaverse. Reconfiguring the *technical* perceptions of virtuality and reality through these pieces of art helps draw a new baseline of digital mediation that foregrounds a path for pertinent revision on how we should conceptualise, experience and govern media that relate the physical to the digital. Thus, this section first offers physical evidence to inspire reframing electric-atomic divides when conceptualising the futures of real, digital, interaction. And it does so through an unusual technical approach: art critique.

On a warm spring night the sun set on Austin, Texas, and patrons shuffled in to dadaLab to watch lasers dance away distinctions between the virtual and real. The lasers were the art of Alberto Novello, in a work called 'blacklight' [premiered 2023] that questions the difference between photon, pixel, or pigment. His work can be described as laser sculpture and leverages computer controlled pattern precision to bounce laser light off a special phosphor laced canvas. It is not just the laser's light that makes the show. The canvas extends space and time for the laser's trace in novel physical form. After their ephemeral existence, intricate paths of laser light hold on the canvas, and then slowly fade away in an atomic dance that opens questions to the physical reality of digital-photonic forms of real-time display technologies.

Here, digital information in a lightbeam, while maybe a 'virtual' sculpture, also actually physically resonates with and shifts the atoms of a canvas in real time for the observer—offering something between the 'permanence' of physical reality ink and the ephemeral nature of digital patterns. Neither a projection nor a pigment, 'blacklight's ability to mediate with physical with the digital shows how 'reality' is always constructed through mediation'. And not in a sociological sense, but via hard physics and chemistry, as digitally directed photon emitters materially relate their information on canvas that emits its own glow in its own time.

Phosphorescent materials work through the absorption and re-emission of light energy at an atomic level. Novello's digital laser display technology offers photons to excite the electrons within the quantum structure of the canvas. They do not overlay the physical with pigment [ink]. Nor is their display the ephemeral electron flows of circuits that render for an instant as pixels on screen or in your eye. Photons excite the electrons of the canvas' atoms and move them to a higher metastable energy state due to the specific chemical structure of the material. Over time, the electrons slowly release the stored energy as photons, resulting in a prolonged glow. This emitted light is what we perceive as the material glowing in the dark.

The intricacies of quantum level transitions of electrons, specifically the interaction between electronic states, energy levels, and the probabilities of various transitions, allow various timeframes for phosphorescent 'displays' to relate the photonic to the physical. Note that the painter Anders Knutsson has previously experimented with these timings in his luminous painting, using pigments with variable energy states to create a physically changing reality of pigment-based art. Knutsson's art reveals its very real 'luminous state' on the canvas when excited. Novello's work also incorporates digital via precise laser control to create luminous states of exquisite patterns and explicitly shows the malleable relation of pigments and real-time displays. The work makes explicit the digital's capacity to change the physical world. Photons do not 'overlay' these atoms, they excite them in digital patterns, spinning electrons to new states in ways that anticipate their decay and generation of light. Novello's work engages photons and atoms to deconstruct a spectrum between virtual and real. It offers the quantum reality of laser-media as both particle and wave, emitting and mediating reality of the canvas back to us in a state of semi-permanent controlled decay.

It might be tempting to consider a similar spectrum to virtuality-reality by this example, with phosphorent displays in the middle of line from pigment to pixels. However, doing so creates division through category, where we should instead be focussed on how atomic and electric combine. And this is why deep dive into the physics of a phosphorescent laser light art is merited. It shows it is the relation between elements that mediates perceptions of reality. It is not digital display overlayed on physical reality, it is photons interacting with atoms to spin up their electrons, relating digital information into quantum states that shift the surrounding environment, so that humans might perceive reality, augmented. Reality is 'extended' in this sense not by virtual tricks or overlays, but by the relationship between digital information and physical information; quantum energies exchanged and exchanged again to produce perceptions of what reality is. Here the digital is made physical, and perceived as luminous, emanating from physical reality, rather than a layer of virtuality superimposed.

The second art example to consider is Yamagami Yukihiro's installation titled *Shinjuku Calling* [2014]. The installation of 'mixed media' *shows* how a layered divide between analogue reality and digital virtuality offers a poor explanation of our lived—and mediated—experience.

Yukihiro's work cleverly integrates hitherto divided atomic and electronic information. Yukihiro painstakingly pencilled a streetscape of Shinjuku Station across about 2.5 meters of white plywood. Onto these physical graphite pigments, pixels are projected that give a *virtual* 'real life' video of pedestrians and cars navigating the canvas; neon glows augment the pencil lines of stencilled crossing lines and sunset makes the buildings glow. The 'virtual' imbues life as we expect and experience it, past the monotone and material sketch. The size, detail, and movement make it a breathtaking work that shifts viewers into a real-time perception of a distant space as they physically walk along the two dimensional—physical but unreal—pencilled detail of a static street scape.

One way to consider the work is the technical 'magic' of graphite layered on plywood, with photons dancing on top, which makes something new through layers of virtual and material representations. Yet, the work is not powerful by overlaying the virtual on the physical.

Its power is to make real by relating electrons to atoms: we perceive it as a real-space in full, through the analogue line art and pixelated ghosts of movement and light. Further, we might imagine the 'real' inhabitants of Shinjuku, walking across the road, seeing both pigments and pixels via the advertisements around them—would they consider which of these signals is virtual or real? The experience of Yukihiro's work opens up how pixels relate to pigments, and electrons to atoms, to make reality. It also helps focus discussion how we might think about AR as mediating the real, instead of a confusing layering of terms around virtuality, reality, physical, and digital.

The 'display technologies' of these pieces of art allow us to use inductive reasoning to quickly list different ways that humans can perceive reality for our sample of n = 2. These are not meant to describe reality, merely show how we can perceive it through linked 'display technologies' of atoms and photons that mediate our physical existence with the world. None of the categories below speaks to virtual or real, they speak to mediating relations between electrons and photons, both very much a part of reality, whether directed at the environment, from screens, or to eye balls, etc. (**Table 1**).

These two distinct art forms—a gallery hung installation and a laser-DJ experience—were selected to show how common conceptions of the physical are not synonymous with the real. The environments we live in do not suffer from stark digital-analogue divides. Their physics do not suffer from virtuality-reality divides. At play in these forms of art is the relationship between photons and atoms, including how one directs the other, and what that allows us to perceive.

While artwork—laser or pencil based—might seem far off from conceptual tools to explain data-mediated environments, that point is that reality is sprung in these works not across a spectrum of what is virtuality and what is reality, but from how data comes to be mediated via the environment: pigment, pixel, or otherwise. There is a relationship between data and the physical environment that will come to define the metaverse in ways that differ from how data and the environment define the world wide web, newspapers, laser art, or other media.

Name	Event	Perception
Pigment	Atoms reflect ambient photons	'Physical media'
Phosphoric	Atoms store and release directed or ambient photons	'Conceptual art'
Projected	Atoms reflect directed photons	'Screen media'
Pixel	Atoms direct photons	'Screen media'

Table 1.
Inductive typology of displays of reality, per relations between atoms and photons as observed across two art projects.

Past the physics of display, the science of perception itself can also be considered as we contemplate reality after the metaverse. Various disciplines outside display or computer science are happy to break common assumptions of what makes reality. For instance, a divide between atoms and electrons equating to the physical and not is less than accurate in understanding the human experience from neuro-evolutionary perspectives. Hoffman [20] argues that our physical reality is only perceived in particularly useful ways to keep life going. Neuro-biological reality is mediated by receptor cells, neural pathways, and bodies in ways that have provided best 'fit' to succeed, even if this means physical reality itself is not perceived directly or accurately by human minds. Instead, our perceptions are shaped in ways that are particularly useful for survival and reproduction, rather than providing a true representation of an external world. Away from biological imperatives on reality, Harari [21] suggests that sapiens are unique in their capacity to 'transmit information about things that do not really exist, such as ... nations, limited liability companies, and human rights'. This has been done through verbal language, written documents, social institutions, etc. The argument here is that we have never been merely physical. Or, putting it another way, *Real Life* as human experience must be mediated. Key is that media do not just carry or translate information, they create. Reality is media that we consensually hallucinate into being. Where we share these hallucinations, society exists.

4. Some new products in extending reality (after the metaverse)

The classic societal hallucination of the digital age comes from William Gibson. He describes cyberspace via a 1984 lens that engendered a whole genre of cyberpunk futures:

> *'Cyberspace. A consensual hallucination experienced daily by billions of legitimate operators, in every nation...Lines of light ranged in the nonspace of the mind, clusters and constellations of data.' [22]*

'Real' iterations of cyberspace, through the world wide web, a corporatised 'Web 2.0' that enabled social media, and more recently, questioning the duality of cyber separate from other 'spaces' of interaction [18, 19] have opened concern around the technologies that mediate our existence in socio-technical categories. While mirroring Green's [12] political economy critiques of VR, the 'technology' of cyberspace is receding into the background via terms like 'spatial computing' and 'wearables' that create embedded, embodied and everyday [19] experiences of connectivity that define human perception and cognition. Even without terms like spatial computing or the metaverse, we can understand how contextually relevant data [computed in geospatial or temporal relations] are already endlessly integrated into our everyday by, for instance, mobile phone messages and use of GPS enabled screen maps. In this sense, real and virtual are not accurately defined through mirrors of themselves [23] in terms of what they do or how they relate. They instead form complex intra-relations [24] where the physical is infiltrated by computational surveillance of space and bodies in generative feedback loops. Below we unpack intra-relations, but for now consider how current 'non-metaverse' technologies allow a good life from users finding a good restaurant from their car, feeling reminders on their wrists, or automatically alerting authorities to their car crash.

These two latter haptic feedback loops [triggering alerts for authorities via your car crash, or a gentle tapping on wrist as a reminder of an appointment] are both features of the consumer wearable Apple Watch. Note this watch also 'connects' your own computed probability of an irregular heart rhythm and other biofeedback to the network.

The argument could be made that the Apple Watch is the first consumer product understand reality 'after the metaverse'. Gone are concerns directed toward how virtuality and reality overlay each other by designing for fidelity and 'presence' in a VR-like product. Instead, this wrist-internet-connected consumer devices witnesses how data-mediated environments can be perceived in real physical life—it extends our perceivable reality into a metaverse of perceptual and persistent data-body-environment of compute. Past the latent biospatial surveillance of rapid de-acceleration or heart irregularities—what is also called bio-inferred data—there is an intentionality of physical-digital feedback loops that are not unidirectional. Apple Watch now uses what the company calls a 'double tap gesture' that registers a 'touch' of the formerly-screen-based interface by double tapping your finger to your thumb in the air—in a space previously known to be outside the screen interface. In their language:

'[The device] processes data from the accelerometer, gyroscope, and optical heart sensor [and] detects the unique signature of tiny wrist movements and changes in blood flow when the index finger and thumb perform a double tap' [Apple 2023].

Apple Watch shows how physical digitality exist in the metaverse in ways that present physical manifestations of digital logics, economies, and programmable media in complex media flows [25]. In this sense, Apple Watch shows the metaverse is already here, if very unevenly distributed to discrete packages of accelerometers and linear actuators that connect your wrist to automated emergency services and other networks, as it monitors your bio-signals for intentional input. The metaverse requires media that relate the physical world with persistent computed data that Apple is providing to your wrist.

Moreover, current auditory mediation technologies have a space in the metaverse that is often overlooked. Auditory Augmented Reality [AAR] [26] was an early descriptor of digital-physical interactions, but now offers a dearth of conceptualisation—with some exceptions [see 27] on how sound can relate computation to the physical environment. Nevertheless, audio mediation makes an interesting case study on how reality is 'augmented'. If information is presented aurally, we assume such media are very much part of reality—lest we consider 'virtual' the Doppler of a mechanical siren passing on the street, or for that matter, the music in your ears from noise cancelling/adaptive headphones. The audio company Bose experimented with Bose AR that offered an audio-first approach to augmented reality but was later discontinued. The industry of other hearables that augment the perceived environment [28] is growing, while binaural beats are marketed as 'digital drugs' [29] that hack the brain's perceptions and neural feedback loops. To what extent these experiences are tied to networks of spatial computing or the economic or social 'worlds' aligned with persistent computing will remain a political task as much as it is a technical one.

While spatial computing products are mostly thought about visually, haptics, auditory, and neurologic cues can all augment reality and mediate computer generated data into our perceptions. It is not then sufficient to describe the metaverse through new forms of a virtuality-reality continuum originally based off display technologies constraints. The metaverse offers a sustained relation of digital information to physical information that can be multifarious. So while in some regards novel or immersive display technologies might be useful to explain or continue research on the metaverse, they are only so far as they works offer novel experiences to relate digital data and the physical environment in ways that make the virtual 'disappear', to borrow from Billinghurst et al. [14]. Whether from haptics and auditory stimulants to the visuality that most AR technologies are defined through, we can then suggest that layering the virtual onto the physical is a category error to explain AR and open discussion about the metaverse. It is less about managing the visibility of 'virtual' and 'real' objects and environments and more about relating computed environmental information back into the biospatial—our biological and physical environments – and vice versa. Specifically, AR generates novel relations through computational surveillance of space and bodies in generative feedback loops—whether this is presented via 'display technology', haptic sensations, auditory cues or otherwise. Augmenting each of these perceived senses again shows how a 'layer' of digital information might not be the best metaphor to understand augmented reality with. For clarity, the novel ways how AR 'layers' onto extant environments in the display-science sense remains an interesting field of research, and one that continues to be innovated on.

So the point this chapter will keep coming back to is that life is not lived in layers, or categories of virtuality and reality, but in what these connect. Otherwise, our descriptions of life suffer a latent digital dualism [18], which cleaves our mediated perceptions of life into atomic and electronic domains to the detriment of understanding the perceived environment, which is also to the detriment of future metaverse research and regulation in that service. So, the remainder of this chapter offers some initial thoughts on what can be done to serve as a corrective to virtual-real divides in AR research and products that open promising avenues in both technical and social terms.

To show one final example of work that reconstructs how AR is real and creates data-mediated environments, consider the work of Humane in the mid-2020s. Humane produced a wearable 'AI Pin' in 2024 that allows us to consider what it might mean if AR media, instead of focusing on screens, fidelity, and measures of virtuality, instead were considered in terms of radically relational accounts of perceptible life. For some context note that Humane's AR product 'pivoted' to AI as the near real time generative AI interactions that LLMs provide were accelerating through 2023. Among other issues, this pivot seemed to muddy the product's launch and reception. Nevertheless, Humane's 'AI pin' is worth bringing up as an alternate entry point to the metaverse than classic imaginings of VR, AR or other screen-based media.

Humane offered an alternative imagined materialisation of how the metaverse actually works and what AR media offer. Humane's patents, pitches, and product were proud to ditch the technology of 'displays' and directly present symbols onto surfaces in and as part of the environment. While its clear their technology happens to flick out particles light rather than ink, as above, it is not that we should focus on whether photons would be any more 'real' than pigments, but that each luminates perceptions that users get to 'hallucinate' into meaning.

Humane's product and patents offer a unique way to consider data-mediated environments 'after the metaverse' that is not aligned to the virtuality continuum. Here is how Humane describes its own use of lasers and the environment: 'The laser projection can label objects, provide text or instructions related to the objects and provide an ephemeral user interface... [to among other things] share and discuss content with others' [30]. In the patent image (**Figure 2**), hands glow with instructions or interfaces. After the machine's vision recognises a thermostat on the wall, the hand shows relevant controls. These types of interaction also require biospatial surveillance [8] of users' bodies and environments to infer cues, and radicalise relations between the physical and digital data flows.

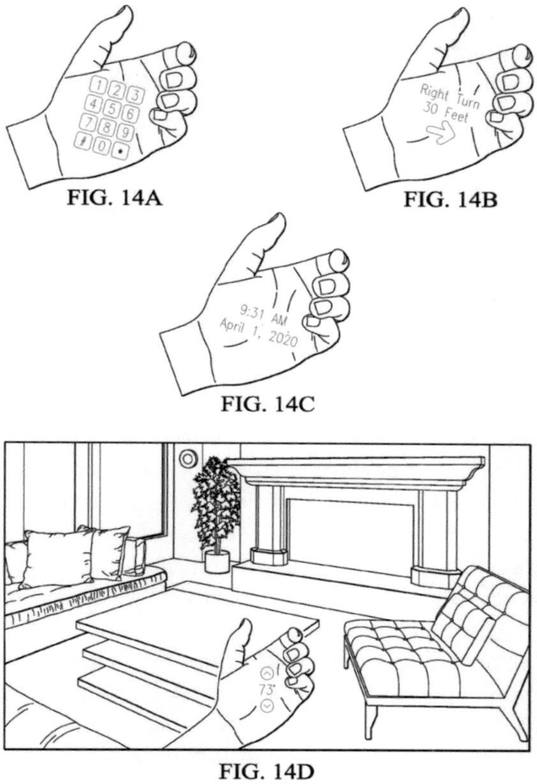

Figure 2.
Patent WO 2020/257506 A1; Chaudri et al.

Considering how Humane mediates relations of data-objects in the world shows the new relations available through AR's mediation of environment with data; ephemeral and real time—it offers a different reality to life than one dictated by newsprint and billboards. I would not describe it as virtual, however, or as layering information on the physical. It is mediating environmental features together [data and form] that we previously could not perceive. Their work considers the way AR can mediate that other media cannot. It derives from a conception of metaverse that is not caught in janky avatars, or display 'screen doors' that ruin immersion. Instead, it relates digital information to the environment in radical ways. Its machine vision responds to the environment and user, and luminesces the pigments of users own hands bridge the electronic-atomic divide.

Considering how technologies like Apple Watch, Humane's AI-Pin and even advanced headphones mediate, and extend reality offers a new path to understand what is real, and how we can create radical relations of data and environment. To drive the point home let us reconfigure how Gibson [22] described cyberspace. Classically we have 'A consensual hallucination experienced daily by billions of legitimate operators, in every nation...Lines of light ranged in the nonspace of the mind, clusters and constellations of data'.

To configure what is really different about AR media, we might remix the definition to Augmented Reality: consensual hallucinations experienced daily by billions '... [where] Lines of light are ranged in what we perceive, opening the mind to clusters and constellations of our data-shared environment', though even here the visual bias remains.

AR media are then better described as relations between computing-data and environment made perceptibly real. Divides across physical media and non-physical media are subsumed with radically relational accounts of what is perceptible in our mediated reality.

5. So what? some thoughts on regulation and theory

This section considers the regulator and theoretical implication of rebooting the metaverse as data-mediated environments. Simply put, understanding AR as mediating the real is crucial when forming relevant governing regimes now and to bring about a just future. Augmenting reality is not considering limits on a virtual layer on life, it is 'Real Life', considered by mediation. On the one hand, this flip helps focus regulatory power where state institutions like courts, parliament, and regulators are comfortable, removing the 'cyber'-layer that might misdirect away from what is real.

For instance, this would mean that traditional regulations that separate physical and digital realms may become obsolete. Policies should be designed to govern a unified AR environment where digital augmentations are as impactful as physical objects, and physical and digital data that pertains to the biospatial are equivalent to 'cyber-bullying'. This would mean data privacy and security regimes that understand the data collected, processed, and displayed in and by metaverse environments must be protected under robust privacy laws akin to medical information rather than consumer information. The work of XRSI Privacy and Safety Framework 2.0 is indicative of how to frame such questions and will hopefully be of use in guiding practitioners and politicians into the future.

At the least, such work needs to address how data is gathered, who owns it, and how it can be used, when we think of data not as separate to, but indicative of our real life. The normative guides from which future recommendations can be built need to be positioned to support those who create XR [31] to enhance accountability, as much as legal frameworks need to be targeted to policy opportunities that offer control. Such policy also needs to remain technologically neutral, meaning applicable consistently, regardless of the specific interfaces, economies, and products used to create AR experiences that relate digital to physical. Technological neutrality is also useful when considering holistic approaches that encompass the physical and digital as interconnected parts of our single reality. This will require effective governance with the involvement of multiple stakeholders, including technologists, ethicists, policymakers, market actors and the public—with this last category inclusive of individuals and communities. Any specific recommendations must come from this wholistic environment, lest industry or government mis-define the envelope of possibility and responsibility.

Finally, we can ask on more theoretical grounds what happens when we conceptualise AR as something other than display technologies that are often based on virtual/real definitions. Here, I am less concerned with product or organisational critique but in considering the 'augmented subjectivity' [32] that references the co-production of physical and the digital to define [post-]human experience. Such intellectual concern is, for example, focussed on how AR media offer real-time computationally mediated perception [33].

We can take these social concerns and come full circle via the quantum nuance of what was an erroneous electronic-atomic divide explored above. We begin with the philosophy of physicist Karen Barad. With apologies to Barad's [24] insights in quantum mechanics, my theoretical interest here is in the radically relational accounts of perceptible life that AR can make visible and knowable after metaverse that relates data to the environment in ways that previous media could not. To simplify a bit, reality for Barad is a dynamic process of becoming, where relations and entities are continuously co-emerging and co-constituting each other through the combined intra-actions. It is not that a virtual and real exist and then interact. Instead, it is more productive to borrow from Barad's view of intra-action and describe the way entities *emerge* through their relationships with one another. This is opposed to understanding entities as existing independent to each other that can then interact. In our example, it is not that the virtual affects the real and vice versa, rather, it is that reality comes into being through mutual entanglement—measured via relating photons and atoms and the mediation of that environment. Philosophically, questions then become centred on a shift away from the categories of entities and toward processes and relationships that create entities. AR is relational.

While Barad's work on intra-action and radically relational existence provides frameworks for rethinking how we understand the nature of reality, they can, when considering how reality is mediated, also emphasise the co-constitutive nature of our data-mediated environments. In this sense, media mediate social reality away from categories of 'virtual' or 'real' and instead serve as 'knowledge objects' that mediate what was previously perceptually inaccessible to humans [34]. This mediation creates and is constrained not just by technical factors but also the imagined publics [or networked publics or refractions therein] that emerge and the economic systems that grind along in ways that might or might not produce a corporate 'metaverse' of experiencing reality. As Couldry [35] points out, media offer an ecology of 'infrastructures' that make and distribute content in forms that carry particular contexts with them. Maybe this is a tap on the wrist, or maybe a platform for immersive attention seeking designed by Meta. Regardless, as these contexts surveil and distribute biospatial environments to data flows, and then re-constitute into reality, we see [and hear and feel] how reality after the metaverse will be.

6. Conclusion

This chapter redefines Augmented Reality [AR] not as overlay of virtual elements onto the real world but as a relational medium that integrates digital data with our physical environment, ultimately challenging the traditional virtual-reality continuum. Doing so allows us to reconsider what the metaverse does, and how it comes to be. Key points included critiquing the longstanding dichotomy between the virtual and the real in mediating the world through quantum art critique, and related limitations of existing typologies like Milgram and Kishino's continuum. Past critique, the chapter proposes a relational understanding that focuses on how digital and physical elements co-constitute our experience of reality as a starting point to understand, experience, and regulate the metaverse. This perspective reveals that AR and the metaverse are already part of our lived environment, as seen through current case studies of Apple Watch and Humane's AI Pin, which seamlessly integrate digital data into our daily lives.

Like any claims to knowledge, this work has several limitations. Conceptually, while redefining AR challenges entrenched perspectives, it may oversimplify the nuanced experiences of virtuality and reality, as well as the technical work that makes these experiences possible. The relational approach does not seek to fully capture the diversity of user interactions and test for empirical validation via varying degrees of immersion and presence experienced in various AR environments, nor their effects. Furthermore, the theoretical basis, while potentially innovative, could now consider empirical validations that substantiate claims across different contexts and applications. Specifically, future research should address these limitations by conducting studies to test the proposed relational framework outside the lab and in the lived experiences across visual, audio, and haptic mediation. This will require interdisciplinary approaches that combine insights from physics, philosophy, and social sciences—not to mention interaction design and display science—to provide a more holistic understanding of AR's place in mediating reality. By addressing these avenues, we can better understand and navigate the evolving landscape of data-mediated environments and their impact on our perception and regulation of reality.

Author details

Luke Heemsbergen
Deakin University, Melbourne, Australia

*Address all correspondence to: luke.h@deakin.edu.au

References

[1] Milgram P, Kishino F. A taxonomy of mixed reality visual displays. IEICE Transactions on Information and Systems. 1994;**77**(12):1321-1329

[2] Heemsbergen L, Cadman S. Commercial and research clustering of augmented reality: Discourses and divides between ar apps and applications. AoIR Selected Papers of Internet Research. 2021

[3] Naimark M. Elements of real-space imaging: A proposed taxonomy. In: Stereoscopic Displays and Applications II. International Society for Optics and Photonics; 1991

[4] Mann S, Wyckoff C. Extended Reality. Cambridge, Massachusetts: Massachusetts Institute of Technology; 1991. pp. 4-405

[5] Mann S. Phenomenological augmented reality with the sequential wave imprinting machine [swim]. In: 2018 IEEE Games, Entertainment, Media Conference [GEM]. New York: IEEE; 2018

[6] Milgram P, Takemura H, Utsumi A, Kishino F. Augmented reality: A class of displays on the reality-virtuality continuum. In: Telemanipulator and Telepresence Technologies. International Society for Optics and Photonics; 1995

[7] Haraway D. A manifesto for cyborgs: Science, technology, and socialist feminism in the 1980s. Socialist Review. 1985;**15**(2):65-107

[8] Heemsbergen L, Bowtell G, Vincent J. Conceptualising augmented reality: From virtual divides to mediated dynamics. Convergence. 2021;**27**(3):830-846

[9] Heemsbergen L, Bowtell G, Vincent J. Making climate change tangible in augmented reality media: Hello my black balloon. Environmental Communication. 2022;**16**(8):1003-1009

[10] Liao T. Is it 'augmented reality'? Contesting boundary work over the definitions and organizing visions for an emerging technology across field-configuring events. Information and Organization. 2016;**26**(3):45-62

[11] Liao T. Definitional Realities. Sydney: CAVRN; 2023. p. 2

[12] Green N. Disrupting the field: Virtual reality technologies and "multisited" ethnographic methods. American Behavioral Scientist. 1999;**43**(3):409-421

[13] Azuma RT. A survey of augmented reality. Presence: Teleoperators and Virtual Environments. 1997;**6**(4):355-385

[14] Billinghurst M, Clark A, Lee G. A survey of augmented reality. Foundations and Trends® Human–Computer Interaction. 2015;**8**(2-3):73-272

[15] Liao T. Mobile versus headworn augmented reality: How visions of the future shape, contest, and stabilize an emerging technology. New Media and Society. 2018;**20**(2):796-814

[16] Geels FW. Regime resistance against low-carbon transitions: Introducing politics and power into the multi-level perspective. Theory, Culture and Society. 2014;**31**(5):21-40

[17] Geels FW. Technological transitions as evolutionary reconfiguration processes: A multi-level perspective and a case-study. Research Policy. 2002;**31**(8-9):1257-1274

[18] Jurgenson N. Cyborgology. 2011. Available from: https://thesocietypages.org/cyborgology/2011/02/24/digital-dualism-versus-augmented-reality/

[19] Hine C. Ethnography for the Internet: Embedded, Embodied and Everyday. London: Bloomsbury Publishing; 2015

[20] Hoffman D. The Case against Reality: Why Evolution Hid the Truth from our Eyes. New York: WW Norton and Company; 2019

[21] Harari YN. Sapiens: A Brief History of Humankind. New York: Random House; 2014

[22] Gibson W. Neuromancer. New York: Ace Science Fiction Books; 1984

[23] Kelly K. AR will spark the next big tech platform—Call it mirrorworld. Wired. 2019

[24] Barad K. Meeting the Universe Halfway: Quantum Physics and the Entanglement of Matter and Meaning. Durham: Duke University Press; 2007

[25] Heemsbergen L, Bowtell G, Vincent JB. Physical digitality: Making reality visible through multimodal digital affordances for human perception. In: Materializing Digital Futures: Touch, Movement, Sound and Vision. London: Bloomsbury; 2022. p. 187

[26] Bederson BB. Audio augmented reality: A prototype automated tour guide. In: Conference Companion on Human Factors in Computing Systems. New York: ACM; 1995

[27] Dam A, Siddiqui A, Leclercq C, Jeon M. Taxonomy and definition of audio augmented reality [AAR]: A grounded theory study. International Journal of Human-Computer Studies. 2024;**182**:103179

[28] Boisvert I, Dunn AG, Lundmark E, Smith-Merry J, Lipworth W, Willink A, et al. Disruptions to the hearing health sector. Nature Medicine. 2023;**29**(1):19-21

[29] Barratt MJ, Maddox A, Smith N, Davis JL, Goold L, Winstock AR, et al. Who uses digital drugs? An international survey of 'binaural beat' consumers. Drug and Alcohol Review. 2022;**41**(5):1126-1130

[30] Chaudhri IA, Gates P, Relova M, Bongiorno B, Huppi B, Chaudhri S. Wearable multimedia device and cloud computing platform with laser projection system. Google Patents. 2021

[31] Norval C, Cloete R, Singh J. Navigating the audit landscape: A framework for developing transparent and auditable XR. In: Proceedings of the 2023 ACM Conference on Fairness, Accountability, and Transparency. New York: ACM; 2023

[32] Rey P, Boesel WE. The web, digital prostheses, and augmented subjectivity. In: Rey PJ, Boesel WE, editors. Routledge Handbook of Science, Technology, and Society. NY: Routledge; 2014. pp. 173-188

[33] Chevalier C, Kiefer C. What does augmented reality mean as a medium of expression for computational artists? Leonardo. 2020;**53**(3):263-267

[34] Bleeker M, Verhoeff N, Werning S. Sensing data: Encountering data sonifications, materializations, and interactives as knowledge objects. Convergence. 6 Dec 2020;**26**(5):1088-1107

[35] Couldry N. Media, Society, World: Social Theory and Digital Media Practice. Cambridge; Malden, MA: Polity; 2012

Chapter 2

Web3 – The Heartbeat of the Open Metaverse

Jane Thomason

Abstract

The term "Metaverse" itself is derived from the fusion of "meta" (signifying "beyond") and "verse" (an abbreviation of "universe"), suggesting a realm transcending physical reality. It foreshadows a networked constellation of virtual worlds wherein individuals can engage in various activities, including work, recreation, and social interactions. Web3, in conjunction with AI, will be integrated into Metaverses, where people can interact, learn, exchange, and have new immersive experiences. A profoundly transformational aspect of Web3 Metaverses will be the creation of community-owned economies, known as decentralised autonomous organisations (DAOs). With blockchain and smart contracts, community rules can be encoded, and digital assets allow members to exchange value within a token economy. The chapter describes a future world of greater decentralisation, a new data economy, and a world where the open Metaverse, powered by Web3, will provide social utility across multiple sectors.

Keywords: Web3, metaverse, decentralised autonomous organisations, token, decentralisation, internet of value (IOV), algorithm, DeFi, NFT, tokenization, decentralized autonomous governance, risk, governance, data, confidentiality, decentralized autonomous organization, blockchain, token economy, immersive, avatars

1. Introduction

While the Metaverse has been the subject of much discussion, there is not yet a universally accepted definition. A recent definition from the ITU Focus Group on Metaverse, which produced a Technical Report [1] that reviewed Metaverse definitions from academia, business initiatives, and international organisational collaborations, aiming to develop a working definition. The term "Metaverse" itself is a combination of "meta" (signifying "beyond") and "verse" (an abbreviation of "universe"), suggesting a realm transcending physical reality. It foreshadows a networked constellation of virtual worlds where people can engage in multiple activities, including work, recreation, and social interaction. A future where individuals may concurrently visit multiple distinct virtual worlds. The analysis emphasises the convergence of technologies, such as artificial intelligence (AI), Web3, blockchain, and digital twins, together with immersive modalities, including virtual (VR), mixed (MR), and augmented reality (AR). Thus, the Metaverse is a digital ecosystem comprising interconnected virtual worlds that provide new digital experiences, facilitate multiple transactions, streamline human-computer interactions, and foster social connectivity. This chapter will describe how the open Metaverse, powered by Web3, will provide social utility across various sectors.

2. The transformative potential of Web3 and AI integration in the metaverse

Web3 offers a transformative iteration of the Internet from "the internet of information" to "the internet of value" [2]. Central to Web3 is the foundational framework of blockchain, which has the capabilities to facilitate the seamless sharing and exchange of information and value through blockchain-based tokenisation mechanisms. The ethos of Web 3.0 incorporates principles of decentralisation, transparency, and enhanced user utility. Outlier Ventures has articulated a modular Web3 toolbox comprising decentralised finance (DeFi), non-fungible tokens (NFTs), decentralised governance mechanisms, cloud services, and self-sovereign identity frameworks [3]. These elements are summarised below.

2.1 Decentralised finance (DeFi)

Decentralised Finance (DeFi) represents a paradigm shift in financial intermediation, facilitating direct peer-to-peer interactions without traditional intermediaries and physical infrastructure. DeFi transcends geographical barriers, enabling widespread access to financial markets via mobile devices. DeFi is underpinned by the programmability inherent in blockchain technology, fostering the proliferation of decentralised financial instruments. These encompass borrowing and lending protocols, options contracts, decentralised exchanges, and automated market makers, which collectively augment market efficiency, transparency, and inclusivity [3].

2.2 Non-fungible tokens (NFTs)

Non-Fungible Tokens (NFTs) offer the digitisation of tangible assets, with a wide array of digital representations ranging from artworks and music to in-game items and cinematic content. NFTs confer digital assets with inherent scarcity, offering novel avenues for asset monetisation and ownership verification. NFTs have been used for collectables, virtual real estate, and gaming, catalysing the emergence of open Metaverse ecosystems. Specialised protocols such as the Boson Protocol have extended NFT functionality to physical assets, facilitating seamless redemption and trade within decentralised Metaverse environments, thereby bridging the divide between virtual and physical realms [3].

2.3 Decentralised autonomous Organisations (DAOs)

DAOs represent a departure from conventional governance structures, empowering communities to codify and automate collective decision-making processes through smart contracts. DAOs foster a distributed governance model where communities delineate and hard code mission statements, values, and operational protocols. This democratic framework facilitates community engagement, incentivisation, and collaboration, transcending geographical boundaries to engender inclusive and participatory governance frameworks. Despite their transformative potential, DAOs also pose inherent challenges and risks, necessitating robust governance frameworks and technological safeguards to mitigate against potential vulnerabilities [3].

2.4 Decentralised cloud

Decentralised cloud computing is a distributed network architecture where user data is stored across multiple providers without centralised control. In contrast to conventional cloud services, decentralised cloud platforms prioritise user sovereignty and data privacy, ensuring that only the user retains access to their stored data. This empowers individuals to monetise surplus computing resources by renting out a storage or computational capacity within the decentralised cloud network, thereby fostering a more equitable and decentralised cloud computing ecosystem [4].

2.5 Self-sovereign identity

Self-sovereign identity frameworks are a foundational tenet of Web3, enabling user sovereignty and self-custody of personal data. Innovations in self-sovereign identity and verifiable claims afford individuals control over their digital identities, enabling identity verification and transactional engagement without divulging sensitive underlying data. These frameworks engender trust, security, and privacy in digital interactions, facilitating seamless identity management and authentication across diverse Web3 platforms and applications [3].

The convergence of Web3 and AI will catalyse profound changes in the emergent landscape of Metaverses. An example of Web3's transformative potential lies in the potential of community-owned economies, a paradigm shift enabled by decentralised autonomous organisations (DAOs) [5]. Empowered by Web3, communities can now come together and establish decentralised structures or DAOs which govern community affairs, codify regulatory frameworks, and facilitate a token-based economic ecosystem. This concept reimagines the democratisation of economic agency and the decentralisation of power structures.

3. Metaverse fundamentals

A fierce debate continues about the merits of an open (Web 3.0) or closed (Meta) Metaverse. An open Metaverse is decentralised and uses blockchain to enable the exchange of value peer-to-peer. This is combined with gaming augmented and virtual reality (AR/VR) to enable users to participate in an immersive meta-economy [3]. Blockchain technologies, including virtual assets and NFTs, enable the transfer of digital assets across virtual borders. Increasingly generative AI will be incorporated into Metaverse experiences. The Metaverse is the next frontier for online interaction.

3.1 Metaverse stakeholders

The development of the Metaverse involves diverse stakeholders, including BigTech companies, the gaming industry, government and industry sectors, and Web 3.0 communities, each contributing to its creation through various initiatives. Big tech firms such as Meta and Microsoft are investing substantial resources in Metaverse development, with Meta alone committing $10 billion to VR-related hardware and software acquisitions [6].

The video gaming industry has long used virtual and augmented reality and has a huge user base, many of whom are young and understand the value of digital goods [7]. Thus, the gaming industry, valued at USD 195.65 billion in 2021, is poised to drive Metaverse adoption through GameFi integration, offering players opportunities to spend, earn, and exchange digital assets within games [8]. This industry's expansion is facilitated by technological advancements and improved infrastructure, ensuring seamless digital asset storage and distribution for gamers [9]. Governments worldwide are also exploring Metaverse applications, with initiatives ranging from Neom's planned virtual city in Saudi Arabia to Seoul's municipal Metaverse and Singapore's utilisation of advanced gaming systems for urban planning. Additionally, Web 3.0 companies like Decentraland and Dapper Labs aim to foster Metaverse interoperability through initiatives like The Open Metaverse Alliance, emphasising decentralised governance and the integration of technologies such as DeFi and NFTs to enable asset exchange within interconnected virtual worlds [10]. These efforts collectively underscore the multifaceted nature of Metaverse development and its potential implications across various sectors.

3.2 Metaverse assets

There are three types of assets in the Metaverse. These are: 1. Physical Assets - space, objects, avatars, 2. Economic assets - currency, financial instruments, marketplaces, and 3. Content assets - media and data assets [3].

3.2.1 Physical assets

In a Metaverse, users can acquire space and various objects, such as in-game assets. They can also create 3D digital identities or Avatars as a virtual representation of themselves in games and Metaverses. Users can create Avatars and, enter a virtual world and can communicate with each other and other's Avatars from anywhere in the world [11].

3.2.2 Economic assets

MetaFi refers to the elements that enable peer-to-peer financial interplay within a Metaverse. It uses the key blockchain tools of NFTs, DAOs, and digital assets, as well as two of DeFi's main characteristics: unstoppability and composability. The combination of mutualisation of risk, gamification of finance, increased availability of financial tools, and a functional DAO are enablers [11]. MetaFi is expected to incentivise developers globally to actively participate in the new ecosystem [12].

MetaFi will be driven by four main factors. (i) Decentralised NFT platforms enable content creators to negotiate the conditions of creative exchange with users. (ii) These NFT platforms can provide recurrent income for content creators. (iii) MetaFi will open the doors to collect digital asset value and flow in open free marketplaces. (iv) Play-to-earn games and monetisation of data will attract users and complement and boost Metaverse's functionality [9].

Using the example of sports, clubs provide fan tokens which confer special benefits and privileges to fans. MetaFi can simplify the process of creating, purchasing, and trading fan tokens. In video games, there is often a feature of playing and earning, where players earn tokens for their participation, which can create an in-game economy, in which capital and labor are linked to produce value [13].

3.2.3 Content assets - media and data assets

Many millions of content developers, using self-sovereign identity, will be able to control how their content is used and monetise their data [3]. Existing blockchain NFT markets like Open Sea, Magic Eden, Rarible, and LooksRare enable the exchange of non-fungible goods such as art, music, gaming collectables, avatar skins and virtual clothing. In the future, MetaFi markets will list every single asset type from multiple chains, allowing collectors to access all NFTs on a single platform and boosting the efficiency of digital asset exchange.

3.2.4 Protocols

The Metaverse offers developers new horizons. Physical assets, such as avatars, serve as identities within the Metaverse, offering users immersive experiences across diverse virtual spaces. Avatars, often generated en masse through Profile Picture Projects (PFPs), afford users unique interactions, including communication with other players globally. Economic assets, categorised under MetaFi, facilitate financial transactions within the Metaverse, leveraging Blockchain technology to enable the exchange of non-fungible and fungible tokens. MetaFi platforms, characterised by their composability and unstoppable nature, empower developers to create decentralised finance (DeFi) applications and innovative financial instruments. Moreover, the convergence of DeFi and NFTs in the Metaverse fosters novel opportunities for community-based engagement and value creation. As the Metaverse continues to evolve, the interoperability of virtual worlds and the facilitation of decentralised commerce remain critical areas for further exploration and consensus-building.

3.3 Governance in the metaverse

There is no doubt that Metaverse economies will demand a rethinking of governance. Web3 makes it possible to create leaderless, decentralised organisations. Automation and smart contracts will require a deep analysis of each network, its objectives, decision rights, incentives, and accountabilities. Web 3 Metaverse decentralisation facilitates the shift from centralised human governance to decentralised algorithm governance. DAO governance is an area which requires further experimentation and research, as there can be information asymmetries and a lack of transparency about participant ambitions, motivations, values, and priorities.

As there are risks with digital assets generally, these will be replicated in the Metaverse. For example, volatility, smart contract vulnerability, market manipulation, money laundering, terrorist financing and consumer protection. When smart contracts fail or are hacked in a decentralised economy, there is no recourse to a central authority. As with digital assets, the jurisdictional boundaries of the Metaverse need to be determined as they can cross multiple physical borders.

Many Metaverse users will freely share data across multiple devices without understanding that their data may be transferred or monetised. This is an increased risk in an immersive environment with sensitive data, like long-term brain wave data. This poses the risk of "biometric psychography", which is the gathering and use of biological data to reveal intimate details about a user's likes, dislikes, preferences and interests [14]. In immersive worlds, algorithms record users' subconscious emotional reactions to specific situations through features such as pupil dilation or change in facial expression.

3.3.1 Digital identity and representation

The Metaverse's jurisdictional delineation, like physical borders, raises questions regarding regulatory oversight and accountability mechanisms. Ethical concerns regarding data privacy and identity authentication underscore the need for standardised decentralised identity systems and robust data protection protocols. Digital Rights Management (DRM) technologies also assume significance in safeguarding data integrity and intellectual property rights within the Metaverse [15]. Ultimately, digital education initiatives and governance frameworks are essential for mitigating risks and fostering responsible practices within the Metaverse ecosystem.

4. Web3 and metaverse use cases

An open Web3 Metaverse embodies a decentralised experience using blockchain to create a virtual experience with a meta-economy with its own currencies that can be exchanged peer-to-peer. The open Metaverse will impact many sectors, which are demonstrated in the following industry cases which exemplify the power of the Web3 Metaverse.

4.1 Gaming

Web3 Gaming encompasses not only playing games but also the growth of communities, social integration, and the facilitation of meaningful connections among people. Antler estimates the addressable market for Web3 Gaming to be valued at approximately $200 billion, indicative of its burgeoning significance within the digital ecosystem. The total transaction volume for blockchain games surged to $5.41 billion in 2022, with a projected compound annual growth rate (CAGR) of 68.9%. This exponential growth is further evidenced by a 2000% increase in Web3 gaming activity from 2021 to 2022 [16].

Play-to-earn (P2E) games emerged during the pandemic but encountered criticism due to inherent challenges such as unsustainable tokenomics, volatile inflation and deflation dynamics of in-game tokens, and a skewed emphasis on income generation at the expense of gameplay quality [9]. In response to these challenges, the Play-and-Earn (PAE) model has emerged as an alternative, marrying the financial incentives of P2E gaming with immersive gameplay experiences. Emphasising sustainable tokenomics and long-term viability, PAE games prioritise enjoyable gameplay, fostering a more inclusive gaming environment. Notably, PAE games are increasingly adopting free-to-play models to broaden their audience appeal, with notable titles such as Illuvium, Guild of Guardians, Sidus Heroes, Shrapnel, and Big Time exemplifying this trend, which craft exceptional games that seamlessly integrate NFTs and enhance user value without necessitating explicit blockchain knowledge.

Web3 technologies also present many opportunities for Esports, including integrating NFTs to facilitate cross-platform asset utilisation, tokenised rewards distributed based on players' performance, and establishing decentralised autonomous

DOI: http://dx.doi.org/10.5772/intechopen.1006342

organisations to democratise governance structures. Fan tokens offer enthusiasts a stake in their favourite teams, enabling active participation in decision-making processes and exclusive engagement opportunities. Additionally, tokenised crowd-funding mechanisms empower teams to raise capital by offering ownership or revenue-sharing rights to investors and fans, thereby aligning incentives and fostering community engagement.

Web3 gaming enhances player agency, equitable participation, and new economic paradigms. As the Web3 gaming ecosystem evolves, stakeholders will face inherent challenges such as tokenomics sustainability, regulatory compliance, and user adoption to unlock its full potential. Concerted efforts to address barriers to adoption and foster inclusive, transparent, and ethical gaming environments will be paramount in realising the transformative vision of Web3 gaming. The promise of Web3 gaming is to empower players as owners, facilitate tokenised economies, and redefine traditional gaming experiences.

4.2 Healthcare

Metaverse platforms tailored for healthcare purposes are attracting significant attention because of their potential to enhance healthcare practices. Immersive experiences derived from real surgical procedures are being recreated, with surgeons receiving real-time guidance through integration with surgical navigation systems and fusion of data from multiple imaging sources. Avatars are employed to facilitate realistic consultations, personalised care, and treatment, leveraging data interconnectivity and digital twin technology. Gamification strategies are being employed to foster connectivity between healthcare providers and patients, particularly in wellness and fitness domains, where augmented reality enhances workout experiences with guidance from virtual instructors. The monetisation of health data presents new economic opportunities, and education stands to become immersive, rewarding and precision-targeted through data analytics. The culmination of these advancements is envisioned in the creation of a comprehensive meta health ecosystem within the Metaverse, representing a significant leap forward in healthcare innovation and delivery [17].

Collaborative Work in the Metaverse: In the Metaverse, health professionals can seamlessly collaborate using 3D avatars alongside digital tools such as whiteboards and workstations, facilitating face-to-face interactions without the need for complex conferencing equipment. Leveraging the expansive capabilities of the Metaverse, virtually any object or environment can be three-dimensionally modelled, with real-world specifications replicated through digital twin technology. This enables the testing of machinery, systems, and procedures through digital twins, affording the opportunity to detect potential failures and refine processes before implementation in physical settings. The Metaverse fosters collaboration and knowledge exchange, exemplified by platforms which incorporate Metaverse interfaces to facilitate collaborative learning activities. Learners are ranked based on their engagement and performance, enabling the formation of groups with similar proficiency levels. Incentivising intra-community collaboration through token rewards further enhances the collaborative learning experience.

Education: Innovations in AR and VR technologies will transform medical education and training, enhancing learning processes and procedural proficiency. VR enables immersive journeys within the human body, providing learners with panoramic views of anatomical structures or replicating real-world medical procedures.

AR supplements hands-on learning experiences, allowing students to simulate patient encounters and surgical scenarios, thereby fostering skill acquisition and technique refinement.

Clinical Care: The integration of avatars in clinical consultations introduces a new dimension of personalised care and diagnosis facilitated by data interconnectivity. The Metaverse holds potential for clinical applications, ranging from providing real-time guidance during surgical procedures to enhancing pre- and post-surgical assessments through immersive experiences.

Gamification: The gamification of healthcare in the Metaverse connects patients and healthcare providers, particularly in wellness and fitness domains, where AR enhances exercise regimens with virtual instructors. Concepts such as "move-to-earn" incentivise physical activity, promoting healthier lifestyles through interactive gaming experiences.

The convergence of Blockchain technology and GameFi models in the Metaverse creates new avenues for monetising health data and fostering economic opportunities through concepts such as "learn to earn" and "move to earn."

4.3 Education in the metaverse

The Metaverse is projected to play a pivotal role in shaping the future of education. Forecasts indicate that the market for Metaverse Education is poised for robust growth, with estimations pegging it at US$56.73 million by 2023 and projecting a compound annual growth rate (CAGR 2023–2030) of 44.98%, culminating in a value of US$763.70 million by 2030. This trajectory reflects the growing recognition of the Metaverse as an instantaneously accessible, cost-effective educational platform, potentially emulating the "Uberization" phenomenon in the transportation industry. The metamorphosis towards a "Bricks and Mortarless" educational narrative becomes increasingly pronounced, reflecting a world where education is ubiquitous and handheld.

The globalisation of education coupled with internet connectivity serves as the linchpin for this borderless education, facilitating real-time collaboration and knowledge exchange among students irrespective of their geographic dispersion. Integral to the realisation of a seamless, borderless Metaverse will be interoperability across disparate jurisdictions and a robust framework of Self-Sovereign Identity. This framework will serve as a gateway to virtual worlds, ensuring the veracity of transactions, the legitimacy of educational platforms, and the validity of credentials conferred upon learners and professionals.

The integration of Web3 "Learn to Earn" games incentivises student engagement through token rewards, aligning incentives with educational objectives. The Metaverse empowers educators to tailor virtual learning environments to individual learner profiles, fostering personalised learning pathways boosted with quests, missions, and social interaction opportunities. This, combined with generative AI in education, with avatar instructors and tutors leveraging advanced algorithms to offer personalised learning experiences tailored to individual learner profiles, will enable highly curated. Real-time assessments, automated grading mechanisms, and curriculum refinement will be facilitated by AI algorithms, creating an educational environment characterised by adaptability, responsiveness, and learner-centricity.

VR and AR technologies offer educators tools to overcome traditional barriers to learning, affording students immersive and realistic experiences. For instance, Curiscope's Virtuali-Tee, an AR T-shirt, enables students to explore anatomical structures in the human body with unprecedented depth and interactivity [18]. Similarly, VR simulations provide a safe and cost-effective means for students to engage in high-risk scenarios, such as experiments related to radioactivity in virtual environments like Second Life [19]. VR facilitates hands-on training in contexts characterised by prohibitive costs or logistical challenges, exemplified by Boeing's Aircraft Maintenance Metaverse, where professionals and trainees utilise VR headsets to simulate aircraft maintenance procedures [20].

Traditional modes of virtual learning are also undergoing paradigm shifts, transitioning from passive consumption of recorded lectures to dynamic and interactive experiences. Projects like the VoluProf initiative aim to enhance online lectures by integrating mixed-reality applications featuring lifelike avatars, thereby fostering direct interaction between students and lecturers [21]. Virtual classrooms within the Metaverse afford students immersive interactions with peers and instructors, access to course materials, and engagement in collaborative learning activities [22]. The Metaverse transcends geographical constraints, enabling students to embark on virtual field trips to museums, historical sites, and culturally significant locales, thereby enriching learning experiences and catering to diverse learning needs [23].

The Metaverse stands poised to democratise access to education, ensuring inclusivity and accessibility for individuals constrained by geographical, physical, or socioeconomic barriers, giving rise to an educational landscape that is immersive, globally accessible, gamified, and generative in nature.

4.4 Metaverse tourism

The tourism industry is witnessing a profound transformation-driven demand for experiential tourism, sustainable tourism, and digitalisation, each of which underscores the industry's need to cater to the evolving needs and desires of modern travellers. Experiential tourism incorporates active engagement, where travellers seek authentic, immersive experiences that foster a deep connection with the destination's cultural setting [24]. By facilitating meaningful interactions and personalised narratives, experiential tourism offers travellers a profound sense of place and belonging. In response to mounting environmental concerns and societal imperatives, sustainable tourism has also emerged as a cornerstone of responsible travel practices [25] by prioritising environmental conservation, community empowerment, and cultural preservation, sustainable tourism endeavours to minimise negative impacts while maximising the positive contributions of tourism to host destinations.

4.4.1 Metaverse and tourism opportunities

Technological advancements within the Metaverse are democratising access to travel experiences, enabling individuals to virtually explore destinations. The immersive nature of the Metaverse facilitates deeper consumer engagement through personalised, interactive experiences tailored to individual preferences. By enabling travellers to preview destinations, activities, and accommodations within a virtual environment, the Metaverse influences decision-making processes and augments customer satisfaction and loyalty. AR and VR enable virtual tours, historical reconstructions, and experiential simulations, which redefine the boundaries of spatial exploration and cultural immersion within the tourism domain. The integration of Metaverse technologies streamlines various operational aspects of the tourism industry, from virtual booking systems to AI-driven customer service. By leveraging digital twins and decentralised platforms, tourism operators can optimise resource allocation, enhance scalability, and mitigate operational inefficiencies.

4.4.2 Web 3 as an enabler of metaverse tourism

At the heart of technological innovation lies Web 3.0, an emergent paradigm that integrates decentralised finance, non-fungible tokens, and self-sovereign identity within the fabric of the internet [26]. By empowering travellers with decentralised access to virtual experiences, personalised reviews, and digital assets, Web 3.0 catalyses the evolution of Metaverse tourism towards a more inclusive, equitable, and participatory ecosystem.

Blockchain technology underpins the secure, transparent exchange of value within the Metaverse, facilitating transactions, ownership verification, and digital asset management [citation needed]. Non-fungible tokens (NFTs), as unique digital assets authenticated on a blockchain, imbue virtual experiences with scarcity, ownership, and value, thereby revolutionising the economics of digital tourism.

Digital twins serve as virtual replicas of physical entities, ranging from cities to landmarks, within the Metaverse. By simulating real-world environments with unparalleled accuracy and fidelity, digital twins enhance the authenticity and immersion of virtual tourism experiences, enabling travellers to explore destinations with unprecedented depth and detail.

Metaverse tourism empowers travellers with an unprecedented agency, enabling them to personalise their experiences, engage with destinations, and co-create value within a decentralised ecosystem]. By fostering community-owned economies, social tokens, and decentralised governance mechanisms, the Web3 Metaverse catalyses a paradigm shift towards participatory tourism models characterised by trust, transparency, and inclusivity.

Shanghai's ambitious endeavour to integrate Web 3.0 technologies within the tourism sector underscores the city's commitment to innovation, sustainability, and cultural preservation [27]. By leveraging blockchain, AI, and VR environments, the project aims to deliver immersive, decentralised travel experiences that showcase the city's rich heritage while embracing the digital future.

Airlines are harnessing the power of the Metaverse to enhance pre-travel experiences, streamline operations, and attract tech-savvy travellers [28]. By offering virtual previews of flights, airports, and destinations, airlines facilitate informed decision-making and foster deeper engagement with their brand, thereby redefining the boundaries of customer experience and loyalty.

Hotels are venturing into the Metaverse to reimagine the hospitality experience, offering virtual tours, immersive events, and digital replicas of physical properties [29]. By leveraging the Metaverse as a platform for brand engagement, community building, and experiential marketing, hotels are transforming how guests interact with their properties, both online and offline.

Metaverse technologies offer novel solutions for training and operations within the tourism and hospitality sector, exemplified by case studies such as KLM's virtual fleet tours [30]. By leveraging immersive simulations, 360° imagery, and real-time data optimisation, organisations can enhance staff training, streamline operations, and optimise guest experiences, thereby driving operational efficiency and customer satisfaction.

A recent report from ITU [31] drawing upon recent surveys, industry insights, and technical literature, highlights the transformative potential of the Metaverse in reshaping the tourism experience, enhancing consumer engagement, optimising operational efficiency, and fostering sustainable practices. The paper concludes that by harnessing the transformative capabilities of blockchain, virtual reality, and Web 3.0 technologies, Metaverse Tourism promises to revolutionise every aspect of the tourism value chain, from consumer engagement to destination management.

4.5 Web3 and the industrial metaverse

The Industrial Metaverse is poised to grow [32]. In the aviation sector, the industrial Metaverse enables a transformative approach to aircraft design and manufacturing processes through the convergence of virtual and augmented realities. Digital twins, virtual replicas of aircraft created within the Metaverse, allow exhaustive testing and simulation protocols, leading to substantial cost savings and safety risk reduction. Digital twins also play a crucial role in optimising factory operations, serving as dynamic models that simulate manufacturing environments. They enable preemptive identification of inefficiencies and strategic planning of facility development, leading to increased efficiency and reduced resource consumption. Similarly, in electric vehicle manufacturing, the industrial Metaverse accelerates production timelines and enhances operational efficiency by enabling virtual design and refinement of production facilities, thus minimising risks and ensuring project success.

In building operations and construction sectors, the industrial Metaverse enhances operational methodologies through a synergy of VR, AR, and digital twin technologies.

The industrial Metaverse enhances workforce training methodologies within the automotive and manufacturing sectors by offering a sophisticated platform for developing simulation-based training modules. The Metaverse enables remote training, customisable scenarios, continuous learning, safety and risk management, technical skill development, and data-driven insights, ensuring the seamless integration of digital proficiencies within the workforce.

The emergence of the industrial Metaverse represents a paradigm shift towards advanced digital integration, with blockchain technology playing a pivotal role in establishing a decentralised, secure, and transparent framework for operations. Blockchain ensures transactional integrity and fosters trust among participants by facilitating immutable transaction records. Smart contracts, a feature enabled by blockchain, automate processes and enforce agreements without intermediaries, thereby streamlining operations and enhancing efficiency. Furthermore, blockchain facilitates asset management and interoperability, allowing for the seamless transfer of digital assets and information across disparate platforms. Consequently, Web3 and blockchain emerge as a foundational technology within the industrial Metaverse, underpinning its integrity and efficacy within this growing digital ecosystem.

4.6 Payments in the metaverse

The structure of payment systems in the Metaverse depends on whether the model for the Metaverse is centralised or decentralised. The decentralised model of the Metaverse is based on the idea of Web 3.0, which seeks to decentralise the Internet based on blockchain and open protocols [33]. Payments in a decentralised Metaverse could work through blockchain technology. If the native token of these systems has as base protocol a token standard, for example, ERC-20 from Ethereum, then the so-called currency is interoperable, standardised and consistent with the functionality of the native blockchain. Users in decentralised systems have some direct control over the rules of the platform. In some cases, this translates into voting rights directly in the system's policies.

As the Metaverse expands, the adoption of stablecoins and cryptocurrencies, particularly in blockchain-based applications, emerges as a prominent trend. According to a survey commissioned by PayPal, a significant percentage of Metaverse users express a preference for using cryptocurrencies and stablecoins for purchases and transactions within virtual environments, indicating a growing acceptance of digital currencies in the Metaverse ecosystem [34]. The same survey found Metaverse users preferred to be paid in cryptocurrency (76% of respondents) with fiat currency (69%). NFTs are growing in popularity in the open Metaverse because they provide proof of ownership of products and property bought in the platform.

Cryptocurrencies and stablecoins will allow for seamless, fast and secure transactions on a 24/7 basis globally. Programability of digital assets will enable contingent payments and the tokenisation of real and financial assets. By building interoperability and eliminating barriers between assets in different ecosystems, MetaFi payment platforms could thus serve as an important infrastructure function for a broader virtual economy.

In decentralised Metaverse models aligned with the principles of Web 3.0, blockchain technology serves as the foundation for payment mechanisms. These infrastructural developments not only cater to the payment needs of Metaverse applications but also facilitate seamless, secure, and programmable transactions, paving the way for the tokenisation of real and virtual assets. While end-users may not directly perceive the underlying technical complexities, these payment platforms play a crucial role in promoting interoperability and driving the evolution of a vibrant virtual economy within the expanding Metaverse landscape.

5. Challenges, risks, and open questions

Despite its promise, the Web3 metaverse has many challenges and risks. There will continue to be a dynamic interplay between regulation and technological advancement in the Web3 ecosystem. This section summarises some of the challenges, risks and open questions to be solved.

5.1 Legal and governance challenges

Regulators are working to balance innovation with investor protection, understanding the regulatory impacts of DAOs and the need for adaptive regulatory frameworks, international collaboration, and the economic and societal impacts of Web3 regulations.

In the metaverse, governance by DAOs and algorithms poses unique challenges. These virtual worlds can have jurisdictional boundaries as significant as physical borders, complicating legal and regulatory compliance. Jurisdictional and regulatory requirements remain to be resolved. This includes which jurisdictions need to be considered and which regulatory bodies are involved.

5.2 Financial risks

Participants in the metaverse will face risks familiar to the digital asset space, including market manipulation, volatility, impermanent loss, liquidation, technical issues and price risks.

5.3 Data privacy

Data privacy will be an even larger issue with the collection of biological data and subconscious emotional reactions through indicators like pupil dilation and facial expressions. This raises significant legal and regulatory challenges, including data privacy and intellectual property rights. Establishing clear legal frameworks and regulations is essential for building trust in the Web3 ecosystem.

5.4 Intellectual property protection

The metaverse will generate new forms of intellectual property, such as virtual goods, digital assets, NFTs, and experiences. Ensuring these assets are protected is essential for the ecosystem's growth.

5.5 Digital identity and authentication

Digital identity is complex and will require identity authentication and verification. Secure and trustworthy identity systems will be essential for user safety and trust.

5.6 Technical issues

Key technical considerations for metaverse platforms include security, scalability, privacy, energy consumption and interoperability.

5.7 Ethical challenges

Digital ethics are not different from conventional ethics, but it is the potential for inadvertent or deliberate automation of unethical conduct at scale that highlights ethical dilemmas for developers, investors, consumers and regulators at the technology, application, and societal levels [35]. Many ethical challenges will arise in the metaverse, including co-creation and co-ownership of digital assets, rights of avatars, potential harm through digital representations, and risks for vulnerable groups, such as children. Establishing guidelines for ethical standards in the metaverse will be needed.

5.8 Education and awareness

Widespread education and awareness are needed to help users understand the benefits, risks, and implications of using Web3 applications.

6. Conclusion

The chapter has described a future world of greater decentralisation, a new data economy, and a world where the open Metaverse, powered by Web3, will provide social utility across multiple sectors. Web3 has created the means to exchange value on a peer to peer basis, while the Metaverse has created the possibility of exchanging value in virtual worlds.

When combined with IoT AI, big data, and data analytics, this creates the foundations for the spatial web.

Distributed Autonomous Organisations (DAOs), with their automated governance, have allowed multi-jurisdictional economies to develop globally. This enables the creation of community-owned economies, which has opened up the world for the peer-to-peer exchange of value using Web 3 and provides opportunities for content creators globally. Gen Z and Gen Alpha will be the users of Web 3.0 and the Metaverse, and they will also be demanding better user experience, that companies take sustainability seriously. They will want a voice in the development of new products and to be remunerated for their contributions.

Interoperable Web3 Metaverses will allow people to interact and exchange value across them. Self-Sovereign Identity will enable people to control access and monetise their data. This will also enable secure cryptographically secured data exchange, making scientific discovery and medical records, for example, far more accessible. Investment knowledge will be decentralised; science will be decentralised. Decentralised developer communities will co-create products instead of companies providing products to customers.

Web3 Metaverse education will provide a means to agilely reskill workers displaced by Artificial Intelligence (AI) and prepare leaders with the tools to thrive in the new digital economies that challenge traditional views of sovereign states, nation-states, and global governance.

The world is only beginning to understand the social utility of the immersive Web3. The Web3 Metaverse will be used for entertainment and commerce, healthcare, research, education, government, and industry. Web3 will power the exchange of all kinds of value in the Metaverse, allowing it to operate a virtual economy within which participants can be rewarded for their efforts and earn in new ways. Web3 holds the promise of a future characterised by accessibility, inclusivity, and value creation for all.

Author details

Jane Thomason
UCL Centre for Blockchain, London, United Kingdom

*Address all correspondence to: jane.blockchainquantumimpact@gmail.com

References

[1] ITU Focus Group on Metaverse. Technical Report: Definition and Requirements of Metaverse. Geneva: International Telecommunication Union; 2023

[2] Burke J. The Web 3 Toolbox. London; 2021. Available from: https://outlierventures.io/research/the-web-3-toolbox/ [Accessed: July 14, 2022]

[3] Tasca P. Internet of value: A risky necessity. Lausanne: Frontiers in Blockchain. 2020;**3**:39. DOI: 10.3389/fbloc.2020.00039

[4] Khan Ali. Decentralized Cloud Computing. Available from: https://www.devteam.space/blog/what-is-decentralized-cloud-computing/ [Accessed: November 14, 2022]

[5] Thomason JA. New Tribes of the Metaverse — Community-Owned Economies. New York: Cointelegraph; 2021. Available from: https://cointelegraph.com/news/new-tribes-of-the-Metaverse-community-owned-economies [Accessed: November 15, 2022]

[6] Rees K. These 8 Tech Giants Have Invested Big in the Metaverse. MakeUseOf. Canada: Montreal; 2022. Available from: https://www.makeuseof.com/companies-investing-in-Metaverse/ [Accessed: November 14, 2022]

[7] Chow AR. Why you Should Be Paying Attention to the Metaverse. New York: TIME; 2021. Available from: https://time.com/6118513/into-the-Metaverse-time-newsletter/ [Accessed: November 14, 2022]

[8] Meilich A, Ordano E, Guide S. What Is GameFi? 'Play-to-Earn' Gaming Explained. Singapore: Crypto.com; 2022. Available from: https://crypto.com/university/what-is-gamefi-play-to-earn-gaming-explained [Accessed: November 14, 2022]

[9] Howell J. MetaFi - Where DeFi Meets the Metaverse. London: 101 Blockchains. 2022. Available from: https://101Blockchains.com/metafi/ [Accessed: November 14, 2022]

[10] Takahashi D. The DeanBeat: Why Web3 Companies Created the Open Metaverse Alliance. San Francisco: VentureBeat; 2022. Available from: https://venturebeat.com/games/the-deanbeat-why-web3-companies-created-the-open-Metaverse-alliance/ [Accessed: November 14, 2022]

[11] Blockchain Magazine. YouTube. 2023. Available from: https://blockchainmagazine.net/lets-meet-Metaverse-avatar-metafi/ [Accessed: June 2, 2023]

[12] Cognizant. What's the Plural for Metaverse? Cognizant. Teaneck, New Jersey, U.S. - Publisher; 2021. Available from: https://www.cognizant.com/futureofwork/article/whats-the-plural-for-Metaverse [Accessed: November 14, 2022]

[13] Amerikayageldim. YouTube. Available from: https://www.amerikayageldim.com/assets/uploads/files/1647380348146-1647331508066.pdf [Accessed: November 14, 2022]

[14] Heller B. Watching androids dream of electric sheep: Immersive technology, biometric Psychography, and the law. Vanderbilt Journal of Entertainment and Technology Law. 2021;**23**:1. Available from: https://scholarship.law.vanderbilt.edu/jetlaw/vol23/iss1/1

[15] Carter S. Online Gaming Has Issues That Only Web3 Can Solve. 2023. Available from: https://www.forbes.com/sites/digital-assets/2023/09/07/online-gaming-has-issues-that-only-web3-can-solve/?sh=17da652a45fb [Accessed: May 13, 2024]

[16] Miller K, Demirbilek M. Instructing AI ethics and human rights. In: Vasiliu-Feltes I, Thomason J, editors. Applied Ethics in a Digital World. Hershey, Pennsylvania: IGI Global; 2022. pp. 59-72. DOI: 10.4018/978-1-7998-8467-5.ch005

[17] Thomason J. MetaHealth-how will the Metaverse change health care?. Available from: https://www.researchgate.net/publication/362035490_MetaHealth_-How_will_the_Metaverse_Change_Health_Care. Journal of Metaverse. 2021;**1**(1):13-16 [Accessed: May 13, 2024]

[18] Kye S, Kang M, Park E. Virtualitee: Using augmented reality to teach anatomy. Interactive Learning Environments. 2021;**29**(5):592-604

[19] Kanematsu H, Taniguchi H, Hirokawa M. Educational use of second life for radioactive decay experiments: A trial study for high school students. Journal of Computer Assisted Learning. 2014;**30**(4):344-355

[20] Siyaev D, Jo J. Virtual reality training for aircraft maintenance: A case study of Boeing's aircraft maintenance Metaverse. Journal of Aviation Technology and Engineering. 2021;**11**(2):28-36

[21] Fraunhofer. Fraunhofer HHI's VoluProf initiative: Enhancing online lectures with mixed-reality applications. 2023. Available from: https://www.fraunhofer.de/en/press/research-news/2023/august-2023/voluprof-facilitates-individual-and-interactive-online-lectures.html

[22] Mystakidis S. Virtual classrooms in the Metaverse: Opportunities and challenges. Virtual Reality in Education Journal. 2022;**15**(3):210-225

[23] Hupont Torres J et al. Virtual field trips in the Metaverse: Enriching learning experiences through cultural immersion. International Journal of Educational Technology in Higher Education. 2023;**20**(1):37-49

[24] National Geographic Society. Is Experiential Travel the Next Big Trend? Washington DC: National Geographic Society; 2023. Available from: https://www.nationalgeographic.com/travel/article/is-experiential-travel-the-next-big-trend

[25] United Nations Department of Economic and Social Affairs. Sustainable Tourism. 2024. Available from: https://sdgs.un.org/topics/sustainable-tourism

[26] Thomason J, Ivwurie E. Introduction to Web 3.0. Hershey, Pennsylvania: IGI Global; 2023. DOI: 10.4018/978-1-6684-6658-2.ch001

[27] Springer. Metaverse for Tourists and Tourism Destinations. New York: Springer; 2023. Available from: https://link.springer.com/article/10.1007/s40558-023-00271-y

[28] Haqshanas Ruholamin. Shanghai Aims to Generate $6.9B Annually with Web3 Tourism Projects. 2023. Available from: https://tokenist.com/shanghai-aims-to-generate-6-9b-annually-with-web3-tourism-projects/

[29] SITA. Metaverse operations, autonomous electric vehicles, and the digital economy set to transform the

travel industry. 2022. Available from: https://www.sita.aero/pressroom/news-releases/Metaverse-operations-autonomous-electric-vehicles-and-the-digital-economy-set-to-transform-the-travel-industry/

[30] Metamandrill. Metaverse hotel; ways for hotels to benefit from the Metaverse. 2024. Available from: https://metamandrill.com/Metaverse-hotel/

[31] Accenture. Why the metaverse (really) matters for travel, Fannelie Gerard. 2022. Available from: https://www.accenture.com/us-en/blogs/compass-travel-blog/metaverse-travel

[32] ITU Focus Group on Metaverse: International Telecommunication Union. ITU ["The future of travel in the Metaverse: landscape and use cases". Technical Report, FGMV-I-WG2-TG-Metaverse-tourism-013, Focus Group on Metaverse]

[33] International Telecommunications Union (ITU) Focus Group on the Metaverse. Landscape and use cases for the industrial Metaverse. FG-MV-I-WG2-TG-industrial-Metaverse-004, Focus Group on the Metaverse

[34] Cantú C, Franco C, Frost J. The Economic Implications of Services in the Metaverse. No 144. Basel, Switzerland: BIS Papers; 2024

[35] Vasiliu-Feltes I, Thomason J. Applied Ethics in a Digital World. Herschey, Pennsylvania: IGI Global; 2021. p. 316. DOI: 10.4018/978-1-7998-8467-5. ISBN13: 9781799884675. ISBN10: 1799884678. EISBN13: 9781799884699. ISBN13 Softcover: 9781799884682

Section 2

Healthcare Innovations in the Metaverse

Chapter 3

AI- and XR-Powered Digital Therapeutics (DTx) Innovations

Alex G. Lee

Abstract

This book chapter explores the transformative advancements in digital health through the integration of artificial intelligence (AI) and extended reality (XR) technologies. Digital Therapeutics (DTx) represent a significant leap in healthcare by using evidence-based software to treat, manage, and prevent a wide range of diseases and disorders, offering non-invasive, personalized, and scalable solutions. AI-powered DTx enhance the diagnosis and treatment of conditions such as Alzheimer's disease (AD), mental health disorders, developmental disorders, and diabetes by leveraging machine learning algorithms and deep learning models to provide real-time, adaptive interventions based on patient data. XR-powered DTx further revolutionize healthcare by creating immersive, interactive environments that enhance patient engagement and therapeutic efficacy for conditions like AD, mental health issues, developmental disorders, neurological rehabilitation, pain management, and behavioral addictions. The convergence of AI and XR in DTx amplifies these benefits, offering personalized, engaging, and intelligent therapeutic solutions that address individual patient needs in real-time. This book chapter underscores the potential of these innovations to revolutionize healthcare delivery.

Keywords: artificial intelligence, extended reality, digital therapeutics, innovation, technology convergence, healthcare, digital health, large language models, virtual reality, augmented reality, mixed reality, spatial computing, commercialization, product design, diagnosis, treatment, disorders, digital twins, precision medicine, clinical trials, genomics, mental health, neurology, neuroscience, oncology, cognitive health, ADHD, autism, pain management

1. Introduction

Digital Therapeutics (DTx) represent a transformative advancement in digital health, leveraging technology to enhance or potentially replace traditional medical interventions. As defined by the Digital Therapeutics Alliance, DTx deliver medical interventions directly to patients using evidence-based, clinically evaluated software to treat, manage, and prevent a broad spectrum of diseases and disorders (for details, see [1]). Unlike conventional healthcare or wellness apps, DTx are designed to have a direct therapeutic impact on specific medical conditions, making them a critical component of modern healthcare.

DTx offer a low-risk profile due to their non-invasive nature, eliminating the complications associated with surgical procedures or drug side effects. They enhance patient engagement by allowing personalized experiences and continuous monitoring, providing valuable feedback on adherence and early detection of issues. The efficacy of DTx is backed by clinical evidence, ensuring consistent and effective treatment across diverse patient populations. Additionally, their digital nature facilitates rapid scalability, cost-effectiveness, and integration with existing healthcare systems. This positions DTx as a complementary or substitutive option for traditional treatments, promoting preventive care and supporting comprehensive healthcare delivery [2].

Artificial intelligence (AI)-powered DTx are revolutionizing healthcare by leveraging AI to provide data-driven insights, automate tasks, and enhance diagnostics, leading to more personalized and efficient patient care. The U.S. digital health sector has experienced substantial venture funding growth through 2023, with billions invested in digital therapeutics. This surge in investment is driving innovation and addressing critical pain points for health systems, such as mental health demands and the shift to value-based care.

AI-powered DTx utilize advanced machine learning (ML) algorithms to adapt treatments to individual patient needs in real-time. The core distinction of these therapeutics lies in their use of digital biomarkers and AI-driven feedback loops, which continuously analyzing patient data [3]. This allows treatment protocols to evolve based on changes in the patient's condition, enabling personalized treatment plans tailored to individual variability in symptoms, behavior, and response to treatment.

The integration of AI in DTx represents a significant shift from traditional therapeutic models to more dynamic, personalized healthcare solutions. This technology does not merely automate existing treatments but actively adapts them, offering a transformative approach to disease management and health maintenance.

Extended Reality (XR)-powered DTx represent a transformative shift in healthcare delivery, emphasizing personalized, immersive, and interactive treatment modalities. XR-powered DTx innovations leverage virtual reality (VR), augmented reality (AR), mixed reality (MR), and other immersive technologies to create novel therapeutic environments that transcend traditional treatment methods. This approach offers a multifaceted platform for enhancing patient engagement, treatment adherence, and overall health outcomes through deeply engaging and personalized healthcare experiences [4].

The core of XR-powered DTx innovations lies in their ability to tailor therapeutic interventions to the individual needs and preferences of each patient. By leveraging XR, healthcare providers can create immersive environments specifically designed to address unique medical conditions and treatment plans. This personalized approach enhances the relevance and effectiveness of the therapy while significantly increasing patient engagement through interactive and captivating treatment experiences [5].

One of the most innovative aspects of integrating XR-powered DTx is its potential to capitalize on the placebo effect, where a patient's positive belief in the effectiveness of a treatment can lead to actual health improvements [6]. By creating immersive virtual environments that align with treatment models, XR technology can activate neurobiological mechanisms related to expectation, reward, and learning phenomena. This not only has the potential to amplify the efficacy of traditional medical treatments but also opens new avenues for exploring how patient beliefs and mental states can influence treatment outcomes.

DOI: http://dx.doi.org/10.5772/intechopen.1006619

XR-powered DTx address critical gaps in patient education and treatment compliance by providing an interactive and engaging platform for patients to understand their medical conditions and the importance of their treatment regimens. Through immersive XR experiences, patients can visually and sensorially explore the effects of their diseases and the mechanisms of their treatments. This aids in demystifying complex medical information and motivates patients toward better health behaviors and treatment adherence. As the integration of XR for DTx continues to evolve, it opens up exciting possibilities for the future of healthcare.

2. AI-powered DTx innovations

2.1 AI-powered DTx for Alzheimer's disease

The integration of AI in the field of Alzheimer's disease (AD) DTx marks a significant leap forward in the diagnosis and treatment of AD. AI technologies, including ML algorithms and deep learning (DL) models, are transforming the early detection, monitoring, and management of AD. By leveraging these advanced technologies, healthcare providers can offer early diagnosis, personalized treatment plans, and continuous monitoring of patients with AD [7]. This not only improves the quality of life for affected individuals and their families but also offers hope for managing a condition that has long been challenging to treat.

Early detection of AD is crucial, as it provides an opportunity for early intervention that can potentially slow disease progression. AI-driven digital diagnostic tools utilize sophisticated algorithms to analyze data from various sources, such as interactions with mobile devices, to identify early signs of cognitive decline. These tools can differentiate between AD and other cognitive conditions, enhancing diagnostic accuracy and allowing for timely and appropriate treatment strategies [8]. For instance, AI algorithms can analyze passive data collected from mobile devices, using ML techniques to detect subtle changes in cognitive functions. By comparing individual performance against benchmarks established from healthy populations, a functional impairment score that reflects the user's cognitive health can be calculated. This approach aids in early detection and monitoring of disease progression over time.

ML algorithms are central to enhancing diagnostic accuracy in AD care. These algorithms can handle complex, multifaceted data to identify patterns indicative of AD. Techniques such as decision trees and convolutional neural networks enable AI to analyze clinical information, images, and even facial expressions to classify cognitive conditions accurately [9]. A unique voting approach among multiple ML algorithms further ensures a more accurate and robust diagnosis by aggregating findings from various sources and methodologies. This multifaceted approach allows for a comprehensive assessment of the patient's cognitive state, facilitating early and accurate diagnosis.

AI technologies provide non-invasive methods for AD diagnosis and monitoring, offering a less stressful and more accessible alternative to traditional diagnostic techniques. Advanced ML techniques analyze images of the subject's head or facial features to detect signs of cognitive decline. Tailoring these models to individual patients enhances the precision of predictions concerning dementia progression and the effectiveness of monitoring efforts [10]. AI-powered DTx innovations excel in personalizing treatment for AD patients. By continuously analyzing patient data, AI algorithms can adapt therapeutic interventions to the individual's specific condition, symptoms, and response to treatment. This adaptive approach ensures that patients receive care tailored to their unique needs, maximizing engagement and the effectiveness of the treatment.

2.2 AI-powered DTx for mental health

AI-powered DTx in mental health represent a transformative shift in diagnosing, managing, and treating mental health disorders, leveraging advanced technology to provide evidence-based interventions. The integration of AI has significantly amplified the potential of DTx, offering innovative solutions that address the limitations of traditional mental health care approaches. By providing personalized, accessible, and effective treatment options, AI-powered DTx have the potential to revolutionize mental health care, making it more responsive to the needs of individuals and society at large-scale [11].

ML models, including natural language processing (NLP) and acoustic analysis, enhance the early detection of mental health issues. These technologies can analyze speech, text, and facial expressions to identify early signs of conditions like depression or anxiety [12]. Continuous monitoring allows for real-time adjustment of treatments, ensuring that interventions are aligned with the patient's current needs. This improves outcomes and potentially prevents the escalation of conditions, offering a proactive approach to mental health care.

One of the AI's most profound impacts in DTx is its ability to personalize treatment. By analyzing extensive datasets, including clinical information and real-time behavioral data, AI algorithms can identify patterns and nuances in a patient's mental health state. This leads to highly personalized treatment plans that are more effective than one-size-fits-all approaches. For instance, AI can tailor digital Cognitive Behavioral Therapy (CBT) programs to address specific negative thought patterns of an individual, enhancing the therapy's relevance and effectiveness [13]. This personalized approach ensures that each patient receives care that is uniquely suited to their needs, significantly improving the chances of successful treatment.

AI-powered DTx are designed to be engaging and accessible. Through interactive elements like games, guided meditation, and behavioral activation tasks, these systems maintain user engagement, which is crucial for the effectiveness of any therapeutic intervention [14]. Accessibility is significantly enhanced as these interventions are available on digital devices, enabling users to access care at their convenience without the stigma or logistical challenges of traditional therapy sessions. This digital availability broadens the reach of mental health care, making it more inclusive and reducing barriers to access.

The multipronged care approach facilitated by AI-powered DTx addresses the complex nature of mental health disorders. By combining various therapeutic methods — from problem-solving therapies to behavioral activation and mindfulness — AI-powered DTx can offer comprehensive treatment plans that cater to the multifaceted needs of individuals [15]. This holistic approach not only targets specific symptoms but also works on building resilience and promoting overall mental well-being. By integrating different therapeutic modalities, AI-powered DTx ensure that treatment is comprehensive and effective.

AI in DTx continuously learns from user interactions, feedback, and progress, allowing these systems to adapt and evolve over time. This dynamic learning capability ensures that the therapeutic content remains relevant to the user's changing needs and preferences. Additionally, detailed tracking and analysis provide personalized insights that can empower users in their mental health journey, promoting a sense of control and involvement in their own treatment. This adaptability and continuous improvement are key strengths of AI-powered DTx, ensuring that care remains effective and up-to-date.

2.3 AI-powered DTx for developmental disorders

Innovations in AI-powered DTx for developmental disorders such as Autism Spectrum Disorder (ASD) and Attention-Deficit/Hyperactivity Disorder (ADHD) represent a significant leap forward in personalized medicine. The development of an AI-powered DTx system to diagnose developmental disorders using ML models marks a pivotal advancement. By analyzing patients' responses and clinical characteristics, this system intelligently predicts the most relevant subsequent questions, significantly reducing the length of questionnaires without compromising diagnostic accuracy. This efficiency is crucial in addressing the extensive time commitment and variability in symptom presentation that challenge traditional diagnostic methods [16].

The integration of ML for diagnosing ADHD addresses a critical need for more accessible and precise diagnostic tools. By evaluating clinical parameters and refining the model's accuracy with data from previously diagnosed patients, this system improves the diagnostic process. This approach not only enhances accuracy but also ensures that the diagnostic process is streamlined and less burdensome for both patients and healthcare providers. The ability to rapidly and accurately diagnose ADHD allows for earlier intervention, which can significantly improve patient outcomes [17].

Wearable devices equipped with AI algorithms for continuous learning from users' environmental and physiological cues represent a novel approach to managing developmental disorders. These devices catalog user-specific cues and resolutions, offering highly personalized support aimed at improving training, comfort, and focus [18]. The use of DL to process data from sensors and cameras further enhances the device's ability to recognize and respond to the user's focus or distraction states, tailoring interventions accordingly. This continuous, adaptive support is particularly valuable for individuals with developmental disorders, as it provides real-time assistance and promotes greater independence.

The incorporation of personalized entertaining elements into therapeutic sessions for individuals with developmental disorders exemplifies the potential of AI in enhancing treatment efficacy. By using visual and auditory stimuli, patient movement tracking, and AI precision, therapy sessions are dynamically adjusted in real time to match patient performance and engagement levels. This personalized approach ensures that therapy remains engaging and effective, addressing the unique needs and preferences of each patient. The ability to adapt therapeutic interventions in real time based on patient responses enhances the overall effectiveness of treatment and promotes sustained engagement.

AI-powered DTx innovations offer promising avenues for improving the diagnosis and treatment of developmental disorders. By leveraging AI, these innovations not only enhance diagnostic accuracy and treatment personalization but also increase the accessibility of care. For patients, this means shorter paths to accurate diagnoses, more engaging and effective treatments, and the potential for better outcomes. For healthcare providers, these innovations promise more efficient diagnostic processes, tools for continuous patient monitoring, and dynamic therapeutic interventions tailored to each patient's unique needs. The integration of AI for developmental disorders holds the potential to significantly improve both patient experiences and clinical outcomes, making care more responsive and effective for those affected by ASD, ADHD, and other developmental disorders.

2.4 AI-powered DTx for diabetes

AI powered DTx for diabetes represent a transformative advancement in managing diabetes and other cardiometabolic disorders. These innovations emphasize the crucial role of personalized and behaviorally focused treatments, addressing the limitations of traditional approaches that often overlook individual behavioral patterns contributing to disease progression [19].

The adaptability of AI-powered DTx is a key advantage in diabetes management. The AI-powered DTx system not only customizes initial treatment plans but also continuously adjusts these plans based on ongoing patient progress. By doing so, it addresses the patient's unique needs more effectively than static treatment protocols. This dynamic customization is crucial for fostering better disease management and improving patient outcomes. Patients receive personalized interventions that evolve with their condition, ensuring that the therapy remains relevant and effective over time.

Healthcare professionals often struggle to keep up with the expanding medical knowledge base and the intricacies of individual patient data. The capabilities within AI-powered DTx can assimilate and apply this vast, often conflicting, array of information, tailoring therapy to individual patient profiles based on biometric and lifestyle data. By analyzing various factors, including clinical and demographic data, ML models can predict user engagement levels, optimizing treatment plans and tailoring outreach efforts to keep patients engaged without feeling overwhelmed.

The integration of AI in diabetes DTx also enhances healthcare providers' ability to make informed decisions based on data-driven insights. This approach not only improves the efficacy of diabetes management but also streamlines the treatment process, making it more efficient and effective. The predictive capabilities of ML models enable the optimization of patient engagement strategies, ensuring that interventions are both timely and impactful. This data-driven approach empowers healthcare providers to deliver more precise and personalized care, ultimately leading to better patient outcomes.

2.5 Large language models for precision digital therapeutics

Large Language Models (LLMs) in Generative AI, such as OpenAI's ChatGPT-4, are highly sophisticated tools capable of understanding, generating, and manipulating human language. These models have shown proficiency in a wide range of language-related tasks, including answering questions, writing essays, summarizing documents, and translating languages. This versatility makes LLMs invaluable across various sectors, particularly in healthcare, where they enhance diagnostics, treatment, and patient management [20].

LLMs are increasingly being utilized in fields like oncology, neurology, and mental health to improve diagnostic accuracy and streamline treatment processes. By integrating with wearable sensor technology, LLMs can analyze vital physiological data such as heart rate variability and step counts. This combination enables predictive healthcare by allowing personalized health monitoring and early interventions for at-risk individuals. For example, continuous monitoring through wearable devices provides real-time data that LLMs can analyze to predict health outcomes, thus facilitating timely and personalized medical interventions. (i.e., "For details, see [21].")

While LLMs hold significant potential, challenges remain in ensuring the accuracy and reliability of their recommendations, especially in complex medical decisions. One major issue is the potential for LLMs to generate biased or incorrect outputs, known as hallucinations. These hallucinations can arise from the vast and diverse datasets on which the models are trained, leading to recommendations that are not always grounded in accurate medical evidence. To mitigate these risks, it is crucial to implement robust validation mechanisms and continuous monitoring. Additionally, the sheer scale and complexity of LLMs pose a challenge for interpretability. With models containing billions of parameters, developing efficient and effective interpretation algorithms is essential to provide meaningful insights without overwhelming healthcare professionals [22].

Precision Digital Therapeutics (PDTx) is an innovative approach that integrates precision medicine principles with digital health interventions. PDTx utilizes sophisticated software-driven therapies tailored to individual patient profiles, based on comprehensive analyses of genetic, environmental, and lifestyle data. This approach aims to enhance treatment efficacy, minimize side effects, and improve overall patient outcomes by delivering highly individualized therapeutic interventions through digital systems [23].

LLMs significantly enhance PDTx by integrating diverse data types to provide a comprehensive view of an individual's health status. This integration allows healthcare providers to offer more effective and personalized care by analyzing various data streams to create holistic health profiles [24].

LLMs excel in processing and analyzing genomic data to identify individual variations that affect treatment responses. This capability allows for the development of personalized treatment plans targeting specific genetic markers associated with diseases. For instance, LLMs can predict pathogenic variants and gene expression, which are critical for designing tailored treatments. These models facilitate a deeper understanding of the genomic underpinnings of diseases, enabling healthcare providers to develop more effective and individualized therapeutic strategies.

In addition to genomic information, LLMs consider environmental exposures and lifestyle habits such as diet, exercise, and stress to tailor interventions. This holistic approach ensures that treatments are not only effective but also sustainable in the patient's daily life. By incorporating data on environmental and lifestyle factors, LLMs help create interventions that align with the patient's real-world conditions, thereby enhancing adherence and long-term success.

LLMs can analyze vast datasets to identify patterns and predict treatment outcomes. LLMs enable the development of highly personalized and adaptive therapeutic interventions, enhancing the precision and effectiveness of treatments. By leveraging LLMs, healthcare providers can uncover insights that inform better clinical decisions and personalized care strategies [25].

Telemedicine including home care and remote monitoring is also a crucial aspect of PDTx, supported by digital systems that facilitate these capabilities. PDTx allows healthcare providers to deliver personalized care and support to patients regardless of their geographic location, improving access to precision therapies. Remote monitoring ensures continuous care management, enabling healthcare providers to track patient health metrics in real time and intervene promptly when necessary. This approach not only enhances patient engagement but also ensures that care is proactive and responsive to individual needs [26].

2.6 AI-powered digital twins for DTx innovation

AI-powered Digital Twins (DTs) in healthcare represent a transformative approach to medical care by significantly enhancing how patient data are used for diagnosis, treatment, and disease management. A DT in this context is a dynamic virtual model that mirrors the physical state of a patient, continuously updated with real-time data from various sources [27].

These DTs integrate complex data sets, including electronic health records (EHRs), genomic data, imaging studies, and real-time physiological measurements from IoT devices. This comprehensive integration enables healthcare providers to view a detailed model of a patient's health status, allowing for more precise and personalized care plans [28].

AI-powered DTs are particularly useful in the development of DTx and in clinical trials. For instance, these models can simulate how different therapies might affect a patient's health, allowing for the optimization of treatment plans before they are applied in the real world. This capability reduces the risk of adverse effects and increases the effectiveness of treatments by tailoring them to the unique needs of each patient [29].

In clinical trials, AI-powered DTs can be used to create highly accurate simulations of patient outcomes. This application, known as TwinRCTs, involves using DTs to forecast potential outcomes for patients in control and treatment groups, thereby reducing the number of participants needed and shortening the time required to reach conclusions. This method not only speeds up the clinical trial process but also enhances the reliability of the results by providing more robust data for analysis [30].

3. XR-powered DTx innovations

3.1 XR-powered DTx for Alzheimer's disease

Utilizing XR technologies can significantly enhance the diagnostic process for AD by engaging patients in an immersive environment. This approach facilitates early detection by assessing cognitive functions in a controlled yet flexible virtual space. The use of digital avatars enhances the sense of embodiment, which is crucial for emotional and cognitive engagement, stimulating brain regions essential for cognitive health. By immersing patients in 3D environments to perform tasks assessing spatial orientation, memory recall, and other cognitive functions, the system offers a realistic and engaging method for early detection of cognitive impairments [31].

XR-powered DTx are being explored for their potential to stabilize and enhance cognitive functions in AD patients through cognitive rehabilitation in a virtual environment. This includes simulating daily living activities for physical therapy, offering a safe and controlled setting for patients to manage physical symptoms and engage in therapeutic exercises. By providing interactive missions and tasks tailored to the user's cognitive abilities and needs, XR can deliver personalized treatment regimens aimed at improving cognitive functions [32].

By simulating real-world conditions and challenges, XR environments can assess and enhance key cognitive functions in an engaging and interactive manner.

Combining XR with emotion recognition technologies offers a novel therapeutic tool for individuals with AD. These devices adjust content in real time based on the user's emotional state, providing a personalized and responsive therapeutic experience. Utilizing XR environments to deliver content that stimulates cognitive functions offers a dynamic approach to therapy [33].

An example of XR-powered DTx for AD treatment is to deliver reminiscence therapy (RT), a form of behavioral intervention that stimulates memory and emotional well-being through the recollection of past experiences. This innovative approach has significant implications for cognitive health, especially in addressing challenges like isolation, mood deterioration, and memory decline in senior patients and those with cognitive impairments. This approach not only stimulates cognitive functions through vivid recollections of the past but also promotes social connections among users. By experiencing XR in groups, elderly patients can share their journeys with peers, effectively reducing the feelings of isolation and enhancing their overall mood and well-being [34].

3.2 XR-powered DTx for mental health

Utilizing XR, through immersive environments and interactive virtual sessions, allows for the simulation of scenarios or the creation of unique, engaging environments tailored to address specific mental health issues like anxiety, depression, PTSD, and more. This personalized approach ensures that therapy is relevant and effective for each individual, enhancing the likelihood of successful outcomes.

Mental health care access is often hindered by factors such as stigma, geographical limitations, and the availability of mental health professionals. XR technologies can significantly mitigate these barriers by making therapy more accessible and less stigmatizing. Individuals can engage in therapy sessions within the privacy and comfort of their own homes, reducing the stigma associated with seeking mental health care. Additionally, XR allows for remote access to therapy, which is particularly beneficial for populations in remote or underserved areas where traditional mental health services are scarce [35].

By creating a multi-sensory environment that adapts in real time to the patient's emotional and cognitive states, XR offers a novel way to address mental health conditions. This closed-loop system, integrating visual, auditory, tactile, and olfactory stimuli, enhances the user's sense of presence in the virtual environment, potentially increasing the therapeutic benefits of the treatment. Sensory immersion can help in creating a more profound therapeutic experience, aiding in relaxation, stress reduction, and overall mental well-being.

XR allows for the incorporation of various therapeutic techniques, including exposure therapy, CBT, and mindfulness practices, within immersive environments [36]. This versatility supports a comprehensive approach to mental health treatment, enabling the addressing of a wide range of conditions with tailored interventions. The ability to dynamically adjust these interventions based on real-time feedback and biometric monitoring further enhances the personalization and effectiveness of treatment. This flexibility ensures that therapy can be precisely aligned with the patient's current needs and progress.

The use of interactive XR content, resembling game-like scenarios, represents a significant innovation in engaging patients with emotional disorders. This approach not only makes therapy more engaging but also helps in diverting the patient's attention toward achievable goals, thereby improving their emotional well-being. The interactive nature of these treatments, coupled with the ability to track progress and adapt interventions, offers a dynamic and effective approach to mental health care. Gamification of therapy can make the process more enjoyable and less daunting, encouraging sustained participation and engagement.

XR Therapeutics, a UK-based XR-powered DTx for mental health product development company, is pioneering a cutting-edge approach to mental health treatment through the integration of VR technology with CBT, offering a promising avenue for individuals grappling with various forms of anxiety and phobias. This innovative treatment methodology is designed to harness the immersive power of VR to create a controlled, safe environment where patients can confront and learn to manage their anxiety triggers under the guidance and support of experienced therapists.

At the heart of XR therapeutics' approach is the use of VR to create highly detailed, lifelike virtual environments within their Immersive Studio [37]. This allows for the simulation of specific scenarios that patients find challenging, from social situations and public speaking to more specific phobias such as fear of heights, insects, or dogs. What sets this treatment apart is the ability of therapists to fully control and customize these digital scenes in real-time, adjusting exposure levels, sound, character interactions, and scene elements to tailor the experience to each patient's unique needs and triggers.

Patients navigate these scenarios, starting with a low level of difficulty and gradually progressing to more challenging levels as they develop coping strategies and become more comfortable facing their fears. This progression is carefully managed by therapists who guide patients through each step, ensuring a supportive and therapeutic experience. For example, a patient with a fear of crowded busses might start by getting on an empty bus in the VR environment, with the scenario gradually including more people as they become ready to face a busier setting.

The ability to create and display interactive virtual environments that closely mimic real-life scenarios, customized to reflect a patient's individual anxiety triggers and cultural preferences, marks a significant advancement in personalized mental health care. This approach not only addresses the specific fears and anxieties of each patient but also respects and incorporates their cultural background and personal experiences into the treatment plan, ensuring a more effective and compassionate therapeutic process.

The following case studies, as illustrated graphically in **Figure 1**, provide a vivid illustration of how XR-powered DTx are making significant strides in the treatment of various phobias and anxieties.

3.2.1 Case study 1: fear of flying

This case involved an adult female with a debilitating fear of flying, especially turbulence, which induced extreme pre-flight anxiety. Through four VR sessions, the patient was gradually exposed to the entire flying process, including the replication of turbulence, with the added customization of a night flight scenario to address her specific fears. Post-treatment, the patient experienced substantial improvement, successfully applying relaxation techniques during a real flight and even planning future travels with enthusiasm. This case exemplifies how VR can safely expose individuals to their fears in a controlled, therapeutic setting, enabling them to overcome anxieties with real-life applications.

Figure 1.
Graphical illustration of case studies (These images are created by the author using ChatGPT 4).

3.2.2 Case study 2: fear of heights

An adult female with a longstanding fear of heights underwent VR therapy, which included exposure to heights in various scenarios, such as a building with a glass balcony and a chair ski lift. This gradual exposure helped her manage her anxiety effectively, resulting in a significant decrease in her fear, thereby broadening her and her family's activity range. Observational involvement of the family during sessions provided them insights into the therapeutic techniques, fostering a supportive environment for the patient. This case highlights the versatility of VR in simulating real-life situations that directly impact a patient's daily life and familial interactions.

3.2.3 Case study 3: fear of open spaces

A professional woman with a fear of open spaces due to past trauma experienced significant lifestyle limitations. Through VR therapy that replicated gradually more challenging open spaces, she learned to manage her anxiety in small, manageable steps. Post-treatment, she reported increased confidence in engaging with previously anxiety-inducing spaces, illustrating the effectiveness of incremental exposure therapy in VR settings. Her ability to now partake in activities with her children in open spaces showcases the profound personal and familial impact of this treatment.

3.2.4 Case study 4: Emetophobia (vomiting phobia)

A 30-year-old female with a severe phobia of vomiting underwent VR therapy, where she was exposed to a hierarchy of feared situations involving vomiting. Through the sessions, she developed the confidence to manage her anxiety and the physical manifestations of her phobia. The significant lifestyle changes post-treatment, including the ability to travel and socialize freely, demonstrate the transformative potential of VR therapy. The involvement of her partner in observing the therapy sessions underscores the importance of a supportive environment in the therapeutic process.

These case studies collectively demonstrate the efficacy of XR-powered DTx in treating a variety of phobias and anxieties. The technology allows for highly personalized and controlled exposure therapy, engaging patients in a safe and supportive environment. The incremental exposure to feared situations, coupled with the development of coping strategies, provides patients with the tools needed to confront and manage their anxieties effectively.

3.3 XR-powered DTx for developmental disorders

For children with ADHD, XR technology offers a unique method for both detecting the disorder and providing targeted training to address specific challenges such as attention deficits, coordination issues, and memory difficulties. By creating multiple virtual scenes tailored to the individual needs of the user, this XR-powered DTx system provides a highly engaging and personalized training experience. The immersive nature of these environments not only increases user engagement but also allows for the continuous monitoring of brainwave signals to assess attention levels in real time. This approach enhances the effectiveness of ADHD treatment by providing targeted interventions designed to improve academic performance, physical coordination, mental health, and overall quality of life [38].

The use of XR technology in treating developmental disorders introduces a dynamic and personalized approach to therapy. By projecting an augmented version of a healthcare professional into the patient's field of vision, XR enables therapy sessions to be conducted in the comfort of the patient's own environment. This method adds a layer of comfort and familiarity to the therapy process, potentially increasing patient engagement and reducing therapy dropout rates.

Imagine a scenario where a person is learning to navigate a busy city street, which can be particularly challenging for individuals with ASD due to the overwhelming sensory input and the need for complex social interactions. This scenario can illustrate the differences among VR, AR, and MR in a learning context for ADS treatment:

In a VR environment, the individual wears a VR headset and is fully immersed in a digitally constructed city street. There are no real-world visuals or sounds – everything the user sees and hears is part of the virtual simulation. The person can practice crossing the street, avoiding obstacles, and interacting with virtual passersby through predefined scripts or cues. The VR setting allows for repeated practice in a controlled environment without the unpredictability of real-life interactions. However, transferring these learned behaviors to the real world might require additional guidance and support, as the sensory experiences and social cues in VR may differ significantly from those in a real city street.

Using AR, the individual might wear smart glasses or use a tablet that overlays digital information onto the real world. For example, as they look at a real city street through their device, they might see arrows guiding them when to cross the street safely or icons above people's heads suggesting appropriate social interactions (like saying "hello" or "excuse me"). AR enhances the real-world experience by adding interactive elements but does not replace the real environment with a digital one. The challenge here is maintaining engagement and ensuring the digital overlays are helpful without becoming distracting or overwhelming.

In an MR setup, the individual might wear a headset capable of blending digital objects with the real world. For example, while standing on a real city sidewalk, they see a holographic guide dog that leads them across the street, teaching them when it's safe to cross while real cars pass by. They might also interact with a mix of real people and holographic avatars that demonstrate appropriate social behaviors. MR offers a more integrated experience, where digital and physical elements coexist, providing a more seamless transition of skills learned in the therapeutic session to real-life situations.

3.4 XR-powered DTx for neurological health

At the forefront of modern therapeutic strategies, XR technologies aim to enhance neuroplasticity – the brain's ability to reorganize itself by forming new neural connections. This capability is crucial for recovery from brain injuries and combating neurodegenerative diseases. XR can simulate real-world environments and tasks in a controlled, immersive setting, which stimulates specific brain regions like the hippocampus, essential for memory and spatial navigation. For example, tasks that mimic real-life challenges can improve spatial learning and memory more effectively than traditional, less immersive methods. This immersive approach provides a dynamic way to engage the brain in rehabilitation exercises, fostering neuroplastic changes and enhancing cognitive functions [39].

The potential applications of XR-powered DTx innovations in treating neurological conditions are vast. For epilepsy, modulating hippocampal activity through tailored virtual experiences could offer new therapeutic avenues. XR-powered DTx innovations extend to cognitive rehabilitation, where the XR-powered DTx system guides patients through exercises designed to rehabilitate spatial attention deficits and improve upper-limb function post-stroke [40]. These innovations employ computational assessments, real-time feedback, and adaptive difficulty levels to tailor the therapy to each patient's needs, ensuring an engaging and effective rehabilitation process.

For instance, a patient recovering from a stroke might use an XR environment to practice reaching and grasping tasks that are progressively more challenging, promoting recovery of motor function. Such approaches can significantly enhance rehabilitation intensity and outcomes compared to traditional methods, providing a more interactive and motivating therapeutic experiences.

MedRhythms, a US-based XR-powered DTx for neurological health product development company, is at the vanguard of neurorehabilitation, blending Rhythmic Auditory Stimulation (RAS) with AR to pioneer a novel approach in the treatment of walking disabilities caused by neurological injuries or diseases. This innovative therapy merges the therapeutic power of music with cutting-edge technology to create a personalized and engaging rehabilitation experience for patients with neurological conditions such as stroke, multiple sclerosis, and Parkinson's disease.

MedRhythms utilizes RAS, an evidence-based intervention grounded in music therapy principles and neuroscience research. RAS has been shown to significantly improve walking impairments by targeting neural circuitry involved in motor function. The MedRhythms platform employs algorithmically generated music and rhythmic cueing, tailored to each patient's biometric data, thereby introducing an interactive element that fosters adherence to therapy protocols and enhances the rehabilitation process [41].

The integration of AR visual content with RAS offers a uniquely immersive therapeutic experience. By creating dynamic 3-D models from images or videos, MedRhythms ensures that each therapy session is not only personalized but also contextually relevant to the patient's specific rehabilitation needs. This approach significantly increases patient engagement by synchronizing personalized AR visual content with beat signals, creating an interactive environment that motivates patients to participate actively in their rehabilitation.

The AR visual content provided by MedRhythms, as illustrated graphically in **Figure 2**, features a virtual treadmill and footprints paced to the music's rhythm, with an animated figure mirroring the intended repetitive motions. This setup, adjustable in real-time to the music's tempo, offers a comprehensive and supportive AR environment that encourages physical engagement and coordination. The dynamic customization of the AR experience, including adjustments to footprints spacing, animation speed, and virtual obstacles, significantly contributes to the rehabilitation process, making it a highly effective and forward-thinking approach to neurological rehabilitation.

As research and development in this field continue to advance, the potential for XR technologies to improve the quality of life for patients with neurological disorders becomes increasingly tangible. These technologies can transform how neurological

Figure 2.
Graphical illustration of AR visual content (These images are created by the author using ChatGPT 4).

DOI: http://dx.doi.org/10.5772/intechopen.1006619

conditions are diagnosed, treated, and managed, offering new hope for effective interventions. The immersive and adaptive nature of XR experiences can address both the cognitive and physical aspects of neurological rehabilitation, making them a versatile tool in the hands of healthcare providers. As these innovations are further refined and integrated into clinical practice, they promise to deliver more precise, engaging, and effective therapeutic options for patients, ultimately leading to better health outcomes and improved quality of life.

3.5 XR-powered DTx for pain management

XR-powered DTx for pain management represents a transformative shift in how pain is approached and treated within healthcare. This innovative strategy leverages the power of XR to offer a non-pharmacological alternative that complements traditional drug therapies, introducing a new dimension of personalized, patient-centered care. By immersing patients in serene, engaging virtual environments, XR provides distraction therapy that can significantly lessen pain sensations and potentially reduce reliance on opioid medications, which are often associated with adverse side effects and a high risk of dependency [42].

At the forefront of XR-powered pain management is the development and application of specialized XR therapy content. Utilizing the unique capabilities of XR, these therapies create immersive experiences specifically tailored for pain relief. These experiences engage the patient's senses through visually rich environments, auditory relaxation scripts, and, when applicable, tactile feedback. By transporting patients to virtual sanctuaries designed to induce profound relaxation, XR therapy offers a holistic, multisensory immersion that makes it a powerful alternative to conventional pain management techniques, which often fail to address the complex needs of patients suffering from cancer-related and chronic pain.

A key component of XR-powered DTx's effectiveness in pain management is its ability to dynamically adjust therapeutic content in real time, responding to the user's physiological and psychological feedback. This adaptability ensures that therapy remains highly tailored and responsive, enhancing its potential to induce desired behavioral and emotional changes. For example, a VR simulation designed to alleviate pain might alter its environment based on the patient's stress levels or pain intensity, providing calming experiences or simulating scenarios that visually represent the healing process or the negative consequences of unhealthy habits like smoking. This real-time responsiveness makes XR therapy a versatile and effective tool in pain management.

3.6 XR-powered DTx for behavioral addictions

XR-powered DTx for behavioral addictions, including Substance Use Disorder, represents a significant innovation in behavioral health care. This cutting-edge approach leverages the immersive and multisensory capabilities of XR technologies to create therapeutic environments that deeply engage individuals in their treatment process. Positioned at the intersection of technology, psychology, and personalized medicine, XR-powered DTx transcends the boundaries of conventional therapeutic methods, which often fall short in terms of interactivity and customization [43].

The efficacy of XR-powered DTx innovations in behavioral addiction treatment is rooted in their mechanism of action, which involves immersing users in virtual environments that adjust continuously based on real-time biometric feedback. This creates a personalized feedback loop that elicits targeted psychological and physiological responses, promoting behavior change. The technology's capacity to monitor and adapt to the user's reactions in real-time enhances both engagement and effectiveness of therapeutic interventions, offering a level of personalization previously unattainable in traditional therapy settings. This personalized feedback loop is crucial for maintaining patient engagement and ensuring that the therapy adapts to their evolving needs.

By simulating real-life scenarios that trigger addictive behaviors, XR therapy allows patients to confront and manage their cravings in a controlled environment, building resilience and enhancing their ability to cope with triggers in the real world. Combining the immersive capabilities of XR with the structured techniques of CBT can create a comprehensive therapeutic approach that addresses both the psychological and physiological aspects of addiction.

4. XR and AI convergence powered DTx innovations

The convergence of XR and AI in DTx marks an advancement in the realm of immersive, personalized, and intelligent therapeutic solutions. This synergy leverages the strengths of both technologies to tailor experiences that are not only deeply engaging but also highly interactive. Particularly in mental health, this integration is instrumental in managing a wide array of conditions, from anxiety and depression to PTSD and ASD. By providing immersive digital therapeutic interventions that prioritize personalization, this combination enhances mental resilience and offers effective management solutions.

4.1 AI for augmenting XR powered DTx

AI plays a crucial role in augmenting XR environments by driving the creation of realistic visual content and crafting immersive storytelling experiences and interactive training programs. AI's capability to generate detailed 3D models, dynamic environments that react in real-time, and lifelike avatars enriches XR applications, making them more engaging and authentic [44]. These technological advancements significantly contribute to the efficacy of therapeutic interventions by making the user experience more immersive and emotionally engaging. For example, in treating PTSD, AI can create safe yet challenging virtual scenarios that help patients confront and process traumatic experiences within a controlled and supportive environment.

As an illustration of AI for the creation of realistic visual content, Senkiva, a US-based DTx innovation company, introduces the Sensory Immersion Vessel (SIV) for various digital treatment delivery, including stress reduction, mood enhancement, and cognitive improvement. The SIV is designed to create a fully immersive sensory environment that dynamically adapts to an individual's emotional and cognitive states. This immersive experience is achieved through a closed-loop system that adjusts the immersive sensory environment in real time using AI to the user's physiological responses [45].

The SIV provides customizable and interactive digital medicine experiences, as illustrated graphically in **Figure 3**, catering to a range of therapeutic needs through four immersive virtual environment categories: Relax, Restore, Meditate, and Transform. Each category is designed to elicit specific sensory and emotional responses, utilizing a diverse array of sensory stimulations for targeted therapeutic outcomes.

Figure 3.
Graphical illustration of digital medicine experiences (These images are created by the author using ChatGPT 4).

In the Relax Category, the focus is on mental and physical unwinding through serene environments. The "Field of Grass" experience immerses users in a tranquil grassy field with synchronized visual, auditory, olfactory, and tactile elements, enhancing relaxation. The "Deep Space" environment transports users to the expanses of space, with sensory stimulations that align with the vastness and tranquility of the cosmos, promoting a state of awe and relaxation.

The Restore Category is tailored to rejuvenate focus and energy. The "Living Painting" environment engages users in a creative zero-gravity space, combining visual, auditory, and tactile stimuli to renew mental vitality. The "Crystal Cave" setting offers a mystical exploration experience, with glowing crystals and a cave setting that restores mental energy through engaging sensory interactions.

In the Meditate Category, the emphasis is on guiding users toward deep meditation and mindfulness. The "Aspen Trees" setting provides a tranquil forest environment, complete with sensory elements that enhance meditation. The "Floating Clouds" experience positions users amidst drifting clouds, facilitating a deep meditative state through synchronized sensory inputs.

The Transform Category aims to alter consciousness and foster a sense of unity and connection. The "Souls Birth" experience offers an abstract journey from darkness to a pulsing womb, using synchronized sensory stimulations for a transformative effect. "Quantum Oneness" immerses users in a quantum field, using particle systems and tactile interactions to create a sense of oneness with the environment.

The collaboration between AI and XR opens up new possibilities in healthcare delivery [46]. AI's ability to analyze XR-generated data presents exciting opportunities, such as developing virtual patient models for enhanced diagnostics and crafting therapeutic gaming experiences that are both fun and beneficial. For instance, AI can monitor a patient's reactions and progress within a virtual reality game designed for CBT, adapting the game's difficulty and content in real-time to ensure optimal therapeutic benefits. This integration underscores the potential for creating highly effective and engaging therapeutic interventions that are tailored to individual patient needs.

4.2 Convergence of XR spatial computing with AI

The convergence of XR spatial computing with AI represents a transformative direction for DTx. Devices like Apple Vision Pro are leading the way, showcasing the immense potential of spatial computing and XR technologies in revolutionizing DTx. By integrating these advanced technologies, healthcare providers can offer more sophisticated, interactive, and effective DTx solutions.

Apple Vision Pro demonstrates how XR spatial computing can redefine interactions between healthcare providers and patients. By leveraging spatial environments, these technologies make treatment plans more understandable and engaging. Applications like Cedars-Sinai's Xaia app, which utilizes Apple Vision Pro for AI-enabled mental health support, illustrate the wide-ranging impact of XR technologies in healthcare. These applications facilitate everything from diagnosis and treatment to mental health and wellness, creating a more immersive and interactive healthcare experience [47].

5. Limitations and challenges in AI- and XR-powered DTx innovations

The integration of AI and XR into DTx offers transformative potential for healthcare. However, several significant limitations and challenges must be addressed to fully realize their benefits and ensure sustainable implementation. Each of these challenges requires careful consideration and strategic solutions.

5.1 Ethical considerations

The implementation of AI and XR technologies in healthcare demands a robust ethical framework to guide their development and deployment. Privacy concerns are paramount, as these technologies must handle sensitive health data with the utmost confidentiality to prevent unauthorized access and breaches. There is also a crucial need for algorithmic transparency. AI algorithms should not operate as "black boxes," but rather, they must be transparent in their decision-making processes, allowing for accountability and fostering trust. Additionally, there is the challenge of minimizing biases in AI algorithms that could lead to unequal treatment or discrimination in patient care [48].

5.2 Data protection and security

The sensitive nature of the data collected through AI and XR applications makes its protection a top priority. This involves implementing and maintaining advanced cybersecurity measures to safeguard patient data from breaches and cyber-attacks. Adherence to global data protection laws, such as the GDPR in the European Union and HIPAA in the United States, is essential as these laws dictate strict guidelines on the handling of medical information. Moreover, the development of data anonymization techniques is critical to allow the use of data for research and improvement of services while ensuring individual privacy is maintained [49].

5.3 Consent and transparency

Maintaining trust through transparent operations and informed consent is critical. Clear communication is essential, providing patients with understandable information about what data are collected, how it is used, and whom it is shared with. It is also vital to ensure that participation in these technologies is voluntary, allowing patients to opt out without losing access to standard care. Furthermore, facilitating mechanisms for patients to provide ongoing consent, especially as technologies or their applications evolve, is necessary to address the dynamic nature of these innovations.

5.4 Technical integration

Integrating new technologies with existing healthcare IT systems presents multiple technical hurdles. Ensuring interoperability between new AI and XR systems and existing EHRs and other healthcare technologies is essential. This might involve upgrading or adapting legacy systems that may not initially be compatible with cutting-edge AI and XR applications. Another significant challenge is developing solutions that can be scaled across different healthcare settings, including those with varying levels of technological advancement.

5.5 Accessibility and adoption

Ensuring wide adoption and accessibility of AI and XR in healthcare involves addressing several factors. The requirement for specific hardware for XR applications, which may not be readily available or affordable for all patients or healthcare providers, poses a significant barrier. Enhancing the digital skills of both healthcare providers and patients is crucial for the effective use of AI and XR technologies. Moreover, overcoming skepticism and resistance to adopting new technologies in traditional healthcare settings is necessary to achieve cultural and social acceptance [50].

5.6 Clinical validation

Proving the clinical efficacy and safety of AI- and XR-powered DTx is essential. This involves conducting extensive and rigorous clinical trials to establish the effectiveness and safety of DTx solutions enhanced by AI and XR. Navigating the complex regulatory landscape to gain approval for new therapeutic technologies can be both time-consuming and resource-intensive.

6. Future directions in AI- and XR-powered DTx innovations

6.1 AI-powered DTx innovations

Future innovations in AI-powered DTx for AD will likely focus on multi-modal data integration, real-time monitoring, and cognitive rehabilitation. Multi-modal data integration involves combining genomic, imaging, and behavioral data to create more comprehensive diagnostic models, which can improve diagnostic accuracy and provide deeper insights into disease progression. Continuous monitoring through wearable devices and IoT sensors will become more prevalent, with AI algorithms analyzing real-time data to adapt treatment plans dynamically, ensuring personalized and timely interventions. AI-driven cognitive training programs tailored to individual needs will gain traction, helping to maintain or improve cognitive functions through personalized exercises and activities.

Future advancements in NLP will enable more nuanced understanding and analysis of patient communications, improving the detection of subtle mental health issues. Combining AI analysis with biometric data from wearables (e.g., heart rate, sleep patterns) will provide a holistic view of mental health, allowing for more accurate and personalized interventions.

AI will create personalized virtual learning environments tailored to each child's specific needs, improving engagement and outcomes in educational and therapeutic settings. Advanced AI algorithms will analyze real-time behavioral data, providing immediate feedback and interventions to support children with developmental disorders. Systems that facilitate collaboration between caregivers, educators, and healthcare providers will ensure a comprehensive support system for children with developmental disorders.

AI models will predict potential complications and recommend preventive measures, enhancing proactive diabetes management. Integration of AI-driven behavioral coaching programs will provide personalized guidance and support for lifestyle changes, such as diet and exercise. Development of interconnected ecosystem where AI-powered DTx systems integrate with other health monitoring systems will create comprehensive diabetes management solutions.

LLMs will increasingly analyze genomic data to develop personalized treatment plans targeting specific genomic markers associated with diseases. Incorporating data on environmental exposures and lifestyle habits will create holistic health profiles and tailored interventions. LLMs will support advanced telemedicine systems, providing real-time, personalized medical advice, and monitoring.

Digital Twins will continuously update with real-time data from wearables and IoT devices, providing up-to-date patient models. Advanced AI algorithms will predict disease progression and treatment outcomes, allowing for proactive and personalized healthcare. Digital Twins will simulate clinical trials, reducing the need for large participant numbers and accelerating the research process.

6.2 XR-powered DTx innovations

Developing more sophisticated XR environments for detailed cognitive assessments, incorporating AI for real-time analysis and adaptation, will enhance diagnostic accuracy. Using XR to facilitate social interaction among AD patients will reduce isolation and improve emotional well-being. Combining XR with advanced emotion recognition technologies will create responsive therapeutic experiences based on the patient's emotional state.

Developing AI-driven XR environments that personalize therapy sessions based on real-time biometric and behavioral data will enhance treatment effectiveness. Enhancing remote access capabilities will ensure that XR mental health therapies are available to underserved and remote populations. Integrating additional sensory modalities (e.g., tactile feedback, olfactory stimuli) will create more immersive and effective therapeutic experiences. XR environments tailored to specific mental health conditions (e.g., anxiety, PTSD) will offer immersive therapeutic experiences, enhancing patient engagement and treatment effectiveness.

Developing XR environments that adapt to the unique needs of each child will provide personalized training and support, improving engagement and outcomes. Creating systems that facilitate collaboration between educators, therapists, and caregivers will ensure a comprehensive support system. Utilizing AI to provide real-time feedback and adapt interventions based on the child's behavior and responses will enhance treatment effectiveness.

Developing more sophisticated XR protocols for neurological rehabilitation, incorporating real-time data analysis and adaptive difficulty levels, will enhance treatment effectiveness. Integrating XR technologies with other therapeutic modalities (e.g., music therapy, physiotherapy) will create comprehensive rehabilitation programs. Using AI to develop patient-specific XR interventions based on individual neurological profiles and rehabilitation needs will improve outcomes.

Developing XR environments that adapt in real-time to the patient's pain levels and emotional state will provide personalized pain relief. Incorporating additional sensory modalities (e.g., tactile feedback, olfactory stimuli) will enhance the immersive experience and improve pain management outcomes. Using wearable devices to monitor patients' pain levels continuously will provide data to adapt XR therapies dynamically.

Developing XR environments that adapt in real-time based on the patient's biometric data will provide personalized addiction treatment. Combining XR with CBT techniques will create comprehensive treatment programs for behavioral addictions. Creating XR systems that facilitate support groups and peer interactions will enhance the therapeutic experience.

6.3 XR and AI convergence-powered DTx innovations

AI will continue to improve the realism of XR environments, creating more engaging and effective therapeutic experiences. AI will use data from XR sessions to predict patient outcomes and adapt therapies dynamically, ensuring personalized and effective treatments. Developing integrated systems that combine XR and AI technologies will provide comprehensive and cohesive therapeutic solutions.

XR spatial computing will enable the creation of fully immersive therapeutic environments that can be tailored to individual patient needs. These environments will provide real-time feedback and adjustments based on patient interactions and biometric data, enhancing the effectiveness of DTx interventions.

By integrating AI with XR spatial computing, treatment plans can be made more interactive and dynamic. Patients will be able to visualize their progress and understand complex medical information through immersive 3D models and simulations, leading to better adherence and outcomes.

6.4 Limitations and challenges in AI- and XR-powered DTx innovations

Implementing robust data protection measures and ensuring compliance with data protection regulations will safeguard patient privacy. Developing transparent AI models that provide clear explanations for their decisions will foster trust among users. Using diverse and representative datasets will minimize biases in AI algorithms and ensure equitable treatment.

Implementing advanced cybersecurity measures to protect patient data from breaches and cyber-attacks will enhance security. Developing techniques for data anonymization will allow the use of data for research while maintaining individual privacy. Ensuring adherence to global data protection laws, such as GDPR and HIPAA, will facilitate compliance.

Providing patients with understandable information about data collection, usage, and sharing will enhance transparency. Ensuring that patients can opt out of using AI and XR technologies without losing access to standard care will protect their rights. Facilitating mechanisms for patients to provide ongoing consent as technologies and their applications evolve will address the dynamic nature of these innovations.

Ensuring interoperability between new AI- and XR-powered DTx systems and existing healthcare IT systems will streamline their integration. Upgrading or adapting legacy systems to be compatible with new AI and XR applications will enhance their functionality. Developing solutions that can be scaled across different healthcare settings with varying levels of technological advancement will increase their impact.

Ensuring that XR hardware is affordable and accessible to all patients and healthcare providers will increase adoption. Enhancing the digital skills of healthcare providers and patients to effectively use AI and XR technologies will improve their usability. Addressing skepticism and resistance to adopting new technologies through education and advocacy will facilitate cultural acceptance.

Conducting extensive clinical trials to validate the efficacy and safety of AI- and XR-powered DTx solutions will ensure their reliability. Navigating the regulatory landscape to gain approval for new therapeutic technologies will facilitate their adoption. Implementing continuous monitoring to ensure the ongoing efficacy and safety of AI- and XR-powered DTx solutions will maintain their effectiveness.

7. AI- and XR-powered DTx innovation's commercialization

The commercial potential of AI- and XR-powered DTx innovations is vast, spanning diverse health conditions and offering a modern approach to treatment. These innovations involve developing commercial DTx products that can be effectively marketed and integrated into the healthcare ecosystem. The commercialization journey of these DTx innovations is comprehensive and structured, encompassing several critical phases from ideation to real-world application as illustrated in **Figure 4**.

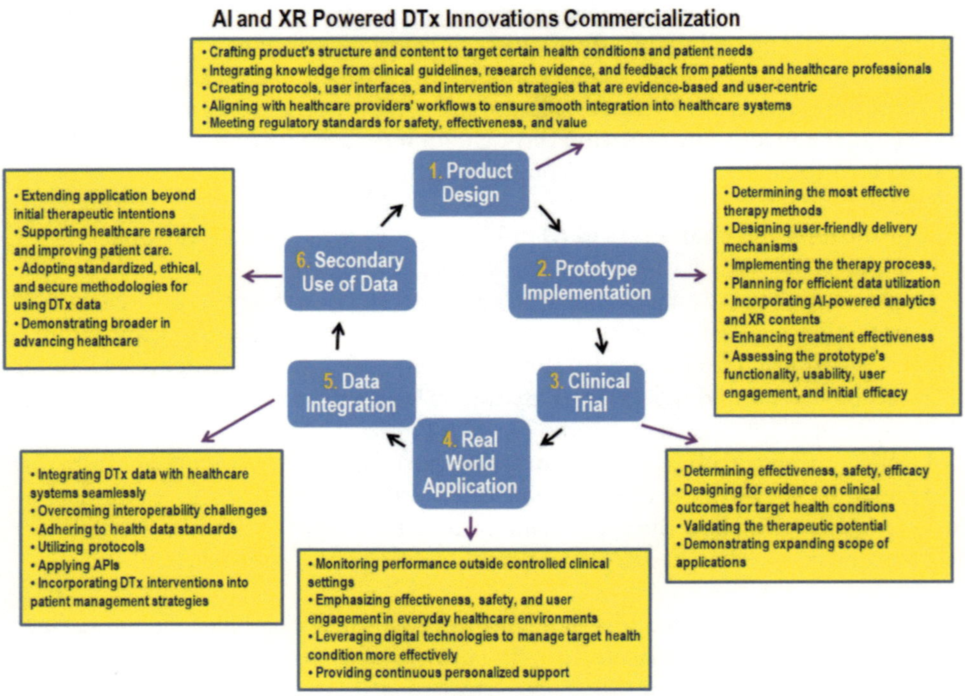

Figure 4.
Commercialization process of AI- and XR-powered DTx innovations.

7.1 Product design

The product design is the foundational step in the commercialization process, where the structure and content of DTx products are meticulously crafted to address specific health conditions and patient needs. This involves integrating clinical guidelines, research evidence, and feedback from patients and healthcare professionals. The goal is to create evidence-based and user-centric protocols, user interfaces and intervention strategies. By aligning these designs with healthcare providers' workflows, DTx products ensure smooth integration into existing healthcare systems. This not only benefits providers and patients but also meets regulatory standards for safety, effectiveness, and value. The emphasis on a user-centric approach ensures that the DTx products are both practical and beneficial in real-world settings [51].

7.2 Prototype implementation

In the prototype implementation, the focus shifts to developing DTx prototypes that cater to patients' unique needs while seamlessly integrating within the broader healthcare ecosystem. This is characterized by an iterative and adaptive process, combining elements such as therapy methods, user-friendly delivery mechanisms, and data utilization plans. Advanced AI-powered analytics and innovative XR content creation enhance treatment effectiveness and patient engagement. Preliminary testing is crucial, assessing functionality, usability, user engagement, and initial efficacy. This stage is underscored by user-centric design principles, rigorous ethical standards, and flexible assessment methodologies. The objective is to develop evidence-based, cost-effective DTx products that promise improved healthcare quality and efficiency [52].

7.3 Clinical trials

Clinical trials play a pivotal role in the DTx commercialization process, determining the effectiveness, safety, and overall efficacy of the products. These trials, often randomized controlled trials (RCTs), are designed to gather clinical evidence across various health conditions. The process involves a comprehensive review and analysis of clinical literature, focusing on target health conditions, and demonstrating the expanding scope of DTx applications. Rigorous assessment during clinical trials is crucial for validating the therapeutic potential of DTx products and fulfilling regulatory requirements. This underscores the potential of DTx to offer effective, evidence-based treatment options through digital systems, paving the way for their commercialization and clinical integration [53].

7.4 Real world application

The real-world application monitors DTx products' performance outside controlled clinical settings, emphasizing effectiveness, safety, and user engagement in everyday healthcare environments. This phase provides invaluable insights into the actual impact of DTx on health outcomes and its integration into standard care practices. Continuous monitoring, personalized support, and leveraging digital technologies are essential for managing health conditions more effectively. This highlights the importance of real-world data in refining and validating DTx products' efficacy and safety in diverse healthcare settings [54].

7.5 DTx data integration

Integrating DTx data with healthcare systems is critical for enriching patient records and providing comprehensive care. Overcoming interoperability challenges involves adhering to health data standards, utilizing protocols, and applying APIs for seamless integration. This integration facilitates a holistic view of patient health for healthcare professionals, incorporating DTx interventions into patient management strategies. Effective data integration ensures that DTx products are seamlessly embedded within existing healthcare infrastructures, enhancing their utility and impact [55].

7.6 Secondary use of DTx data

The secondary use of DTx data extends its application beyond initial therapeutic intentions, supporting healthcare research and improving patient care. By adopting standardized, ethical, and secure methodologies for using DTx data, stakeholders can unlock insights into disease patterns, treatment efficacies, and patient behavior trends. These data can significantly enhance public health strategies and personalized medicine. The broader impact of DTx data in advancing healthcare and treatment paradigms demonstrates its potential to contribute to a deeper understanding of health conditions and improve overall patient outcomes [56].

8. Conclusion

AI- and XR-powered DTx innovations represent a significant leap forward in modern healthcare, offering personalized, immersive, and intelligent solutions that enhance patient engagement, treatment efficacy, and overall health outcomes. By continuing to explore and refine these technologies, the healthcare industry can unlock new potentials for improving patient care and transforming the therapeutic landscape, ultimately leading to a more responsive, effective, and patient-centered healthcare system.

As we look to the future, the continuous advancement of AI and XR technologies promises to further revolutionize healthcare delivery. Future research should focus on expanding the range of conditions that can be effectively managed using AI- and XR-powered DTx, improving the precision and adaptability of these technologies and exploring new therapeutic modalities that leverage their unique capabilities.

Additionally, addressing ethical considerations and ensuring robust data protection, as well as challenges in technical integration, accessibility, adoption, and clinical validation, will be crucial for maintaining patient trust, safeguarding privacy, and successfully commercializing innovations. Transparent data management practices and rigorous consent protocols are essential to uphold patient rights and ensure the responsible and ethical deployment of these advanced therapeutic technologies.

Acknowledgements

The author acknowledges the use of ChatGPT (https://chatgpt.com/) for language polishing and creating figures of the manuscript. This tool contributed to improving the quality and clarity of the manuscript's language.

DOI: http://dx.doi.org/10.5772/intechopen.1006619

Author details

Alex G. Lee
TechIPm, Lexington, MA, USA

*Address all correspondence to: geunholee@gmail.com

References

[1] Digital Therapeutics Alliance. Understanding DTx, digital therapeutics alliance. Available from: https://dtxalliance.org/understanding-dtx/ [Accessed: May 29, 2024]

[2] Park K, Lee S, Lee E. Can digital therapeutics open a new era of sleep medicine? Chronobiology in Medicine. 2021;**3**(4):142-148. DOI: 10.33069/cim.2021.0028

[3] Eapen SA, Saha MK, Chakravorty D, Philip P. Going digital: Emerging potential of digital biomarkers and AI/ML in healthcare. Available from: https://www.excelra.com/blogs/going-digital-emerging-potential-of-digital-biomarkers-and-ai-ml-in-healthcare/ [Accessed: May 29, 2024]

[4] Weinstein D. AI and XR: Two technologies extending reality to millions XR today. Available from: https://www.xrtoday.com/mixed-reality/ai-and-xr-two-technologies-extending-reality-to-millions/ [Accessed: May 29, 2024]

[5] Qu Z, Lau C, Simoff S, Kennedy P, Nguyen Q, Catchpoole D. Review of innovative immersive technologies for healthcare applications. Innovations in Digital Health, Diagnostics, and Biomarkers. 2022;**2**(2022):27-39. DOI: 10.36401/IDDB-21-04

[6] Benedetti F, Mayberg H, Wager T, Stohler C, Zubieta J. Neurobiological mechanisms of the placebo effect. Journal of Neuroscience. 2005;**25**(45):10390-10402. DOI: 10.1523/JNEUROSCI.3458-05.2005

[7] Diogo V, Ferreira H, Prata D, et al. Early diagnosis of Alzheimer's disease using machine learning: A multi-diagnostic, generalizable approach. Alzheimer's Research & Therapy. 2022;**14**:107. DOI: 10.1186/s13195-022-01047-y

[8] He Z, Dieciuc M, Carr D, et al. New opportunities for the early detection and treatment of cognitive decline: Adherence challenges and the promise of smart and person-centered technologies. BMC Digital Health. 2023;**1**:7. DOI: 10.1186/s44247-023-00008-1

[9] Patil V, Madgi M, Kiran A. Early prediction of Alzheimer's disease using convolutional neural network: A review. The Egyptian Journal of Neurology Psychiatry and Neurosurgery. 2022;**58**:130. DOI: 10.1186/s41983-022-00571-w

[10] Gillani N. Intelligent sensing technologies for the diagnosis, monitoring and therapy of Alzheimer's disease: A systematic review. Sensors. 2021;**21**(12):4249. DOI: 10.3390/s21124249

[11] DelveInsight. Delve insight role of digital therapeutics (DTx) in mental health management. Available from: https://www.delveinsight.com/blog/digital-therapeutics-for-mental-health [Accessed: May 29, 2024]

[12] Zhang T, Schoene A, Ji S, et al. Natural language processing applied to mental illness detection: A narrative review. npj Digital Medicine. 2022;**5**:46. DOI: 10.1038/s41746-022-00589-7

[13] Maricich Y. Neurology live the potential of digital therapeutics and cognitive behavioral therapy for insomnia. Available from: https://www.neurologylive.com/view/potential-digital-therapeutics-cognitive-behavioral-therapy-insomnia-yuri-maricich [Accessed: May 29, 2024]

[14] Ford J, Buchanan M, Azeez A, Benrimoh A, Kaloiani I, Bandeira D, et al. Taking modern psychiatry into the metaverse: Integrating augmented, virtual, and mixed reality technologies into psychiatric care. Frontiers in Digital Health. 2023;**5**:1146806. DOI: 10.3389/fdgth.2023.1146806

[15] PositivePsychology.com. Revolutionizing AI therapy: The impact on mental health care. Available from: https://positivepsychology.com/ai-therapy/ [Accessed: May 29, 2024]

[16] Song C, Jiang Z, Liu D, Wu L. Application and research progress of machine learning in the diagnosis and treatment of neurodevelopmental disorders in children. Frontiers in Psychiatry. 2022;**13**. Introduction pp.01-02 and Discussion pp. 05-07. DOI: 10.3389/fpsyt.2022.960672

[17] Maniruzzaman M, Shin J, Hasan M. Predicting children with ADHD using behavioral activity: A machine learning analysis. Applied Sciences. 2022;**12**:2737. DOI: 10.3390/app12052737

[18] Vijayan V, Connolly P, McKelvey N, Gardiner P. Review of wearable devices and data collection considerations for connected health. Sensors. 2021;**21**:5589. DOI: 10.3390/s21165589

[19] Chawla R, Krishnakumar A, Khatry V, Shah A, Joshi S, Pardiwala B, et al. Capturing clinical trends and lifestyle behaviour data of patients with diabetes using an AI-powered digital therapeutic in India. Diabetes. 2019;**68**(Supplement_1):928. DOI: 10.2337/db19-928-P

[20] Mumtaz U, Ahmed A, Mumtaz S. LLMs-healthcare: Current applications and challenges of large language models in various medical specialties. arXiv:2311.12882. 2024. 1. Introduction pp. 1-3. DOI: 10.48550/arXiv.2311.12882

[21] Kim Y, Xu X, McDuff D, Breazeal C, Park H. Health-LLM: Large language models for health prediction via wearable sensor data. arXiv:2401.06866. 2024. 1. Introduction pp. 1-2. DOI: 10.48550/arXiv.2401.06866

[22] Towhidul Islam Tonmoy M, Mehedi Zaman M, Jain V, Rani A, Rawte V, Chadha A, et al. A comprehensive survey of hallucination mitigation techniques in large language models. arXiv:2401.01313. 2024. 2. Hallucination Mitigation pp. 2-8. DOI: 10.48550/arXiv.2401.01313

[23] Research Triangle Institute. The value of digital therapeutics: Personalized, cost-effective care. Available from: https://healthcare.rti.org/insights/value-of-prescription-digital-therapeutics [Accessed: July 31, 2024]

[24] Belyaeva A, Cosentino J, Hormozdiari F, Eswaran K, Shetty S, Corrado G, et al. Multimodal LLMs for health grounded in individual-specific data. arXiv:2307.09018. 2023. 4. Discussion pp. 13-14. DOI: 10.48550/arXiv.2307.09018

[25] Arif A. The power of medical large language models (LLMs) in healthcare. Available from: https://www.johnsnowlabs.com/the-power-of-medical-large-language-models-llms-in-healthcare/ [Accessed: July 31, 2024]

[26] AHIMA. AHIMA policy statement: Telehealth and remote patient monitoring technologies. Available from: https://www.ahima.org/advocacy/policy-statements/telehealth-and-remote-patient-monitoring-technologies/ [Accessed: July 31, 2024]

[27] McCowan A. AI & Digital twins: The future of disease detection & treatment.

Available from: https://hitconsultant.net/2024/03/25/from-concept-to-care-exploring-intelligent-digital-twins/ [Accessed: July 31, 2024]

[28] Vallée A. Digital twin for healthcare systems. Frontiers in Digital Health. 2023;**5**:1253050. DOI: 10.3389/fdgth.2023.1253050

[29] Wang R, Milani S, Chiu JC, Zhi J, Eack SM, Labrum T, et al. PATIENT-Ψ: Using large language models to simulate patients for training mental health professionals. arXiv:2405.19660. DOI: 10.48550/arXiv.2405.19660

[30] TwinRCTs. Available from: https://www.unlearn.ai/twinrcts [Accessed: July 31, 2024]

[31] Almeida OFX. Early and specific detection of Alzheimer's disease: More than a (virtual) reality? Brain Communications. 2024;**6**(1):fcae014. DOI: 10.1093/braincomms/fcae014

[32] Faria AL, Andrade A, Soares L, Badia ISB. Benefits of virtual reality based cognitive rehabilitation through simulated activities of daily living: A randomized controlled trial with stroke patients. Journal of Neuroengineering and Rehabilitation. 2016;**13**(1):96. DOI: 10.1186/s12984-016-0204-z

[33] Marín-Morales J, Llinares C, Guixeres J, Alcañiz M. Emotion recognition in immersive virtual reality: From statistics to affective computing. Sensors (Basel). 2020;**20**(18):5163. DOI: 10.3390/s20185163

[34] Lu Z, Wang W, Yan W, Kew CL, Seo JH, Ory M. The application of fully immersive virtual reality on reminiscence interventions for older adults: Scoping review. JMIR Serious Games. 2023;**11**:e45539. DOI: 10.2196/45539

[35] Navas-Medrano S, Soler-Dominguez JL, Pons P. Mixed reality for a collective and adaptive mental health metaverse. Frontiers in Psychiatry. 2024;**14**:1272783. DOI: 10.3389/fpsyt.2023.1272783

[36] Lee S, Yoon J, Cho Y, Chun J. Systematic review of extended reality digital therapy for enhancing mental health among south Korean adolescents and young adults. Soa Chongsonyon Chongsin Uihak. 2023;**34**(4):204-214. DOI: 10.5765/jkacap.230046

[37] Immersive Studio. Available from: https://xrtherapeutics.co.uk/how-it-works/ [Accessed: July 19, 2024]

[38] Goharinejad S, Goharinejad S, Hajesmaeel-Gohari S, et al. The usefulness of virtual, augmented, and mixed reality technologies in the diagnosis and treatment of attention deficit hyperactivity disorder in children: An overview of relevant studies. BMC Psychiatry. 2022;**22**:4. DOI: 10.1186/s12888-021-03632-1

[39] Yuan TF, Li WG, Zhang C, et al. Targeting neuroplasticity in patients with neurodegenerative diseases using brain stimulation techniques. Translational Neurodegeneration. 2020;**9**:44. DOI: 10.1186/s40035-020-00224-z

[40] Abbadessa G, Brigo F, Clerico M, De Mercanti S, Trojsi F, Tedeschi G, et al. Digital therapeutics in neurology. Journal of Neurology. 2022;**269**(3):1209-1224. DOI: 10.1007/s00415-021-10608-4

[41] Rhythmic auditory stimulation (RAS). Available from: https://medrhythms.com/ [Accessed: July 19, 2024]

[42] Wang Q, Shun X, Guo B, Yan X, Weixin L. Virtual reality as an adjunctive non-pharmacological therapy to

reduce pain in school-aged children with burn wounds. Journal of Burn Care & Research. 2023;**44**(4):832-836. DOI: 10.1093/jbcr/irac149

[43] Stanciu CN. Digital therapeutics for substance use disorders: From research to practice, psychiatric times. Available from: https://www.psychiatrictimes.com/view/digital-therapeutics-for-substance-use-disorders-from-research-to-practice [Accessed: May 29, 2024]

[44] Ramteke S. A new Frontier – Exploring the intersection of generative AI and extended reality, persistent.AI. Available from: https://www.persistent.com/blogs/a-new-frontier-exploring-the-intersection-of-generative-ai-and-extended-reality/ [Accessed: May 29, 2024]

[45] Theory A, Gazzaley A, Jensen J. Sensory immersion vessel (SIV). Available from: https://patents.google.com/patent/US11527318 [Accessed: July 19, 2024]

[46] Nicoll M. How AI combined with XR can transform healthcare, simulation magazine. Available from: https://www.simulationmagazine.com/how-ai-combined-with-xr-can-transform-healthcare/ [Accessed: May 29, 2024]

[47] Moors S. Cedars launches Xaia for Apple Vision Pro. Available from: https://www.dhinsights.org/news/cedars-launches-xaia-for-apple-vision-pro [Accessed: July 31, 2024]

[48] Trotta A, Ziosi M, Lomonaco V. The future of ethics in AI: Challenges and opportunities. AI & SOCIETY. 2023;**38**:439-441. DOI: 10.1007/s00146-023-01644-x

[49] Upwork. 6 Ethical considerations of artificial intelligence. Available from: https://www.upwork.com/resources/ai-ethical-considerations [Accessed: July 19, 2024]

[50] Refract Technologies Pte Ltd. AI-Powered: The Future of VR and XR experiences. Available from: https://axisxr.gg/ai-powered-the-future-of-vr-and-xr-experiences/ [Accessed: July 19, 2024]

[51] Stevens E. The product design process explained: The 2024 guide. Available from: https://careerfoundry.com/en/blog/product-design/product-design-process/ [Accessed: July 31, 2024]

[52] Hutanu A. Innovation in practice: Navigating through proof of concept, prototypes, pilots, and MVPs. Available from: https://www.pentalog.com/blog/tech-trends/innovation-practice-from-prototype-to-mvp/ [Accessed: July 31, 2024]

[53] Morse J. Digital therapeutics and decentralized trials: A match made in clinical. Available from: https://www.appliedclinicaltrialsonline.com/view/digital-therapeutics-and-decentralized-trials-a-match-made-in-clinical [Accessed: July 31, 2024]

[54] Research Triangle Institute. Harnessing the value of real-world evidence for digital therapeutics. Available from: https://healthcare.rti.org/insights/digital-therapeutics-real-world-evidence [Accessed: July 31, 2024]

[55] KMS Healthcare. Data integration in healthcare: Guide & best practices. Available from: https://kms-healthcare.com/blog/data-integration-in-healthcare/ [Accessed: July 31, 2024]

[56] DataFinz. A guide for optimizing patient care through healthcare data integration. Available from: https://datafinz.com/healthcare-data-integration/

Chapter 4

An Immersive Collaborative Virtual Environment for Surgical Planning: Project VR-Surgical

Pierre Boulanger

Abstract

This chapter describes VR-Surgical, an immersive collaborative virtual reality environment designed to assist medical teams to perform surgical planning. This prototype is designed to improve surgical planning between medical teams in both remote and co-located settings. The system makes it possible to define, adjust, and annotate virtual resections of organs' 3D surfaces and 2D image slices from MRI and CT scans. By integrating Insight Toolkit (ITK) core capabilities with VR-Surgical, it is possible to process, register, and visualize various imaging modalities during the meeting. This chapter discusses the fundamental components of a prototype system and a small pilot usability study conducted by two teams of radiologists and surgeons. It shows significant improvements in time and accuracy of the surgical planning process.

Keywords: collaborative virtual environment, surgical planning, medical visualization, surgical training, surgical simulation

1. Introduction

The use of medical collaborative virtual environments (MCVEs) is revolutionizing surgical planning by giving medical professionals immersive, interactive, and real-time platforms to collaborate, visualize, and simulate surgical procedures. Pre-operative strategies can be improved, and surgical outcomes can be enhanced by remote MCVE over the Internet. Surgical teams' interactions and preparation can be significantly impacted by this approach, especially when dealing with complex cases. Let us take a closer look at the components and advantages of this technology:

- *Remote collaboration*: In MCVE, surgeons and other medical specialists from different locations can meet in an interactive immersive virtual environment. This is particularly advantageous for complex cases where multiple specialists are needed. Despite their physical separation, they can view and discuss plans for the procedure together by utilizing 3D patient-specific models that can be manipulated in real time by team members. The system enables the annotation of 3D models, performs resection, modifies transfer functions, and processes data using the Insight Segmentation and Registration Toolkit (ITK). Participants can also access medical reports and other remote information using a virtual web browser located in the virtual meeting room. In the end of a session, VR-Surgical can document and save the designed surgical plan in detail.

- *Remote access to expertise*: By using this technology, one can access a wider range of experts that may not be available locally. Collaborating in real-time, discussing strategies, and making decisions together, allows surgeons, radiologists, and other healthcare professionals to create an optimal surgical procedure for each patient.

- *3D visualization and interaction*: Modern MCVEs can render detailed three-dimensional images from patient imaging data, such as CT and MRI scans, which allows surgeons to manipulate and explore these images in a shared immersive virtual space. Clarifying the anatomical complexity of patients can be crucial for planning the surgical approach and predicting potential challenges. Surgeons can benefit from using these models to explore and comprehend complex anatomical structures in a way that 2D images cannot. These 3D models allow surgeons and medical teams to interact to rotate, zoom, and cut through various layers to gain comprehensive insights into the surgical site and its relationship to the surgical procedure.

- *Artificial intelligence (AI) and machine learning*: By analyzing patient data, AI algorithms can help predict surgical outcomes, optimize procedural plans, and identify potential risks. Using this data-driven approach, personalized surgical plans can be tailored to each patient's needs. In some MCVEs, machine learning algorithms are used to automatically segment and analyze medical imaging data, which simplifies the workload of radiology staff before the meeting.

- *Training and education*: Not only can these environments be used for surgical planning, but also for educational purposes. Surgeons and medical students can have an immersive learning experience without the risks associated with actual surgery.

- *Scalability and flexibility*: Since MCVE operates over the Internet, it can be scaled to accommodate various users with wireless G5 connections, allowing collaboration outside the hospital setting. In addition, the system can be integrated with other digital health records for a more comprehensive approach to patient care.

- *Patient involvement*: The system also allows patient involvement, where patients can be guided through their anatomical models and understand the surgical plan, which can help reduce anxiety and improving patient satisfaction and outcomes.

Overall, MCVE for surgical planning over the Internet is not just about enhancing the surgical planning itself, but also improving the entire ecosystem of medical training, patient care, and international collaboration. This chapter aims to provide an overview of VR-Surgical, a prototype MCVE system that enables surgical teams to plan surgeries through immersive networked virtual collaboration.

Section 2 will briefly review the evolution of MCVE for surgical planning. Section 3 will describe the software architecture of VR-Surgical, which is composed of Unity 3D, ITK, and MiddleVR. Section 4 demonstrates the current capabilities of the

VR-Surgical prototype. In Section 5, we present small pilot usability studies of the prototype. We will then conclude by describing the advantages and future of these systems, in Section 6.

2. Literature review

MCVE systems have undergone a significant change from simple virtual reality simulation applications to sophisticated, immersive platforms that are designed for surgical planning. In this review, we will examine the significant advances and technology in MCVEs for surgical planning from 1990 to 2024. This review highlights the significant contributions and technological milestones that have shaped this dynamic field.

During the early 1990s, VR was first used in medicine by the pioneering work of Jaron Lanier [1] with a primary focus on simple simulations that allowed for visualization of anatomical structures. One of the key components was the development of 3D reconstruction techniques such as the marching cube algorithm [2] to accommodate the limitations of graphic processors that could only render triangles. Initiatives like the Visible Human Project [3] began using digital anatomical models for training, but they did not have the interactivity of later systems.

During the late 1990s and early 2000s, advancements in imaging techniques like MRI and CT scanners allowed for the creation of more detailed and accurate 3D models of patients. In addition, advances in faster graphic processors by Silicon Graphics were essential to display these more precise surgical models. Using these advancements, early surgical planning tools were developed by Gibson [4] and Smith [5]. The introduction of networked environments has also contributed to enabling multiple users to interact within the same virtual space, resulting in collaborative planning and training sessions among surgical teams. The work by Shapiro et al. [6] and Harrisson et al. [7] were instrumental to demonstrate the capabilities of MCVE. In addition, the introduction of haptic feedback devices provided tactile sensations necessary to enhance the realism of surgical simulations by allowing users to feel textures and resistances akin to real-world surgical environments. Most notably the works of Salisbury et al. [8] and Lin et al. [9] were instrumental in demonstrating how haptic devices can improve the ability to perform surgical training.

The precision of surgical planning was significantly improved in 2010 thanks to further advancements in computational power and imaging technology, which resulted in high-quality 3D patient-specific models. This was demonstrated by the work of Johnston et al. [10] and Chen et al. [11]. The integration of real-time patient data into collaborative virtual environments has enabled dynamic adjustments to surgical plans based on live data from the operating room [12]. The integration had a significant impact on adapting to changes during surgery [13]. The development of devices such as the Microsoft HoloLens helps to introduce Augmented Reality (AR) technologies in the operating room to overlay critical information and 3D models onto the physical world, aiding surgeons in planning and executing procedures with enhanced spatial awareness. A review of AR in surgery can be found in [14, 15]. Real-time collaborative surgical planning became more feasible and effective using cloud computing, which facilitated efficient data sharing and collaboration across different locations. Smith et al. [16] and Wang et al. [17] describe the benefits of cloud-based solutions in surgical planning.

Today, surgical planning is now being assisted by AI and machine learning algorithms, which offer predictive analytics, automatic segmentation of medical images, and enhanced decision support. These innovations have significantly improved the accuracy and efficiency of surgical planning. Wang et al. [17] and Zhang et al. [18] provide an overview of the application of AI to surgical planning. The development of highly immersive VR Head Mounted Displays (HMDs) with video-based tracking and high-resolution displays has also significantly changed the use of VR HMDs in surgical planning environments [19]. With the help of advanced interactivity, such as gesture recognition and voice control, the usability and effectiveness of collaborative virtual environments have significantly improved. Brown et al. [20] evaluated the impact of immersive VR on surgical planning. In [21], there is a review of VR platforms for surgical training and planning. Patient-specific models based on genetic information and other personalized data can now be used in collaborative virtual environments to create highly tailored surgical plans that consider individual patient characteristics as described in [22, 23]. The increasing acceptance and regulatory approvals of VR and AR tools for surgical planning have led to their broader adoption in clinical settings, ensuring that these technologies meet safety and efficacy standards. A review of such standards is described in [24, 25]. The recent rollout of 5G technology has improved the speed and reliability of data transfer, making real-time collaboration more seamless and efficient. Effective implementation of CVEs in surgical planning requires this development. The impact of 5G on surgical planning and collaboration has been studied and can be found in [26, 27].

3. VR-Surgical software architecture

Our system is built around a pragmatic approach that brings together immersive VR capabilities from Unity 3D, medical imaging processing from Insight Segmentation and Registration Toolkit (ITK), and robust networking and data management functionalities from Middle VR. **Figure 1** depicts the system's concept diagram. The system's design is explained in detail here.

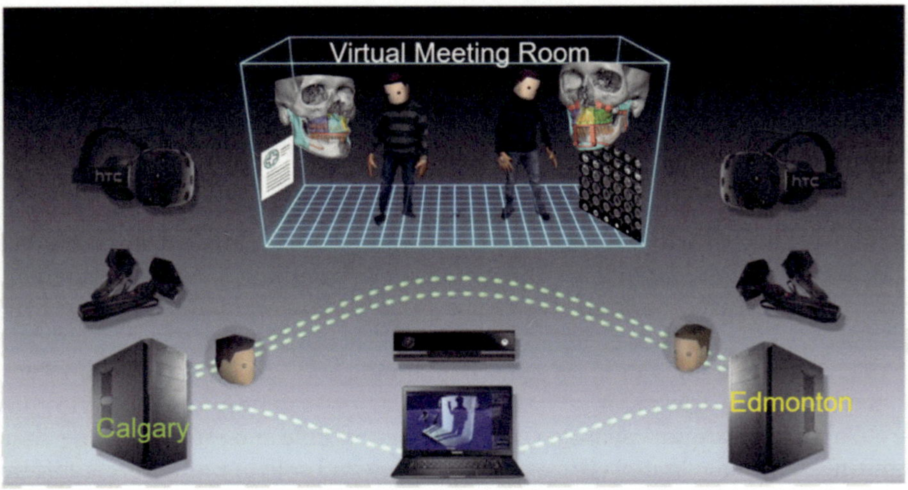

Figure 1.
VR-Surgical concept.

3.1 System overview

Creating an intuitive, efficient, and conducive interface and user experience for surgical planning software is crucial to ensuring high-quality patient care. Here are some essential principles and considerations we used to create VR-Surgical:

- *User-centered design*: We conducted extensive studies during the project to comprehend the needs, workflows, and pain points of surgeons and medical staff to plan surgeries using current tools. Our design process was guided by detailed user personas to ensure that the software meets the needs to perform surgical planning more efficiently.

- *Intuitive and clean interface simplicity*: Our objective was to create an immersive interface that is clean and uncluttered, with a focus on essential features and avoids unnecessary complexity. To lower the learning curve for a surgical team, we employ consistent design patterns, icons, and terminology throughout the interface.

- *Efficient workflow integration*: The software was designed with the aim of seamlessly integrating with existing hospital systems, including electronic health records and medical imaging formats such as Digital Imaging and Communications in Medicine (DICOM).

- *Accessibility and usability*: Our medical collaborators and us conducted usability testing regularly at each stage of development to identify and address issues and ensure that we meet their expectations.

A VR-Surgical system prototype was created based on those design principles. VR-Surgical aims to demonstrate how multiple surgeons and medical practitioners can work together in a virtual environment to create and plan surgeries that are specific to each patient. Using Unity 3D and the Middle VR plugin, a client-side application was developed to support various VR hardware and manage immersive user interactions. The ITK library is employed for the processing of medical images. **Figure 2** shows the software architecture of a VR-Surgical client.

3.2 VR-Surgical is based on unity 3D

Unity 3D is a game engine and development platform that is both powerful and versatile. It is commonly used to create interactive content in video games, simulations, and visualizations. The excellent VR and AR capabilities make it an excellent choice for VR-Surgical. The core features of Unity 3D that we used in this project are:

- *Multiplatform support*: Unity's comprehensive platform support makes it a great choice to develop applications for over 25 platforms, such as Windows, macOS, Linux, iOS, Android, and various VR and AR devices. Our application requires this flexibility because participants may have different types of devices, such as mobile phones and laptop computers. While some devices are VR compatible, others, such as mobile phones and desktop computers, may only be capable of displaying 2D rendering.

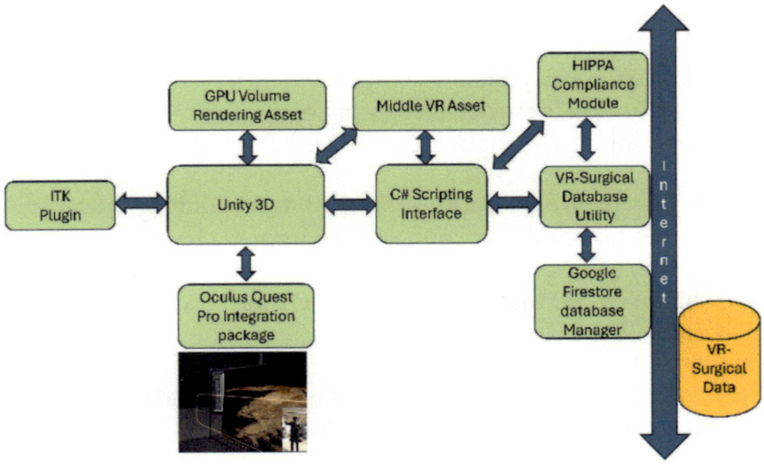

Figure 2.
Software architecture of VR-Surgical client.

- *Integrated development environment (IDE)*: Unity has a comprehensive IDE that combines all the necessary tools for VR development. Importing assets, writing scripts in C#, and assembling scenes can all be done within a user-friendly interface. VR-Surgical functionalities were made possible using C# scripting. These scripts are responsible for handling DICOM readers, processing medical images with ITK, creating avatar animations of the participants, accessing databases, and other tasks.

- *Graphics rendering*: Unity's powerful graphics engine allows it to render 2D and 3D graphics. For medical image rendering, we used one of the volume rendering assets from the Unity store. Its capabilities include: easy import of volumetric data mainly in DICOM format; interactive visualization functionalities such as rotation, zoom, and slicing; a set of shaders for different rendering techniques such as direct volume rendering and iso-surface rendering; functions to define transfer functions to enhance the visibility of different materials or structures based on their densities; and finally GPU-based rendering and multi-threading support to handle large datasets efficiently. Another key advantage of Unity 3D is its extensive support for VR and AR development, providing a range of tools and APIs to create immersive experiences for surgical planning and eventually image- guided surgeries.

- *Physics engine*: The robust physics engine in Unity 3D allows for the realistic simulation of physical interactions in surgical simulation. In this prototype, the physics engine is mainly used for collision detection and rigid transformation of medical image objects. Using this physics engine, we are currently developing extensions to VR-Surgical that can perform basic surgical simulations.

3.3 VR-Surgical and middle VR

Middle VR is a powerful middleware for developing and deploying virtual reality applications, particularly well-suited for collaborative applications like ours where high levels of interactivity and multiple user engagement are required. By providing

DOI: http://dx.doi.org/10.5772/intechopen.1006344

robust support for various VR hardware and seamless integration with Unity 3D, Middle VR enabled us to build sophisticated VR applications like VR-Surgical that are both accessible and scalable.

The core elements of Middle VR used in VR-Surgical are:

- *VR device integration*: Middle VR can support a wide range of VR devices, such as HMDs, motion trackers, 3D mice, and haptic devices. By combining Meta Quest Pro with Middle VR, we were able to significantly improve the quality and efficiency of virtual reality experiences in our application. Meta Quest Pro headsets can operate independently and process everything on the device. Due to the absence of the need for an expensive computer or complex setup, they are more accessible and easier to use than PC-tethered VR systems. The headset and controllers offer 6 degrees of freedom for users to move around and interact with the virtual environment realistically. VR-Surgical most recent release employs the Meta Quest Pro's capabilities to conduct hands-free tracking, enabling users to interact with VR content without the use of hand controllers. The Meta Quest Pro is enhanced by high-resolution OLED screens that offer clear and vibrant visuals, contributing to a more immersive VR experience. The Meta Quest Pro's built-in speakers deliver spatial audio, allowing users to hear the voices of the participants without the need for external headphones.

- *Multi-user support*: Middle VR's uniqueness lies in its support for multi-user environments. This feature allows multiple users to interact with various devices in real-time within the same virtual space. If a participant connects to the system with a mobile phone, Middle VR can adapt the capability of VR-Surgical to deal with its limitations, i.e., 2D display instead of 3D and mouse navigation instead of hand tracking, etc.

3.4 VR-Surgical and ITK

The primary purpose of ITK, which was created through collaboration between different institutions, is to process and analyze visual data in medical imaging applications. Written in C++ its integration with Unity 3D, necessitates the development of custom plugins that can directly utilize ITK's processing capabilities. This allows for on-the-fly image processing in the VR-Surgical environment. Once data is imported in Unity 3D one can use shaders, materials, and Unity's volume rendering capabilities to visualize the data. The primary use of ITK in VR-Surgical is to register various imaging modalities and filter volumetric data.

3.5 VR-Surgical data server

The VR-Surgical data server is a key element of the system. It manages data and processes user inputs, thus ensuring the virtual environment state is maintained across multiple sessions. It consists of:

- *Data management service*: Handles storage, retrieval, and management of medical imaging data. The current system supports DICOM data CT, MRI, PET, Ultrasound, Fluoroscopy, and Radiography; Medical reports as PDF; Patient outcome information as PDF; and Current patient's physiological condition.

- *Real-time collaboration manager*: Manages interactions and updates across client applications while coordinating activities between multiple users. Separation between client interfaces and data processing and management tasks handled by the server is made possible using a client-server architecture. Our system's architecture is based on a microservices architecture, where each server component (data handling, user management, and real-time collaboration) can operate independently. The result is enhanced scalability and maintenance ease. Our implementation is based on the Google Fire Store database, which is a flexible and scalable database for mobile, web, and server development. As the successor to Firebase Realtime Database, it offers enhanced data structuring and more robust querying.

- *Interaction flow*: The interaction between surgeons takes place on the Unity-based client application platform. The server receives inputs, such as rotations, annotations, patient's reports and patient-specific 3D models. By processing these inputs, the server updates the virtual environment's state and sends it back to all connected clients. Synchronization is ensured by the Middle VR by keeping a consistent state across all user interactions. It is also responsible for updating the position and gestures of the participants' avatars using the HMD position/orientation to locate the avatar in the meeting room as well as hand tracking to animate the avatar interaction such pointing and signaling.

3.6 VR-Surgical security and ethical considerations

Creating a data server for healthcare requires careful consideration of various technical, regulatory, and ethical aspects. A healthcare data server is typically responsible for handling sensitive information, such as patient records, medical imaging data, and operational data from different healthcare departments. VR-Surgical created a strong data server that adhered to the rules listed below.

- *Scalability*: Increases in data volume can be handled by the server without affecting performance. Middle VR capabilities enable the expansion of scalable cloud solutions or modular hardware architectures as needed.

- *Reliability and availability*: High availability is necessary in healthcare, as system downtime can affect patient care. Even when there are partial system failures, the server is still operational thanks to redundant hardware, failover clustering, and load balancing techniques. We employ a straightforward method in our implementation where we download all datasets (medical images, reports, etc.) locally from a secure Google server before the meeting. The annotated medical images and surgical plans are saved on the same data server after the meeting, which can be used during the surgery or to review the design.

- *Security*: Security is of utmost importance due to the sensitive nature of medical data. Strong encryption for data at rest and in transit was implemented in VR-Surgical, along with robust authentication and authorization mechanisms. Our data server complies with the standards set by the Health Insurance Portability and Accountability Act (HIPAA).

- *Ethics*: Ethical considerations are essential when developing and implementing surgical planning software to ensure patient safety, privacy, and overall well-being. These are the key ethical considerations that were utilized in the development of VR-Surgical:

- *Accuracy and reliability*: To avoid errors that could harm patients during the procedure, it is crucial to make sure the software is accurate and reliable. As VR-Surgical progresses, it is always necessary to regularly assess and mitigate risks associated with its use. It is also important that surgeons and medical staff are adequately trained to use the software effectively and comprehend its limitations. For the first release of VR-Surgical we developed a basic training module for a stent procedure to treat coronary artery disease that was greatly appreciated by the teams and was used during the usability study.

- *Ethical use of AI and machine learning*: VR-Surgical future version must make sure that AI-driven decisions and recommendations are understandable for both surgeons and patients. VR-Surgical should always be supervised by humans when validating and interpreting AI-generated plans and suggestions. It is also important to be open about reporting any issues, errors, or adverse events related to the software.

4. VR-Surgical prototype

The prototype system's functionality will be demonstrated in this section. Before a meeting takes place, the organizer must create a script file that contains the necessary information for the meeting. It includes:

- The number of participants.
- The names and locations of every participant.
- The IP addresses for every participant.
- Usernames and passwords for each participant.
- Medical Imaging file names to be used in DICOM format.
- List of patient reports in PDF format.

Let us look at the functionality of the prototype system by illustrating each stage of a meeting.

4.1 Step 1: connecting with a participant

The first step an organizer must take is to establish a connection with another participant. As illustrated in **Figure 3a**, the organizer must select the networking item from the virtual drop-down menu and then start connecting with the participant. Then he must start a host server (**Figure 3b**). Once connected, the participants will appear on both sides of the meeting as animated avatars. Each avatar's location and hand gestures are defined by the HMD locator and the hand and finger locations (**Figure 3c**) by the Meta Oculus Pro. Once connected, participants can view the meeting information collaboratively or individually (**Figure 3d**). If collaborative visualization is selected a designated participant will control the visualization.

4.2 Visualizing, manipulating, and annotating patient's medical imaging data

One of the key functionalities of VR-Surgical is its ability to share medical imaging data between participants, which can be visualized at various viewing

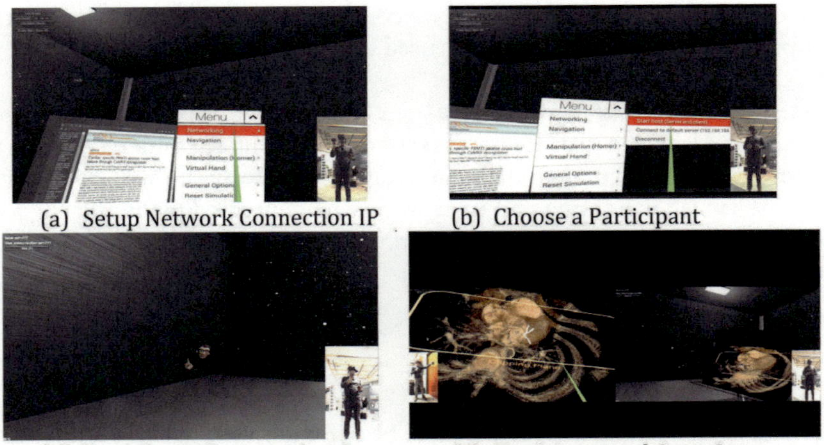

(a) Setup Network Connection IP
(b) Choose a Participant
(c) Participant Connected and Represented as an Animated Avatar
(d) Participant and Organizer Looking at CT Data Collaboratively

Figure 3.
Setting up the network connection and connecting with the participants.

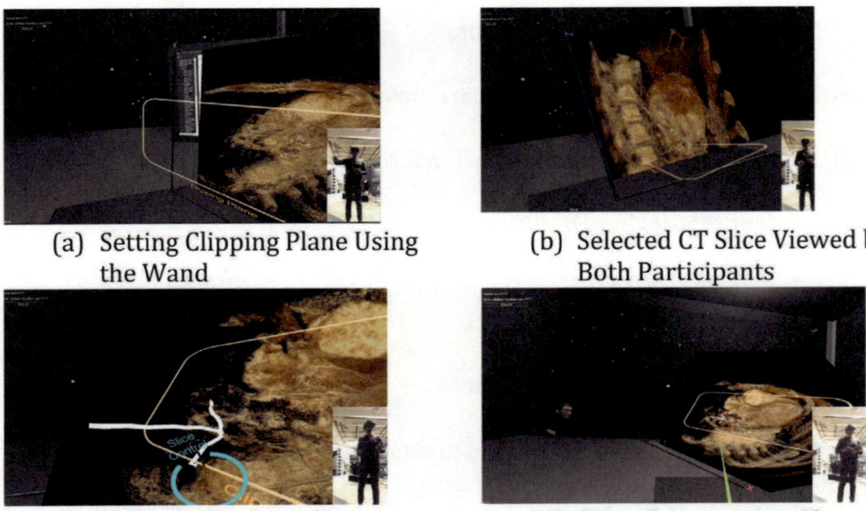

(a) Setting Clipping Plane Using the Wand
(b) Selected CT Slice Viewed by Both Participants
(c) Making a Region of Interest
(d) CT and Annotation Observed by Both Participants

Figure 4.
Manipulating, slicing, and annotating medical imaging data.

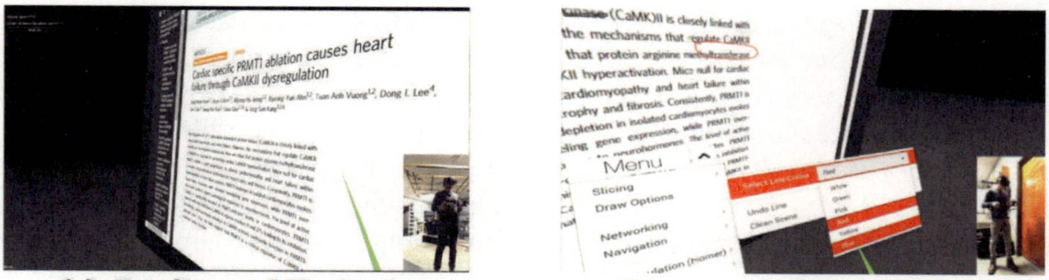

(a) Reading and Navigating Webpages Using a Virtual Web Browser

(b) Using Various Draw Options

Figure 5.
Virtual web browser located in the virtual meeting room.

angles using the wand or hand control (**Figure 4a**). Depending on which participant has control, they can interactively apply a clipping plane to select a slice of volume data (**Figure 4b**).

During their conversation, both participants use pointers to highlight regions of interest in the volume data. Each participant's annotation has a different color that can be selected interactively (**Figure 4c** and **d**). These regions of interest will be saved by the system at the end of the session for future reference.

4.3 Virtual webpage browser

VR-Surgical can display an interactive board in a virtual meeting that functions like a web browser. **Figure 5a** shows how each participant can access information on the WWW or medical databases using this functionality. Because the virtual web browser is the same as a normal web browser, participants can connect to computational services such as Google Collab to process images using Python notebook. The results of the processing are then saved in the VR-Surgical server and can be viewed collaboratively in the virtual environment. Furthermore, Unity 3D natively implements basic ITK functionality for processing locally. Once processed, the information can be saved on the VR-Surgical server and displayed collaboratively. This enables participants to process information separately and then discuss the results in a collaborative manner. In addition, each selected web page can be annotated using the virtual pointer to highlight important information (**Figure 5b**).

4.4 Meeting recording

VR-Surgical can record meetings and save them on the server. It is possible to save all information (including 3D models, participant movements, voices, virtual browser data, etc.). To play back this recording and share information with other participants during a meeting, a participant can use a slider that resembles the one used by video players.

5. Prototype usability study

A small usability study for VR-Surgical was conducted in our laboratory. Due to the challenge of obtaining access at the same time to a radiologist and a surgeon, our study was limited to three teams. We made the decision to present five different cases to each team, generating 15 experimental results. The first case is for training purposes and the four others were actual experiments. The purpose of the task was to plan for a stent procedure. A stent procedure is used to open narrowed or blocked arteries and enhance blood flow. This is typically necessary in conditions such as coronary artery disease (CAD), peripheral artery disease (PAD), and in the arteries of the kidney (renal stenting), among others. The following steps are necessary for pre-operative surgical planning for a stent procedure using a contract-enabled CT scan:

1. *CT scan review*: The contrast CT images are reviewed by radiologists and surgeons to assess the patient's anatomy and the extent of the condition that necessitates stent placement.

2. *Image processing and segmentation:* A detailed 3D model of the relevant blood vessels and surrounding structures is created by using special software to process and segment contract-enhanced CT images. It is also used to highlight the location of blocked arteries.

3. *Measurements and analysis*: After finding blocked arteries, key measurements are carried out, which involve measuring vessel diameters, lengths, and any areas of stenosis or aneurysm. This information is critical for selecting the appropriate size and type of stent.

4. *Stent selection*: Based on the measurements and anatomical considerations, the surgical team selects the appropriate stent type and size.

5. *Procedure planning*: During this step the surgical team discuss where to insert the catheter and to anticipate potential challenges.

The total time for these steps can vary widely depending on the complexity of the case, the availability and experience of the surgical team, and the efficiency of the imaging and planning software. The surgical planning team normally uses FDA-approved TerraRecon, the leading advanced visualization and AI platform on the market. According to our medical team members, the planning process can take on average of 1.0 hour/case using TerraRecon. This includes loading the patient's contrast CT images, processing the information to locate the clots, performing measurements to determine the stent size and type, and finally planning and documenting the procedure.

5.1 The experiment

Each team starts by performing a first surgical planning talk (with three CT images) to become familiar with the interface. Once familiar with the interface a planning session for four medical cases is then presented to them to solve. During the session, the team performance is evaluated using total planning completion time per case (hours) relative to the average time to perform the same tasks using TerraRecon. The accuracy of locating the targets (clot localizations) in mm is also measured. After the five cases, a Likert questionnaire exploring how each team member feels about the performance of VR-Surgical compares to TerraRecon. Using a scale between 0 and 5, the questionnaire assessed how the collaboration between the radiologist and surgeon was perceived for each experiment. The interface's overall user satisfaction was also assessed compared to TerraRecon using a scale ranging from 0 to 5 after each experiment.

The results were:

- *Efficiency*: VR-Surgical allowed each team to finish surgical planning experiments within an average of 2.3 hours, equivalent to an average of 34.5 minutes per case, with an 8-minute variance. Most of the time (16 minutes on average) was dedicated to investigating CT scans to pinpoint the obstructed arteries. Compared to TerraRecon, which takes an average of 60 minutes per case for surgery planning, this is a significant time reduction. The time reduction is primarily attributed to VR-Surgical's capability to collaboratively visualize and annotate contract CT data. VR-Surgical real-time collaboration was also appreciated by them as it likely reduced the need for multiple planning sessions and simplified the decision-making process by improving the ability to choose the best stents for each clot and to plan better the catheter insertion route.

- *Accuracy*: The accuracy of localizing the clot was on average 2.5 mm with a standard deviation of 0.25 mm, which corresponded to the actual resolution of the CT volume images. Our teams determined that this was sufficient to accurately select the stent size and type for each clot. They mentioned that using the enhancement of 3D visualization and interactive tools in VR-Surgical it possible to obtain better stent selections and a better understanding of intricate anatomical structures to reach the clots. TerraRecon has similar capabilities for planning, but due to the limitations of 2D display, anatomical information is more difficult to interpret, which necessitates a higher level of expertise and may result in errors for novice users.

- *Collaboration*: According to our medical testing teams, VR-Surgical improved collaboration and communication. The participants' evaluation of VR-Surgical compared to TerraRecon was on average 4.7 out of 5 better with a standard deviation of 1.2. VR-Surgical was perceived as a more effective communication tool for interdisciplinary collaboration than TerraRecon, allowing for immediate feedback and adjustments during the planning phase.

- *User satisfaction*: When comparing the VR-Surgical system to TerraRecon, users expressed average satisfaction scores of 4.0 out of 5 with a standard deviation of 1.2. The user-friendly interface, 3D medical image interaction, and overall planning improvement were all appreciated by participants and was considered a significant improvement over TerraRecon session especially when virtual meetings are necessary. They mentioned that other pointing techniques should be utilized because the current version is difficult to control. They also mentioned that the virtual web browser can be useful to bridge virtual meetings with their day-to-day practice, for example by showing patient records, emails, and agendas.

Based on this limited pilot study, it is apparent that we are on the right track. Our plan is to conduct a long-term study to observe how VR-Surgical usage affects surgical outcomes and gather more comprehensive data on its effectiveness.

6. Conclusion

VR-Surgical demonstrates how surgeons and medical teams can collaborate remotely, no matter their geographical location, to carry out surgical planning. The small usability study shows that VR-Surgical can indeed improve decision-making before surgeries, but more testing and improvements are necessary before deployment in clinical environments. The key advantage of the current version of VR-Surgical is its ability to deliver immediate feedback and discussion through real-time interaction that relies on shared visualizations of patient data and surgical plans. VR-Surgical advantage lies in its integration of not only being able to visualize immersivity imaging data, but also to bring to the planning room physiological data, genetic information, and real-time intraoperative data by using the virtual web browser. Adopting this holistic approach allows the team to have a better understanding of the patient's condition and optimize surgical strategies.

Future development of VR-Surgical will incorporate AI capabilities to enhance decision-making by analyzing complex datasets and suggesting optimal surgical plans based on the framework developed during this project. This can include predicting outcomes based on historical data and recommending personalized approaches tailored to individual patient characteristics. The use of advanced technologies will lead MCVEs to revolutionize surgical planning, improve outcomes, reduce risks, and enhance the overall quality of patient care.

Author details

Pierre Boulanger
University of Alberta, Edmonton, Canada

*Address all correspondence to: pierreb@ualberta.ca

References

[1] Lanier J, Smith A, Brown B. Virtual reality surgical simulator: An introduction. Journal of Medical Simulation. 1993;**10**(3):123-135

[2] Hinckley K, Doe J, Roe M. Application of virtual reality to the construction of anatomical models. Journal of Medical Simulation. 1994;**12**(4):567-579

[3] Ackerman MJ. The visible human project: A three-dimensional anatomical knowledge base. Journal of Medical Informatics. 1991;7(2):45-53

[4] Gibson DJ. Three-dimensional visualization and surgical planning. Journal of Surgical Simulation. 2001;**15**(1):78-89

[5] Smith D. Advances in medical imaging technology. Journal of Medical Imaging. 2005;**22**(3):145-159

[6] Shapiro G, Lee R, Nguyen T. Networked virtual environments for collaborative surgery. Journal of Surgical Technology. 2004;**18**(2):99-112

[7] Harrison B, Smith J, Clark R. Collaborative virtual reality environments for surgical training. Journal of Medical Simulation. 2006;**20**(4):210-225

[8] Salisbury K, Brown J, Patel V. Haptic feedback enhances force skill learning. Journal of Haptic Technology. 2004;**12**(3):134-145

[9] Salisbury K, Lin MC, Otaduy MA. Haptic feedback enhances force skill learning. Journal of Haptic Technology. 2004;**12**(3):134-145

[10] Johnston E, Adams R, Lee S. High-resolution anatomical models for surgical planning. Journal of Surgical Planning. 2011;**23**(4):189-202

[11] Chen D, Smith J, Williams R. Advances in 3D modeling and surgical planning. Journal of Medical Imaging and Surgery. 2015;**30**(2):145-160

[12] Matsumoto R, Kim S, Lopez A. Real-time integration of patient data in surgical planning. Journal of Medical Informatics. 2013;**18**(3):200-215

[13] Lee J, Brown P, Nguyen T. Dynamic surgical planning with live data integration. Journal of Surgical Innovation. 2018;**25**(2):110-125

[14] Azuma RT, Johnson L, Smith M. Augmented reality in surgical practice: A review. Journal of Medical Augmented Reality. 2012;**15**(1):45-67

[15] Navab N, Bichlmeier C, Wang X. Applications of AR in surgical procedures. Journal of Augmented Reality Surgery. 2015;**18**(2):102-118

[16] Smith K, Johnson L, Davis R. Cloud-based solutions for surgical planning. Journal of Surgical Technology and Innovations. 2017;**21**(3):150-165

[17] Wang L, Chen D, Lee J. Efficient collaboration in the cloud for surgical teams. Journal of Cloud Computing in Healthcare. 2019;**27**(4):198-212

[18] Zhang W, Li X, Yang M. AI in surgical planning: Current. Journal of Artificial Intelligence in Medicine. **33**(1):50-65

[19] Nguyen H, Tran P, Smith A. Machine learning for surgical decision support. Journal of Medical Informatics. 2022;**28**(3):123-137

[20] Brown S, Johnson R, Lee M. Evaluating the impact of immersive VR on surgical planning. Journal of Virtual Reality in Medicine. 2021;**35**(2):210-225

[21] Martinez J, Smith A, Lee R. Advanced VR platforms for surgical training and planning. Journal of Surgical Technology and Training. 2023;**42**(1):78-95

[22] Robinson A, Johnson L, Williams P. Integrating personalized medicine into surgical planning. Journal of Personalized Medicine in Surgery. 2021;**29**(2):100-115

[23] Hernandez L, Martinez J, Kim S. Patient-specific models in CVEs for surgery. Journal of Virtual Reality in Surgery. 2022;**18**(1):75-89

[24] Thompson E, Patel V, Gomez R. Regulatory challenges and approvals for VR/AR in surgery. Journal of Medical Regulatory Affairs. 2020;**14**(3):90-105

[25] Jenkins O, Nguyen T, Lee M. Standards for VR/AR surgical planning tools. Journal of Surgical Technology Standards. 2022;**25**(4):120-135

[26] Liu J, Kim S, Rodriguez P. Impact of 5G on surgical planning and collaboration. Journal of Medical Technology and Innovation. 2020;**30**(2):145-160

[27] Kim S, Nguyen T, Johnson R. Enhanced connectivity for real-time surgical collaboration. Journal of Medical Connectivity. 2023;**18**(1):100-115

Chapter 5

Innovative Use of Machine Learning-Aided Virtual Reality and Natural Language Processing Technologies in Dyslexia Diagnosis and Treatment Phases

Fevzi Daş, Emin Taner Elmas and İhsan Ömür Bucak

Abstract

Dyslexia is a common neurological disorder that affects approximately 5–10% of the population, impacting reading, writing, and spelling despite a normal level of intelligence and education. Integrating virtual reality (VR) and natural language processing (NLP) provides an innovative method for diagnosing and treating dyslexia. This method uses the interactivity of VR and the analytical potential of NLP to make accurate predictions, real-time feedback, and individualized learning experiences. Based on this research, we developed a system architecture called disVRtech that diagnoses and treats dyslexia. The VR technology offers interactive diagnosis and specific tasks, while NLP programs track user progress patterns, which are used in giving detailed and person-oriented responses. A dedicated reading passage helps diagnose dyslexia and targets specific challenges such as follow-up tasks, phonemic awareness exercises, word-definition games, and fluent reading practices. The major goal of disVRtech is to develop an efficient method for diagnosing and treating dyslexia in its early stages. This approach allows dyslexia sufferers, educators, health professionals, and supporters to benefit from fast, accurate, and effective diagnostics and treatment. The disVRtech provides a new and superior approach to the diagnosis and treatment of dyslexia, improving the quality of people's lives and solving learning problems.

Keywords: virtual reality, machine learning, natural language processing, dyslexia, Unity 3D

1. Introduction

Dyslexia is a common neurologically-based disorder characterized by a deficiency in reading, writing, and spelling abilities despite normal intelligence and adequate training. It is estimated to affect approximately 5–10% of the population, making it one of the most common learning disabilities. The basic problem lies in the processing of phonology, which hampers the decoding and automatic word recognition skills. This deficit leads to slow and laborious reading, frequent spelling mistakes, and writing difficulties [1]. Dyslexia manifests itself in many different ways, and, therefore, enormous variability exists between individuals. Sometimes, it is the area of word recognition, whereas other times it is spelling or writing that can pose significant difficulty. Although dyslexia has a significant impact on educational performance and personal development, it often brings about frustration, low self-esteem, and poor academic performance [2].

Early diagnosis of dyslexia is important for the correct intervention. The earlier the condition is diagnosed, the higher the chances of successful intervention. Early intervention can harness the plasticity of the young brain and excite the skills of reading and other linguistic skills through informative education [3]. Children going undiagnosed and unsupported concerning their dyslexia are at high risk of long-term failure at school, leading to long-term educational and social misery. The traditional methods of diagnosing dyslexia usually require lengthy and expensive assessments and also place stress on the child. These often involve standardized testing through reading accuracy and understanding, phonological processing tasks, and assessment of cognitive abilities [4]. Although effective, they do not always capture the full scope of the individual's difficulties nor engage young learners.

Technological innovations seem to be without a break, under the medical panorama of the present scenario. They have, indeed, significantly changed the treatment applied to dyslexia; otherwise, they have to provide diagnostic and therapeutic procedures that offer accurate and effective, very comprehensive representations. Two such technologies that promise to revolutionize dyslexia diagnosis are virtual reality (VR) and natural language processing (NLP), which enable highly individualized intervention. VR is an artificially created environment that is experienced interactively through the use of a computer; that is, it is almost a real phenomenon. Therefore, the use of VR technology in the diagnosis and treatment of dyslexia will provide a simulated reading environment as close as possible to the real environment. This will give the educator or therapist the understanding and skills to recognize how dyslexic people will behave toward the text under different lighting conditions, fonts, or background noises [5]. Doing things that are particularly difficult or stressful can effectively utilize the fully immersive nature of VR with children. Children are involved in the assessment process and through gamification; this process is easily de-stressed, mainly because children feel that they are part of the test and not participants. An example case could well be a virtual environment that supports an activity such as interactive reading games to explore issues of language processing, word recognition, or reading flexibility. In most of the research, it is known that adding games increases the intensity of the experience. For example, game complexity can be a determinant of the effectiveness of a learning experience for the user [6].

NLP deals with artificial intelligence applied to the interaction of computers with humans using human language. NLP can examine large amounts of text data to detect patterns of abnormal language use and thus become a powerful tool for assessing the reading and writing skills of a person with dyslexia. For the diagnosis of dyslexia, NLP algorithms applied to the user's reading passages can give a detailed profile of the reader's reading ability as well as identify pronunciation, syntax, and even grammatical errors. Another area where NLP is useful is in the evaluation of written language through the analysis of spelling, sentence structure, and consistency in identifying difficult areas. Other areas taken into account are the action of untying the spelling, hallucinations, and personality factors, as well as a clear profile of learning and performance level [7].

Such models highlight the integrity inherent in VR and NLP technology in the diagnosis and treatment of dyslexia, and from this point, provide an in-depth understanding of the person's reading and writing problems. VR can therefore be applied to create interactive diagnostic environments and NLP can be applied to assess the use of language, enabling educators and therapists to create individual treatment plans that focus on the specific needs of each student. For example, VR applications can place a user in a virtual classroom completing multiple tasks in reading and writing, and NLP applications can analyze that user's performance in real-time, provide immediate feedback, and detect specific problems. This would facilitate a more user-centered approach and improved decisions on the most appropriate interventions [8]. Combining both technologies is a major advancement in the diagnosis and treatment of dyslexia. Thanks to the immersive and interactive nature of VR and the analytical capabilities of NLP, very attractive, engaging tools can be created with a high level of effectiveness. This integrated approach has further improved the sweep of subtypes of dyslexia, particularly those related to phonological processing, and has led directly to more accurate and individually appropriate interventions that improve the educational and life outcomes of people with dyslexia.

The outline of this paper is as follows: Section 2 deals with the VR in dyslexia diagnosis and treatment. In Section 3, NLP will be discussed in the diagnosis and treatment of dyslexia, especially the importance of NLP techniques in analyzing language patterns will be emphasized, and NLP applications in education will be briefly touched upon. Next, Section 4 is devoted to describing the integration of VR and NLP comprehensively. The main contribution of this paper is introduced in Section 5. The model application, 'Virtual Dyslexia Diagnostic and Treatment System' (abbreviated to 'dysVRtech'), will be introduced in detail. Finally, the concluding remarks are given in Section 6.

2. Virtual reality in dyslexia diagnosis and treatment

VR can be defined as a computer-aided simulation of a three-dimensional environment that appears real or physical in the user's field of view. It is an immersive technology that allows users to be deeply immersed in a three-dimensional environment simulated using appropriate headsets and motion sensors, allowing users to explore and interact with this environment. Realistic images, sounds, and other sensations result from the software technologies used to create the immersive experience [9]. VR is used in a variety of disciplines, including education, medicine, entertainment, and professional training. The appropriate use of VR for dyslexia may provide new avenues for the detection and treatment of reading and writing problems through the creation of interesting, interactive worlds that can make the necessary adaptations. VR's ability to change traditional diagnosis and treatment is part of its potential to provide intense, controlled, multi-sensory learning experiences that are also immersive.

The application of VR in education and therapy is highly advantageous. However, it has several benefits for people with learning difficulties such as dyslexia:

- The VR environment is highly interactive and engaging, thus maintaining the user's attention and motivation when performing learning activities. One of the targeted participants will be children with dyslexia and therefore they are likely to have little in common. It is crucial for children to provide further reinforcement as research has shown that interactive VR experiences significantly increase engagement and learning outcomes [10].

- VR provides a safe and controlled environment for learning, where one can practice and develop skills without fear of making mistakes in the real world. As a result, this reduces the anxiety of experiencing and learning and helps dyslexic individuals improve their self-confidence in reading and writing.

- Customizable Learning Scenarios: The simulated scenarios and environments in VR can be programmed to the needs and abilities of individuals by teachers and therapists. Customization of the VR environments helps to make the interventions more effective by adjusting to the unique challenges experienced by each student. For example, in VR environments, it is possible to simulate different reading conditions to observe how people with difficulty are able to perform under different scenarios [11].

- Multi-sensory learning experience: VR is a multi-sensory system that allows learners to activate their senses of sight, hearing, and touch. The multi-sensory approach in VR can be particularly useful for people with dyslexia, as it strengthens the overall approach of using different senses for similar types of information during learning. VR incorporates multisensory experiences to strengthen the neural connections that contribute to reading and language skills. VR also supports this process through multisensory engagement [12].

- Instant Feedback and Progress Tracking: VR systems can provide immediate feedback on performance to enable users to understand and learn from their mistakes in real-time. In addition, by tracking progress over time, the VR platform can provide valuable data to trainers and therapists on how effective the intervention is and how much better users are getting.

The use of VR technology in the field of diagnosis and treatment of dyslexia has been made through various studies and practical applications. Specific examples include:

- VR Diagnostic Tools: These tools diagnose the effectiveness of phonological processing, word recognition, and reading speed in an immersive reading condition. Research in this field has developed tools to simulate different types of reading conditions and record how a dyslexic person interacts with the utterances in question.

- For example, it has been proven that VR through classroom simulation of interactive reading activities can provide valid assessment of children with reading difficulties [8]. In this framework, participants will be asked to read words or solve word puzzles while monitoring and analyzing their performance at some point. This will enable a reading diagnosis of their abilities in a controlled, dynamic environment.

- Therapeutic VR Applications: VR can also be used to create a therapeutic environment that can actively engage and interact with the reading and writing skills of dyslexic people. This software application has reading activities aimed at reading various texts and word games. The design leads to the development and improvement of phonological awareness and reading performance. According to Rodríguez-Cano et al. [13], VR is highly effective in developing or improving reading skills as a residue of gaming on the system, which is more enjoyable and stimulating than the traditional methods used by dyslexic children. But as an example of a therapeutic application, there is a magical world where they go through different situations. Thus, children can cross libraries in VR, where they have to find a series of books to read, or they can find themselves on a treasure hunt where they have to solve word puzzles [13].

- Enhanced Accessibility: VR reduces differences in access to therapeutic activities as the participant can perform it from home or a similar remote location. In this way, this solution will greatly target those who, for various reasons, find it difficult to receive specialized educational services. Thanks to head-mounted VR displays and mobile devices, diagnoses and treatments can be carried out at the participant's convenience, thus reducing dependency on specialists and the number of visits they have to make to them [8]. For example, VR at home means that children can participate in reading and in games targeting literacy skills. It allows parents to keep track of children's development and provide the necessary additional support, and this information is shared with teachers and therapists for further analysis.

- Integration with Traditional Methods: VR supports and enriches traditional methods of diagnosis and treatment by adding quality, interactivity, and immersion. Thus, traditional reading assessments can be extended with VR simulation scenarios that very closely mimic reading challenges, such as signage on crowded streets or following written instructions in noisy classrooms, among others. Integration can reveal the full scope of the reader's abilities and challenges [14].

Such integrated treatment may include hybrid assessments, where one is assessed in a traditional setting followed by VR-based tasks that can be performed, giving further insight into how the learner (student or patient, depending on the situation) copes with different reading environments. Such an approach to manageability can help educators and physicians make more effective intervention decisions. Finally, with the integration of VR into the diagnosis and treatment of dyslexia, there are many benefits of increasing learner engagement and motivation, and a safe environment can be controlled and adjusted for use.

3. NLP in dyslexia diagnosis and treatment

Artificial Intelligence is a very broad scientific field that includes a sub-discipline called Natural Language Processing (NLP), which acts as the interface between human (natural) language and the computer. NLP is a set of protocols and models that define algorithms, enabling the computer to understand human language and stimulate some meaningful speech at a certain level. NLP covers a wide range of activities from sentiment analysis and translation to speech recognition and text analysis [15].

NLP provides powerful tools to diagnose and treat dyslexia. NLP significantly enhances support for dyslexics through analysis of reading and writing patterns, real-time feedback mechanisms, and personalized learning interventions. The incorporation of NLP into both educational and therapeutic measures will lead to greater accuracy in diagnosis and better outcomes in treatment planning, thus leading to improved educational outcomes and quality of life for individuals affected by this condition.

3.1 NLP techniques for analyzing language patterns

NLP uses a variety of methods for the study and processing of languages, many of which are of particular importance for the recognition and treatment of dyslexia. Key techniques include:

Tokenization: The process of breaking a text into individual words or tokens. This is a fundamental process in many applications of NLP, allowing detailed analysis of every word in a text.

Part of Speech Tagging: The process of identifying which words belong to which grammatically (e.g. nouns, verbs, adjectives, etc.). In terms of syntax, it helps to understand the structure of the sentence.

Named Entity Recognition (NER): NER is the process of identifying and classifying entities in the text, such as names of people, organizations, locations, dates, and other important items.

Parsing: The process of analyzing the grammatical structure of sentences to understand the relationships between words and phrases.

Sentiment Analysis: This refers to the application of text analysis techniques to extract subjective information from the words used, which is more meaningful when trying to understand a dyslexic person's emotional reactions when reading and writing.

Speech Recognition: The ability to transcribe spoken words from a person. This is useful for testing a person's reading skills, which can be done by comparing that person's reading of any written text with the original reading of the text.

Text to Speech and Speech to Text Conversion: These two tools play a big role in researching and supporting the person suffering from dyslexia, as it is easy to switch from text to speech and vice versa.

NLP technologies can be applied in a variety of ways to support the diagnosis and treatment of dyslexia. By analyzing reading and writing patterns, NLP can provide detailed insights into the specific difficulties faced by dyslexic individuals.

3.2 Applications of NLP in educational assessments

3.2.1 Diagnostic applications

The application of NLP technologies in both the diagnosis and treatment of dyslexia can be of great importance; NLP will provide detailed information about the specific difficulties of the dyslexic individual through patterns analyzed in reading and writing.

Reading Assessment: NLP algorithms can process oral reading samples to identify typical signs of dyslexia phonological errors, mispronunciations, and omissions. By comparing the written text with the spoken text, NLP can find the exact points where the person faces difficulties.

Writing Analysis: Written samples can be analyzed for spelling mistakes, grammatical errors, and syntactic complexity through NLP tools. NLP tools are used, for example, to detect patterns that may suggest dyslexia (e.g. frequent reversals, substitutions, and inconsistencies in word usage) [16].

Automated Screening Tools: NLP-based screening tools can be developed to screen large numbers of people for dyslexia quickly and effectively. They can provide an initial screening showing potential cases of dyslexia for further detailed assessment by specialists.

3.2.2 Therapeutic applications

NLP can also play an important role in the treatment of dyslexia by providing personalized and adaptive learning experiences:

Interactive Reading Programs: NLP can provide interactive reading programs that adapt to different levels of difficulty depending on how well or poorly the user is performing. Such meaningful personalized exercises will enable the easy delivery of real-time feedback on the main areas of fluency and comprehension of reading texts.

Writing Assistance Tools: NLP-enabled writing assistants can provide real-time corrections and suggestions for improving the writing skills of dyslexics. They offer phonetic suggestions for misspelled words, correct grammar, and provide options for alternative expressions [17].

Speech Recognition for Phonological Training: This will help a person with dyslexia to develop phonological skills. He can learn strong reading by getting immediate feedback on his pronunciation and reading aloud fluency, while the software speech recognition will check his pronunciation and fluency levels.

3.3 Case studies of NLP applications in dyslexia

There are several case studies in the literature that highlight the effectiveness of NLP technologies in supporting dyslexic individuals:

Project LISTEN's Reading Tutor: This project is an early example of the use of NLP for dyslexia. The student reads aloud and the system gives feedback on how reading skills can be improved. The system uses speech recognition technology to detect errors in reading and give hints and corrections to guide the student to use a better-functioning reading method [18].

Writing Analysis Systems: Like Grammarly and other NLP-based tools, writing analysis systems are customized for educational purposes to support dyslexic learners. These tools correct students' writing in the text if there are any misspelled words, grammatical errors, or sentence structure errors, thus providing corrective feedback in real-time, including suggestions for improving word style.

Personalized Learning Platforms: Platforms such as Lexia Learning, leverage NLP to create a personalized learning experience that would appeal to dyslexic learners. They use interaction data to tailor the difficulty of the text and the type of reading and writing practice in order to personalize classical support and identify exactly what the learner needs to lead to growth [19].

4. Integration of VR and NLP: a comprehensive approach

Overall, VR and NLP can be seen as an all-encompassing, state-of-the-art approach to dyslexia diagnosis and treatment processes because, through a blend of the immersive, interactive nature of VR and the analytical potential of NLP, it can strengthen the user's likelihood of accessing accurate insights, real-time feedback, and ultimately the eventual personalized learning experience. These two technologies are being brought together to create a more engaging and effective educational environment leading to better outcomes for dyslexic individuals.

4.1 Combining VR and NLP for advanced diagnostics

The integration of VR and NLP offers a very effective and innovative method for the diagnosis of dyslexia. VR allows users to perform various activities such as reading or writing in a personal and interactive environment. NLP algorithms will then analyze and process the data from the VR environment and reveal the information in detail.

Enhanced Assessment Tools: The integration of VR and NLP can create very comprehensive diagnostic tools. For example, a VR application can replicate a classroom environment, allowing the user to read aloud. To simulate various reading conditions, the VR environment can adjust variables such as text size, background noise, main character, and lighting. As the user reads, NLP algorithms analyze their speech in real-time to detect errors in pronunciation, fluency, and comprehension. This method provides a comprehensive assessment of the user's reading abilities under various conditions [8].

Real-Time Feedback and Adaptation: One of the biggest benefits and unique features of VR and NLP integration is that it gives real-time feedback. For example, if a particular user has a specific problem with a particular word or phrase, real-time feedback can be provided or materials that are easier to read can be suggested. Thus, a more efficient learning experience can be built by adapting to the user's learning abilities and different needs [13].

4.2 Personalized treatment plans using VR and NLP

The integration of VR and NLP allows for the development of personalized treatment plans as well as diagnosis. These technologies can be used to create engaging, customized learning experiences and environments that meet the specific needs of each individual.

Customized Learning Environments: VR can create a multitude of learning environments that are completely tailored to the individual's preference and level of difficulty in which they operate. For example, a child who has difficulty with phonemic awareness can be given phonemic activities to engage with in a VR environment that focuses on vowel-letter correspondence and is supported by interactive games. NLP algorithms will be able to analyze the child's responses and vary the level of complexity so that the activities are challenging and can further enhance the individual's personal development.

Progress Monitoring and Data Analysis: Using NLP, one will get very detailed tracking of progress over time. Analyses of the user's continuous reading and writing performance will be able to highlight areas of growth and persistent confrontation of NLP algorithms. Thus a data-driven approach continuously tracks changes and helps educators and therapists to make adjustments to the treatment plan and make informed decisions about future interventions. For example, more focused exercises can be added to VR sessions if NLP analysis shows a persistent problem with certain phonemes [15].

4.3 Case studies on integrated approaches

Several case studies demonstrate the effectiveness of integrating VR and NLP in the diagnosis and treatment of dyslexia:

Immersive Reading Programs: A study by Maresca et al. [8] revealed how effective and efficient the use of VR environments integrated with NLP analysis is in the diagnosis of dyslexia. Children were given interactive reading sessions in a virtual reality classroom and NLP algorithms marked reading performance in real time. According to the results, better diagnoses were made with this integrated program; additionally, it was more engaging for students [8].

Adaptive Learning Platforms: Programs such as Lexia Learning incorporate NLP into the process of creating customized learning experiences for students with dyslexia. Reading and writing patterns are analyzed through the platform and the content is adapted according to the user's current level. The platform then presents relevant exercises to readers experiencing sensitive struggles. Integrating VR into such a platform will take the level of interactivity much further and increase engagement toward effectiveness as students will be in a virtual world where learning will be seen as a game [19].

Therapeutic Interventions: Rodríguez-Cano et al. [13] used VR and NLP in therapeutic settings to support dyslexic children. The study involved the creation of VR-based activities that were analyzed using NLP to provide feedback on reading fluency and comprehension. Findings showed that children were more motivated to engage in these activities, which led to significant improvements in reading skills [13].

5. Model application: virtual dyslexia diagnostic and treatment system (dysVRtech)

In this section, we will try to explain a system architecture integrated with today's modern technological hardware and completely machine learning-based software, which we call disVRtech abbreviated for 'Virtual Dyslexia Diagnostic and Treatment System', which we designed for application by constantly renewing it as a result of our own experiences in the diagnosis and treatment phases of dyslexia. In this system architecture, it is aimed to provide an immersive environment, as well as seeking qualities such as high efficiency and performance and being user-friendly and interactive with the user in an entertaining manner.

The dysVRtech system architecture aims to create a comprehensive diagnostic and treatment system for dyslexia by integrating VR and NLP technologies. This innovative approach leverages the immersive capabilities of VR environments to engage users in interactive reading and writing activities while using NLP algorithms to analyze performance in real time, providing detailed information and personalized feedback. The general structure of the tools and technologies used in this system architecture is given in **Figure 1**.

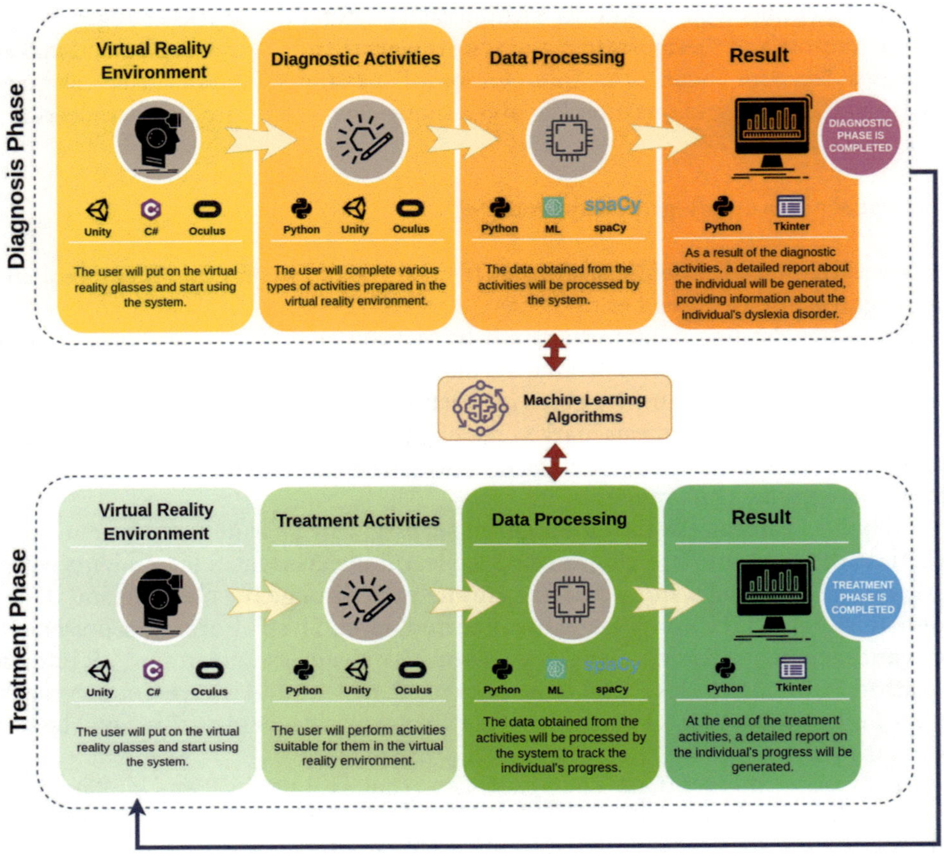

Figure 1.
The general structure of Virtual Dyslexia Diagnostic and Treatment System (dysVRtech).

The VR component of the dysVRtech involves the use of Oculus Go 32GB All in One VR headsets [20], the Unity 3D game engine [21], and the C# programming language to create immersive and interactive environments for users.

Hardware: Oculus Go 32GB Allin One VR headsets are used to provide an immersive experience and allow users to seamlessly interact with virtual environments.

Software: The Unity 3D game engine is used to develop VR environments, providing powerful tools for creating detailed and interactive simulations. The C# programming language is used to code and create interactive components within the VR space.

5.1 NLP in the dysVRtech system architecture

The disVRtech system is designed to integrate advanced VR technology with sophisticated NLP and machine learning algorithms to create an immersive and responsive user experience.

The data acquired from the VR headset application is analyzed using the spaCy NLP toolkit [22]. spaCyc is a sophisticated and effective open-source package specifically created for Python to handle natural language processing. It demonstrates exceptional performance in a range of NLP applications, including tokenization, part-of-speech tagging, named entity recognition, dependency parsing, and text categorization. Using spaCy, the VR headset application data is processed efficiently and accurately, resulting in detailed and insightful text analysis that improves the program's capacity to successfully perceive user interactions and feedback.

Speech Recognition: NLP algorithms convert spoken language into text, enabling the system to analyze reading performance by detecting errors in pronunciation, fluency, and comprehension.

Text Analysis: Written texts produced by users are analyzed to assess spelling, grammar, and syntactic complexity and to identify patterns indicative of dyslexia.

Real-Time Feedback: The developed dysVRtec system architecture provides immediate feedback based on the analysis, helping users correct their mistakes and improve their skills through guided exercises.

5.2 Machine learning and data analysis in the dysVRtec system architecture

Machine learning algorithms are required to process the data collected during the diagnosis and treatment phases. Here, there are many interactive applications for the diagnosis and treatment of dyslexia. Using machine learning methods, diagnostic and therapeutic activities tailored to the individual are determined. The Random Forest machine learning algorithm, an ensemble method based on decision trees, is used to analyze user data and personalize the activities accordingly. By constructing multiple decision trees during training and outputting the mode of the classes (classification) or mean prediction (regression) of the individual trees, Random Forest provides a robust and accurate model for predicting user needs. This approach helps ensure an effective and customized strategy for each user's requirements, as it reduces overfitting and improves generalization by combining the results of many decision trees to produce a more reliable output [23].

In the latter phase, machine learning algorithms are used to process the data collected by spaCy in order to identify if a person has dyslexia and, if so, to calculate the probability that they do. Random Forest and support vector machine (SVM) are the two machine learning techniques we use at this point.

With the use of many decision trees built during training, Random Forest is an ensemble learning technique that produces the mean prediction for regression tasks or the mode of the classes for classification tasks. When dealing with huge and complicated datasets, as those produced by the language features collected by spaCy, this technique performs especially well. Random Forest is a reliable option for assessing a variety of dyslexia-related characteristics since it lowers the chance of overfitting and improves accuracy by averaging the outcomes of multiple decision trees.

In contrast, the supervised learning model SVM finds the best hyperplane to optimize the margin between classes. When it comes to classification problems, this algorithm performs exceptionally well, particularly in high-dimensional spaces created by NLP features. SVM can identify non-linear correlations by using kernel functions, and it can accurately classify dyslexia depending on the data that is extracted.

When combined, Random Forest and SVM provide complementary qualities that enhance the system's overall diagnostic and prognostic skills, guaranteeing a thorough and precise dyslexia evaluation.

5.3 Diagnostic phase

The first phase of the dysVRtech system architecture focuses on the diagnosis of dyslexia. In this phase, users participate in various activities designed to assess their reading and writing skills:

Interactive VR Environment: Users wear Oculus VR headsets and participate in engaging and interactive activities developed using Unity 3D and C#. These activities include reading passages, matching exercises, and orientation tasks that engage multiple senses.

Data Collection: The system collects data from the user's interactions, including audio recordings, written text, and survey responses. This data is then processed using Python, NLP, and machine learning algorithms to evaluate the user's performance.

Accurate Diagnosis: The collected data is analyzed to determine whether the user has dyslexia. The high accuracy of the analysis ensures reliable diagnostic results [7].

5.4 Treatment phase

The second phase of the dysVRtech focuses on treating individuals diagnosed with dyslexia through engaging and effective VR activities:

Interactive Activities: Various interactive and fun activities have been designed in a VR environment to help dyslexia treatment. These activities target different aspects of reading and writing, helping users to improve their skills in a pleasant way.

Data Processing: Similar to the diagnostic phase, the data obtained from treatment activities are processed using Python, NLP, and Machine Learning algorithms. This allows for continuous monitoring and adjustment of the treatment plan according to the user's progress.

Progress Tracking: The system enables continuous tracking of the user's progress throughout the treatment process by recording the results of each activity [8].

5.5 Sample activity materials

The dysVRtech has many different materials for diagnostic and therapeutic purposes. These materials vary according to the knowledge, skills, and level of the individual. **Figure 2** is a reading passage designed to help diagnose dyslexia. This passage contains a mixture of phonetically regular and irregular words, varying sentence structures, and words that may cause difficulty for individuals with dyslexia:

Instructions for using the passage above can be summarized as follows: Read aloud: Have the individual read the passage aloud. Watch for errors in pronunciation, hesitation, and fluency.

Comprehension questions:

- *What did Tom find in the woods?*
- *Describe the hut Tom discovered.*
- *What was written in the mysterious old book?*
- *How did Tom find the treasure?*

Once upon a time, in a small village nestled between two towering mountains. There lived a young boy named Tom. Tom loved to explore the dense forest that surrounded his home. Every day, after school, he would venture into the woods with his faithful dog, Max.

One sunny afternoon, Tom and Max discovered a hidden path that they had never seen before. The path was narrow and winding, covered in fallen leaves and twigs. As they walked deeper into the forest, the trees grew taller and the light dimmer. Tom could hear the rustling of leaves and the distant chirping of birds.

Suddenly, Tom stumbled upon an old, abandoned cabin. The windows were broken, and the door creaked loudly as he pushed it open. Inside, the air was cool and musty. Cobwebs hung from the ceiling, and dust covered the furniture. On a small table in the corner, Tom found a mysterious old book. The cover was worn, and the pages were yellowed with age.

Curious, Tom opened the book and began to read. The words were written in a strange, flowing script that was difficult to decipher. "In the heart of the forest lies a treasure, hidden from those who seek it with greed," the book read. "Only the pure of heart will find it, guided by the light of the moon and the song of the nightingale."

Tom's heart raced with excitement. He knew that he had to find this treasure. With Max by his side, he left the cabin and continued along the hidden path. As night fell, the full moon rose high in the sky, casting a silver glow on the forest. Tom listened carefully, and soon he heard the sweet melody of a nightingale singing.

Following the bird's song, Tom and Max reached a clearing. In the center of the clearing, bathed in moonlight, was a sparkling chest. Tom opened the chest to find it filled with glittering jewels and golden coins. But more precious than the treasure was the adventure he had experienced and the bond he had strengthened with Max.

Tom returned to the village with stories of his adventure. He shared the treasure with his family and friends, and from that day on, he was known as the boy who found the hidden treasure of the forest. And so, the legend of Tom and Max's adventure lived on, inspiring other young explorers for generations to come.

Figure 2.
A sample reading passage used in the system to detect dyslexia disorder.

Error analysis: Analyze the types of mistakes made, such as omission, substitution, and reversal of letters and words.

Follow-up tasks: Based on the errors, create follow-up tasks that target specific challenges, such as phonemic awareness exercises, word recognition games, and fluent reading practices.

This passage and related tasks can help to identify areas where the individual has difficulties and provide valuable information for a comprehensive diagnosis of dyslexia.

5.6 Goals and benefits of the dysVRtech system architecture

The main objective of the dysVRtech is to provide an effective and engaging methodology for the early diagnosis and treatment of dyslexia:

Early Diagnosis: Using VR headsets and interactive activities, the dysVRtech aims to facilitate early and accurate diagnosis of dyslexia, helping to identify the condition before it significantly affects educational outcomes.

Engaging Treatment: A VR-based rehabilitation approach makes the treatment process enjoyable and motivating for users, increasing participation and success rates. Comprehensive Support: The combination of VR and NLP enables users to receive personalized and detailed support, improving reading and writing skills while reducing the stress associated with traditional methods [13].

System feature	Available solutions	Developed system (dysVRtech)
Diagnostic Phase	—	+
Treatment Phase	+	+
VR Technology	+	+
Activity Analysis with NLP	—	+
Analysis with Machine Learning Automatic Update of Difficulty Level	—	+
According to Individual's Progress	—	+
Mobile App	—	+

Table 1.
Comparison of features and solutions of the developed system with other similar systems and/or solutions.

In summary, the disVRtech leverages the latest technologies in VR and NLP to offer a comprehensive solution for the diagnosis and treatment of dyslexia. This innovative approach promises to improve educational and personal outcomes for dyslexic individuals, making learning a more enjoyable and effective experience. When the literature is reviewed, it is seen that various studies have been conducted on dyslexia, especially using VR [8, 6, 13, 24]. These studies are generally related to activities in a VR environment for individuals diagnosed with dyslexia. The features of the solutions in the literature and the system (architecture) developed within the scope of this work are presented comparatively in **Table 1**.

6. Potential limitations and challenges

To successfully implement the disVRtech system, it is necessary to have high-performance hardware in order to guarantee smooth and uninterrupted VR experiences. If the hardware does not meet the required specs, users may encounter latency and frame rate problems, which can negatively impact their entire experience. Moreover, the incorporation of the disVRtech system into current software platforms may provide compatibility obstacles. This frequently requires the creation of customized solutions and the identification and resolution of issues, which can consume a significant amount of time and involve specific technical knowledge.

Regular maintenance and updates are essential to guarantee the system remains operational and up-to-date with technological changes, which presents a continuing operational challenge.

The high learning curve of VR technology can impede novice users. Efficient training programs or materials are crucial in enabling users to develop familiarity with the system and optimize its potential advantages. Ensuring accessibility is a crucial consideration, as the system must be flexible enough to accommodate the requirements of users with different disabilities. This involves guaranteeing that the VR setting is easily traversable for those with physical limitations and that visual and audio information is easily accessible for those with sensory impairments. Moreover, the successful adoption of the system may be impeded by user resistance either from skepticism or a preference for familiar ways.

The initial capital outlay necessary for procuring VR hardware and software is considerable, presenting a notable financial obstacle for several enterprises. This includes the expenses associated with virtual reality headgear, motion-tracking sensors, and high-performance processing systems. Organizations should allocate funds for training programs aimed at instructing users and administrators on the optimal utilization of the technology. In addition to the initial charges, there are continuous costs associated with maintaining the system, such as software updates, hardware maintenance, and prospective upgrades to include newer technology. It is crucial to effectively handle these financial factors in order to guarantee the system's long-term sustainability.

The utilization of VR systems gives rise to significant concerns surrounding data privacy, specifically pertaining to the gathering, retention, and utilization of user data. VR systems frequently gather comprehensive personal information, such as biometric data, which necessitates careful handling to safeguard user privacy. Organizations are required to establish strong data protection procedures and adhere to any privacy legislation in order to protect this information. Ethical concerns also emerge, particularly in delicate domains such as healthcare, where the utilization of VR must be handled prudently to prevent any potential harm. This entails ensuring that VR therapies are grounded in empirical research and that users are provided with comprehensive information regarding the potential advantages and disadvantages. It is of utmost importance to address these ethical and privacy problems in order to establish user confidence and guarantee the proper utilization of VR technology.

7. Conclusion

As seen in the dysVRtech system architecture we have developed, the combination of VR and NLP technologies is very useful in the diagnosis and treatment of dyslexia. It is a new approach that combines the immersive and interactive potential of VR with the data processing phases of NLP, enabling the use of innovative, interesting, and personalized support opportunities for dyslexic people. Diagnosing people with dyslexia in a quick, accurate, and often fun way is a great convenience for both people with the disorder and professionals working in the field, such as teachers, psychologists, doctors, and health professionals. Obviously, this is also true for family members who spend most of their time with individuals with this disorder.

Although the combination of VR and dyslexia brings many benefits, it is clear that there are also some challenges. The first of these challenges is that the development and maintenance of NLP algorithms are based on the data obtained from the VR environment. The design of this process and the processing of the obtained data require quite complex processes and procedures. Experts in the fields of software development, machine learning, and educational psychology will be needed to ensure that these two fundamental technologies can work together seamlessly. In addition, it is critical for the success of the system that the designed environments are adequately tested according to criteria such as different knowledge and skills, age, gender, and different types of dyslexia. Another critical point is the accessibility of such solutions. Especially high-tech and ergonomic VR equipment has limited hardware resources in terms of the computation required to run high-level NLP algorithms. Hardware that offers more resources is expensive. This makes it difficult for families without sufficient financial resources to access these tools. Therefore, future developments need to make solutions in this area more cost-effective and be adopted and supported by a wide range of stakeholders. Another important issue is that educators, therapists, and families need to be fully trained in the use of such tools. An effective understanding of how to read the data provided by NLP and VR systems and how to use this data in a personalized educational plan is crucial to truly reap the benefits that such technology can offer. There are also some ethical challenges. It is important to work on data privacy and security, especially among young children. In addition, the negative effects of intensive VR use on children's physical and mental health and development should be investigated in detail. It is extremely important to further investigate the effectiveness and usability of VR and NLP in different educational models, in different languages and cultures going forward.

Finally, when evaluated through the disVRtech system architecture, the use of VR and NLP together in the diagnosis and treatment of dyslexia, the prevalence of which varies between 2 and 10% in the world, offers great potential in the diagnosis and treatment of this disorder. This approach offers a very interesting, innovative, and original method in the diagnosis process of dyslexia. It is very important in terms of providing a personalized, innovative, and fun environment in the treatment process. Addressing these challenges with future improvements, the disVRtech has a high potential to improve the quality of life and educational outcomes of dyslexic people.

Abbreviations

NLP	natural language processing technologies
VR	virtual reality
dysVRtech	virtual dyslexia diagnostic and treatment system

Author details

Fevzi Daş[1*†], Emin Taner Elmas[2†] and İhsan Ömür Bucak[3†]

1 Computer Application and Research Center, Iğdır University, Iğdır, Türkiye

2 Department of Bioengineering and Bio-Sciences, Graduate School of Natural and Applied Sciences, Iğdır University, Iğdır, Türkiye

3 Computer Engineering Department, Iğdır University, Iğdır, Türkiye

*Address all correspondence to: fevzi.das@igdir.edu.tr

† These authors contributed equally.

References

[1] Shaywitz SE, Shaywitz BA. The neurobiology of reading and dyslexia. ASHA Lead. 2007;**12**(12):20-21

[2] Lyon GR, Shaywitz SE, Shaywitz BA. Dyslexia: Diagnosis, treatment, and prevention. Pediatrics. 2003;**111**(3):763-768

[3] Vellutino FR, Fletcher JM, Snowling MJ, Scanlon DM. Understanding dyslexia: A new approach. Journal of Learning Disabilities. 2004;**37**(2):105-123

[4] Singleton C, Thomas K, Horne J. Computer-based cognitive assessment and the development of reading. Journal of Research in Reading. 2000;**23**(2):158-180

[5] Mikropoulos T. A virtual reality test for the identification of memory strengths of dyslexic students in higher education. Journal of Universal Computer Science. 2013;**19**:2698-2721

[6] Maskati E, Alkeraiem F, Khalil N, Baik R, Aljuhani R, Alsobhi A. Using virtual reality (VR) in teaching students with dyslexia. International Journal of Emerging Technologies in Learning IJET. 2021;**16**(9):291-305

[7] Denckla MB, Rudel RG. Rapid 'automatized' naming (R.A.N.): Dyslexia differentiated from other learning disabilities. Neuropsychologia. 1976;**14**(4):471-479

[8] Maresca G, Leonardi S, De Cola MC, Giliberto S, Di Cara M, Corallo F, et al. Use of virtual reality in children with dyslexia. Child Basel Switzerland. 2022;**9**(11):1621

[9] Trinon H. Immersive Technologies for Virtual Reality-Case Study: Flight Simulator for Pilot Training. [Master Thesis] Liege, Belgium: Liege University; 2019

[10] Huang HM, Rauch U, Liaw SS. Investigating learners' attitudes toward virtual reality learning environments: Based on a constructivist approach. Computers in Education. 2010;**55**(3):1171-1182

[11] Marougkas A, Troussas C, Krouska A, Sgouropoulou C. Virtual reality in education: A review of learning theories, approaches and methodologies for the last decade. Electronics. 2023;**12**(13):2832

[12] Ross M. Virtual reality's new synesthetic possibilities. Television and New Media. 2020;**21**(3):297-314

[13] Rodríguez-Cano S, Delgado-Benito V, Ausín-Villaverde V, Martín LM. Design of a Virtual Reality Software to promote the learning of students with dyslexia. Sustainability. 2021;**13**(15):8425

[14] Elmqaddem N. Augmented reality and virtual reality in education. Myth or reality? International Journal of Emerging Technologies in Learning. 2019;**14**:234

[15] Jurafsky D, Martin J. Speech and language processing: An introduction to natural language processing. Computational Linguistics, and Speech Recognition. New Jersey, USA: Prentice Hall; 2008. pp. 2-9

[16] Denckla MB, Rudel RG. Rapid 'automatized'naming (RAN): Dyslexia differentiated from other learning disabilities. Neuropsychologia. 1976;**14**(4):471-479

[17] Iyer L, Chakraborty T, Reddy KN, Jyothish K, Krishnaswami M. AI-Assisted Models for Dyslexia and Dysgraphia: Revolutionizing Language Learning for Children. 2023. Hershey, Pennsylvania, USA: IGI Global; 2023. pp. 186-207

[18] Mostow J, Aist G, Burkhead P, Corbett A, Cuneo A, Eitelman S, et al. Evaluation of an automated Reading tutor that listens: Comparison to human tutoring and classroom instruction. Journal of Educational Computing Research. 2003;**29**(1):61-117

[19] Lexia. An Adaptive e-Learning Platform for Personalised Education of Children with Dyslexia [Internet]. 2017. Available from: https://www.era-learn.eu/network-information/networks/eurostars-2/eurostars-cut-off-7/an-adaptive-e-learning-platform-for-personalised-education-of-children-with-dyslexia

[20] Popov S, Surchev S, Petkov T, Todorov M, Sotirova E, Sotirov S, et al. Virtual reality as educational technology. In: 2019 29th Annual Conference of the European Association for Education in Electrical and Information Engineering (EAEEIE). Ruse, Bulgaria: IEEE; 2019. pp. 1-6

[21] Wang S, Mao Z, Zeng C, Gong H, Li S, Chen B. A new method of virtual reality based on Unity 3D. In: 2010 18th International Conference on Geoinformatics. Beijing, China: IEEE; 2010. pp. 1-5

[22] Honnibal M, Montani I. spaCy 2: Natural language understanding with bloom embeddings, convolutional neural networks and incremental parsing. To appear. 2017;**7**(1):411-420

[23] Pralhad GP, Joshi A, Chhipa M, Kumar S, Mishra G, Vishwakarma M. Dyslexia prediction using machine learning. In: 2021 International Conference on Artificial Intelligence and Machine Vision (AIMV). Gandhinagar, India: IEEE; 2021. pp. 1-6. DOI: 10.1109/AIMV53313.2021.9671004

[24] Pena N. VR as a tool for students with disabilities. In: Proceedings of July 29, 2022 (VR-REU 2022). New York, NY, USA: ACM; 2022. pp. 1-3

Section 3

Culture and Education in the Metaverse

Chapter 6

Contemporary Apparel and Historical Costume in Metaverse

Victor Kuzmichev and Jiaqi Yan

Abstract

The process of designing, producing, and marketing in the Metaverse will significantly change human interactions with regard to clothing. The development includes each stage of its lifecycle in terms of digitizing the soft skills of fashion industry professionals, simulating and perception of human bodies' activities, and an exhibition of historical costumes. The transformation of 2D objects into 3D virtual clothing will make design more creative. Extended reality technologies require digital twins of human bodies, textile materials, accessories, and sewing patterns. To simulate real sensations and features in the digital system "human body -apparel", all digital twins should be acquired, measured, generated, and validated as the real counterparts. Due to hierarchical information about cultural artifacts, virtual historical costumes will be presented in museums, galleries, and in Metaverse art projects. The Metaverse of contemporary clothing and historical costume has been evolving with more possibilities and greater influence in everyone's life in accordance with the latest technologies such as artificial intelligence, algorithms, and 3D scanning.

Keywords: apparel, artificial intelligence, virtual reality, creativity, cultural heritage

1. Introduction

With the introduction of the Metaverse, virtual clothing has emerged as a distinct category. The new virtual fashion and culture featuring digital artwork, virtual production, and transmission have become popular this year due to the latest technological foundations. Three-dimensional simulation of digital clothing includes the use of several virtual counterparts of soft-bodied objects at once: a human body, textile materials of woven or knitted weaving, and flat textile scans of the parts that will make up the clothing, as well as some solid-state accessories such as buttons, zippers, etc. Modern 3D clothing design systems offer approximately the same scenarios for generating "avatar - apparel" systems with varying degrees of realism and inadequacy to material systems [1].

1.1 Objects of simulation

Depending on the areas of application, these systems are focused on different situations of generating virtual clothing with various requirements:

- design of non-existent clothes (digital fashion),
- presentation of the created apparel (translation of real clothes into a virtual form),
- stylized apparel for the gaming industry.

The development processes of 3D design are activated under the influence of several factors, such as customization (the need for clothing with individual design and a high-quality fit on the body), virtual try-on (before online or offline purchase), as well as special requirements of computer games. The application of virtual clothing and other belongings such as shoes, caps, bags, etc. It includes many directions of human activity such as art and engineering design, marketing, self-presentation, virtual games, museum exhibitions, science, and modeling different situations without real persons. The technology of virtual clothing is a complex multidisciplinary area that operates with a digital form of each element and module combining together the "human body-apparel" system and joining ones after full parameterization. So, scientific research is done with the following objects:

1. Artworks, cyber advertisements, images, videos, and games forming virtual fashion art;
2. Human bodies that should be transformed into like-human avatars. The final result of transformation could be present, first, as an individualized digitized human model with accurate copies of morphological features by means of automatic scanning and intelligently modification and, second, as the artistically styled avatar;
3. Clothing that should be simulated as ready-to-wear (RtW), made-to-measure (MtM), or bespoke real counterpart;
4. Historical costumes or their saved garments which should be accurately virtually reconstructed, generated and repaired according to the precious textile artifacts, photos, paintings, murals, etc.
5. The virtual mirror or fitting room could present a new system "real consumer + virtual apparel" to display the appearance and fit of apparel and give size recommendations by means of artificial intelligence (AI).

All virtual objects could be generated by AI and new algorithms for recognizing colors, shapes, fit of garments, and other attributes of virtual twins classifications. Instead of offline purchasing which takes a lot of time to try on and buy clothing offline, virtual try-on provides a new way of interactive and immersion for consumers. **Figure 1** shows how to use the Gucci AR Sneaker Try-on Application using virtual reality and augmented reality (AR).

DOI: http://dx.doi.org/10.5772/intechopen.1006300

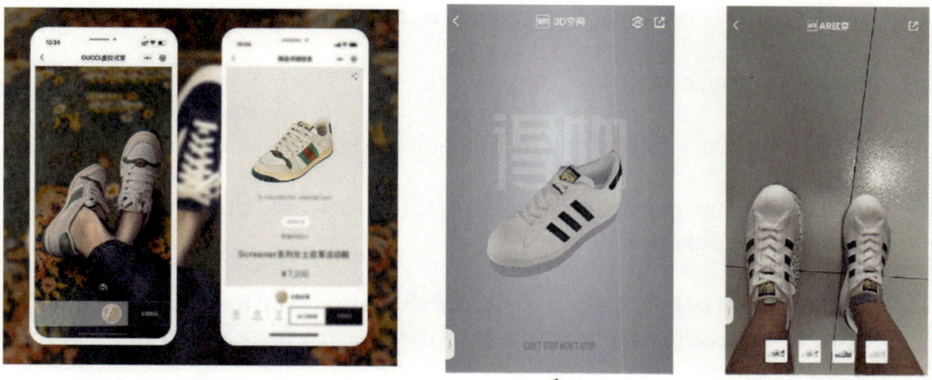

a b c

Figure 1.
VR and AR try-on applications: a - Gucci AR sneaker try-on, b - Poizon VR sneaker exhibition, c - Poizon AR sneaker try-on.

As **Figure 1** shows, consumers can instantly try on the various sneakers using their smartphones, thereby reducing online sales returns and increasing sales volume. Similar online apparel platforms applied VR and AR technologies for 3D exhibitions and virtual try-ons. To present real clothing in the Metaverse, there are basic science and practical directions which are involved in this process and operating with the essential modules composing clothing by means of the technologies laying a solid foundation for Metaverse's development.

1.2 Software for simulation

A series of software are involved in the digital twin of contemporary apparel (DTCA) generating.

In the fashion and computer graphic (CG) industries, the clothing clay model uses virtual fitting systems. These systems can create or modify the two-dimensional (2D) pattern and 3D clothing in virtual space and instantaneously exhibit the simulation of textile materials (TM) draping and shaping, greatly optimizing the efficiency and material consumption. The digital twin of "avatar-clothing" system is supplemented by information links between many elements. In this regard, digitalization relies on software programs that are used to produce twins. The process of twin generation involves many steps, such as the creation of an initial database, human body modeling, pattern drafting, virtual try-on, post-processing, texture painting, rendering, and quality assessment. Each step focuses on different objects and requires special methods to analyze and transform those objects into digital form. For this reason, no single software program can be used throughout the entire process with different objects. The practice shows that IT engineers and 3D modelers use pipelines as a set of software programs due to the initial data overwhelming on its way to the final digital object. This means that different software programs that are part of the pipeline are applied continuously, one after another.

Popular software includes Style3D Studio (China), CLO 3D (Korea), Vstitcher (Singapore), TUKA 3D Fit (USA), Optitex (Israel), 3D Vidya (Germany), and others. These systems usually integrate the following modules: avatar editing, pattern block drafting, virtual fitting, TM editing, rendering, online assets library, etc.

For example, the software Style3D contains the following modules:

1. an avatar editing, edition and output;
2. 2D pattern block (PB) drafting including its modification, import or output;
3. 3D virtual sewing and fitting from 3D PB. The real-time simulation of cloth draping can be observed and evaluated;
4. TM editing: TM exterior appearance and shaping can be imported and edited by specific textures and draping properties parameters, respectively;
5. rendering and output: the complete project can be rendered with editable lights or cameras, outputting static photos, vertical video, runway video, etc.;
6. online assets library: different categories of virtual assets (avatar, TM, auxilliary materials, complete projects, etc.). It can be shared, downloaded and saved;
7. other free body and clothing measuring, Python script, etc.
8. Sometimes, with special requirements, additional software is necessary such as:
9. professional virtual reality TM generating (Style3D fabric) or universal soft Adobe Substance 3D Designer TM's texture maps (texture, normal, smoothness, Metalness, transparency, replacement, etc.);
10. Blender or Zbrush for sculpturing of apparel details.
11. Blender or Unreal Engine for final model outputted for further rendering.
12. 3D CAD/CAM soft is needed, e.g., Rhinoceros, for the investigation of clothing shape.

Published research devoted to digital twins of clothing demonstrates different pipelines in accordance with the functional possibilities of the software. In study [2] AutoCAD, Clo3D and 3dsMax were combined to reproduce the 1840th dress suit. Additionally, the combination of AutoCAD, Autodesk Inventor, Clo3D and 3dsMax was applied to the parametric modeling of historical crinolines and mannequins [3, 4]. A set of 2D pattern drafting systems, computer simulation, and texture painting packages was applied to generate digital twins of Chinese archaeological clothes [5, 6]. Despite encouraging results in using different pipelines, a versatile and systematic approach to creating those pipelines has not yet developed.

The process of choosing software programs that can be used to model virtual clothing includes six steps. The first step is to produce a digital copy of the human body called an avatar. The second step uses 2D computer-aided design (CAD) systems for pattern drafting. The third step utilizes computer simulations to place the garment on the avatar. The fourth step involves post-processing the 3D surface to create a flat surface. During the fifth step, the 3D model is painted in accordance with the colors and textures of textile materials. The sixth step is dedicated to the creation of multimedia materials and the presentation of the digital twin.

Most programs can only be applied once. For example, Make Human and DAZ Studio were developed to model avatars. Seamly2D and AutoCAD are used for pattern drafting. Several software packages, such as Marvelous Designer, Clo3D, Optitex, and Blender are more flexible and can cover two or more steps of 3D modeling. If eight software decisions are available at each step, in accordance with the principles of combinatorics, the above-mentioned software could be organized into 262.144 hypothetic pipelines to generate virtual clothing. The pipelines are not the same; each of them requires resources, namely time, staff, and money. The resulted "avatar-clothing" systems differ from each other as well. The features of clothing can be described using special criteria. To meet those requirements, the software program should be able to reproduce all objects, such as avatars, patterns, textile materials, and the 3D structure of the surface of the garment.

1.3 Apparel in metaverse

The differences between the features of composed modules of "human body (avatar) - clothing" systems in real and virtual reality are shown in **Table 1**.

Design of virtual clothing based on the most essential technologies which are helping to create the scenario for the "avatar + clothing" display. First, the technology of extended reality, namely AR, VR, and mixed reality can present immersive digital information and images generated in the virtual or cyber environments through display, smartphone or wearable computing devices. Second, digital twins can be generated as a virtual replica of the objects or systems for accurate simulation, analysis, and study. Third, AI and automation algorithms can optimize the whole process of

No	Modules of system	Existing and reproducing features	
		Real environment	Metaverse
1	user	1. A real user with individual human body morphological features and dimensions in both static and dynamic, the ability to react on external stimuli. 2. Mannequin (dummy) with standard human body morphological features and dimensions.	An avatar of a human body that should mimic human features, physical behavior, and sensitive reactions.
2	textile materials (TM)	Soft objects with certain exterior textures and physical, mechanical, tactile other properties	A virtual twins with mapping-generated textures and digital (parameterized) physical properties
3	pattern sewing block (PB)	flat details which are reflecting the future clothing style, outline shape and fit	3D details which are locating around an avatar, integrating in apparel by virtual sewing and forming apparel shape due to textile materials properties and other design elements
4	auxiliary materials and accessories	Soft and solid (zippers, buttons, etc.) auxiliary materials and accessories	virtual soft and solid auxiliary materials and accessories;
5	presentation		a scenario for apparel displaying

Table 1.
Special features of virtual and real "human body (avatar) - apparel" system.

clothing designing, generating, marketing, etc., and offer intelligent interactions, automatic operations, and creative personalized experiences. Fourthly, a blockchain can be applied as a tool that helps to ensure a secure, verifiable, and permanent way across a network of computers. https://www.grammarchecker.com/#.

The use of clothing in the Metaverse extends beyond traditional real-world applications:

1. Design: before mass production, it is utilized for virtual design and evaluation;

2. Marketing: virtual images or videos are employed to showcase and promote products;

3. Social interaction: 3D interactive avatars and apparel models serve as representations of consumers or users, engaging in online activities or shopping;

4. Education: virtual software programs can quickly demonstrate clothing-related theories, histories, etc.;

5. Art and entertainment: contemporary apparel and historical costumes are commonly featured in CG artworks, films, television, and video games;

6. Museums or galleries: online and offline exhibitions of reconstructed historical costumes are widespread in museums and galleries;

7. Virtual goods and services: non-fungible tokens (NFTs) are traded online as digital assets.

2. Avatars of human body

The avatar, also known as a virtual human model (VHM), is the digital twin of a human body (DTB). Avatars usually come in two primary styles: realistic and stylish. Obviously, these two styles of avatars differ in many aspects, as shown in **Table 2**. https://chat.gpt-tools.ru/dashboard

First and foremost, realistic avatars are usually reconstructed based on real physical human bodies, looking similar to human appearance and morphology, and their postures in static and dynamic. On the contrary, stylish avatars are designed to be different from physical beings, with variable styles. For instance, super-deformed, cartoon, futuristic, alien. The stylish avatar differs from the real body in that it has a cartoon-styled appearance and abnormal morphological ratios and features. The realistic avatars have the same dimensions as physical human bodies, while the stylish avatars are different. Moreover, both types of realistic and stylish avatars have different skeletons, tissues, etc.

2.1 Avatar types

This section operates with the realistic avatar in detail. The international standard ISO 20497-1: 2021 [10] defines precisely three main types of avatars: virtual clone (VC, scanatar), virtual twin (VT), and virtual fit mannequin (VFM) which are shown in **Table 3**.

As shown in **Table 3**, a scanatar is identical to the real body scanned by a 3D body scanner and equal in terms of the point cloud obtained after scanning, the surface,

Features	**Avatar style**	
	Realistic	**Stylish**
Image		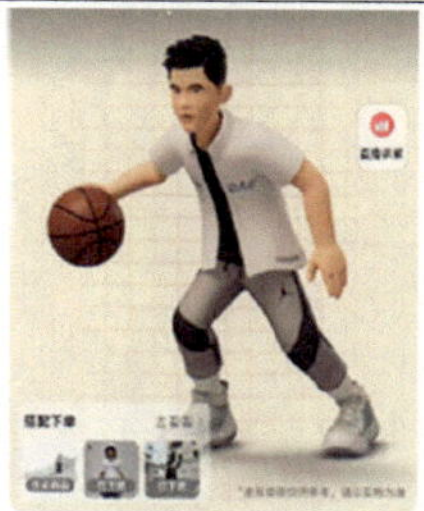
Exterior appearance and morphology	The same as physical human bodies	Different from physical human bodies Generally similar to human, but different in detail
Interior Structure (skeletons, tissues, etc.)	Similar or different from physical human bodies	
Dimensions	The same as physical human bodies	Different from physical human bodies
Type of avatar	1. Standard avatar for ready-to-wear (RtW) clothing design and production, or historical costume reconstruction and exhibition. 2. Individualized avatar for customized clothing (made-to-measure and bespoke), anthropometrical researches and pattern generating methods	Any types exaggerated and expressive appearance
Main application areas	Apparel design, education, scientific research, museum, expressing users' individuality, etc.	Apparel advertisement and marketing, online shopping platforms, social interaction, art and entertainment (3D art, videos, movies), NFT, etc.

Table 2.
Features of two avatar styles [7–9].

and the mesh generated by the software. VC is determined by the actual body, which has the same appearance and morphology. Owing to these features, VC is frequently used in MtM and bespoke clothing processed for designing virtual individualized clothing with a good fit. VC has also paved a broader way for scientific research on human body morphology.

VT is a parametric human body morphed by automatically generated or manually measured body dimensions. When generated automatically, VT is usually the same as the standard body from national or corporation standards. When generated manually, VT is adapted to the typical morphology of an individual. VT is usually generated in specialized software such as DAZ 3D, Character Creator, Style 3D, CLO 3D by means of next options including lengths, girths, fatness, muscle, etc. The face is the part of the body; it has skin, hair, eye, nose, mouse, eyebrow, ear, etc.; skin texture, hairstyle; face expression; static postures and dynamic motions; as gender, age and other features. VT is more flexible than VC in RtW or customized virtual apparel design, exhibition, and advertisement.

VFM is a standard virtual mannequin with standard morphology and dimensions. It is usually generated in advance and kept in the software's asset library. It is mostly

Features	Type		
	VC (scanatar)	VT	VFM
Image	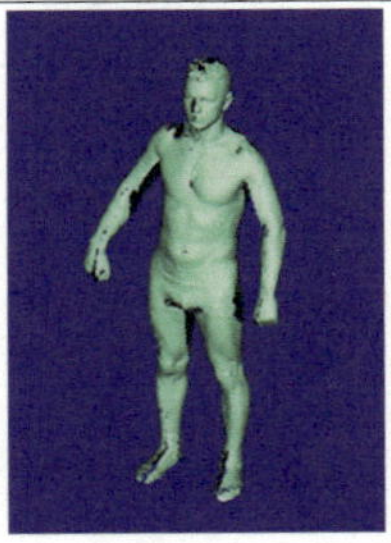	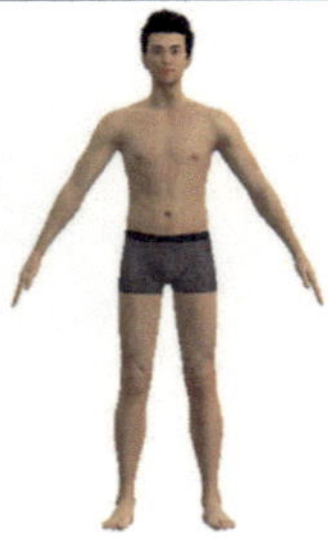	
Description	identical to real physical body and equal to 3D scanned point cloud	a parametric morphed model according to body measurements and acquired through manual or automatic measurements	a copy of physical human body mannequin
Generating method	through 3D body scanning	through avatar generating module modified by standard, individual BM; transformation from a VC	a VC of mannequin; a 3D mannequin model with standard morphology and BM
Exterior appearance	same as an individual real body	looks similar to a real body	looks different from a real body, similar to a real mannequin
Morphology	same as an individual real body	same as an individual or standard real body	partly similar to a standard real body
Adjustable options	None	dimensions, posture, emotion, nationality, hairstyle, age, etc.	None
Main application areas	Virtual fitting of individualized apparel	Virtual fitting of RtW or individualized apparel, virtual display, marketing, etc.	Virtual fitting of RtW apparel

Table 3.
Three types of avatars and their features [11].

used for RtW apparel design and simulation. Standard VFM could be accurately created from samples of VC (the account of VC should be 100 and more) belonging to one size and which is useful for RtW apparel design and fit evaluation.

The avatars are being used in the Metaverse in various aspects.

The most common application of avatars is the creation of virtual clothing for virtual display and marketing, which has shown great satisfaction from consumers and users. Because VC has the same morphology as the scanned real body, it is to help generate customized apparel and realize a new 3D-to-2D method of pattern generating in the opposite of the traditional 2D-to-3D pattern generating method. The new 3D-to-2D method can directly create 3D clothing around the VC and obtain the 2D customized patterns. **Figure 2** shows how to use the scanter and the surface of individual VC to create virtual individual clothing.

The improvement of avatar generation is related to accuracy, practicability, and efficiency in the application of sizing systems from national standards.

To improve the user's experience in Metaverse, the individualized head and face texture were now intelligently generated from an original VT. By putting the user's single frontal face image (a photo), detailed expression capture and animation neural network were adopted to generate the corresponding 3D head model with initial texture. Based on the linear correlation and K-nearest neighbor algorithm, a more

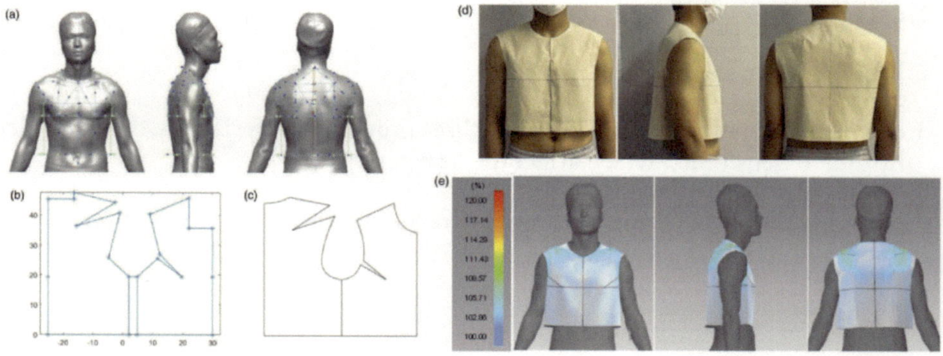

Figure 2.
3D-to-2D PB generating method based on VC: (a) establishment of the prototype wireframe, (b) flattened prototype wireframe, (c) individualized PB, (d) real try-on, (e) virtual try-on [12].

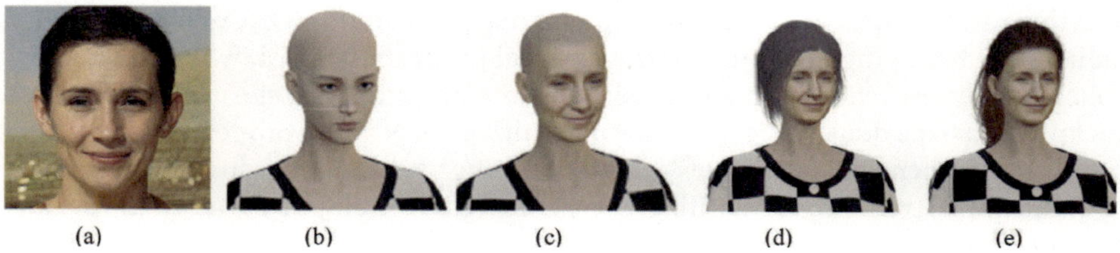

Figure 3.
Individualized head and face texture in Metaverse: (a) user's frontal view, (b) original dressed avatar, (c) user's dressed avatar, (d) user's dressed avatar with short hair, (e) user's dressed avatar with long hair [15].

convenient and efficient avatar can be generated based on semantic-driven parameters through automatic accurate prediction of 12 body dimensions [13].

A multi-sensor information acquisition system (MIAS) can accurately measure 11 key BM and generate a VT without clothes taking off [14].

The final style of the avatar was carried out by a progressive attention manifold alignment neural network. **Figure 3** shows the steps to generate a human face to use in Metaverse.

2.2 Virtual textile materials

One of the most difficult processes is generating a digital twin of TM due to its structural complexity and unknown mechanism of its behavior prediction during the transformation from a flat to 3D. The twin's TM on the surface acquires a complex 3D shape under the influence of physical and mechanical properties and the action of gravity.

The current requirements for a virtual twin of TM include the following schedule that should be similar to real prototypes: coloristic design; surface texture, including interlacing; appearance at the time of draping on the surface of the ball (the most common method of visual representation of material and virtual fabric). The most difficult part is the process of replicating the physical behavior of a real fabric. The shaping of real clothing occurs under the influence of several factors at once, a set of which depends on the shape and structure of the clothing. In real processes of design and manufacturing technology, the following single indicators of geometric, physicomechanical and structural properties are taken into account:

1. drapery,

2. bending stiffness,

3. extensibility under uniaxial loading (three groups of materials are distinguished by their extensibility, which affect the design of parts) [4],

4. changing the angle between the warp threads and the weft or loop columns under the action of shear loads,

5. thickness,

6. change of linear dimensions after thermal treatments,

There are other indicators taken into account when cutting, making clothes, and connecting individual parts with each other, which are not included in the schedule and which may reflect the specifics of the processed fabrics (for example, skewed weft threads, the presence of linear graphic ornament, etc.). ISO 20947-2:2020(E) includes the following indicators of the physical properties of TM, which are controlled during their simulation: extensibility, bending stiffness, shear resistance, thickness, surface density [16]. The indirect influence of these properties is also taken into account when evaluating the "avatar - clothing" system according to the following indicators: stretching of clothing in certain areas, the air gap between the avatar and clothing, the presence of folds.

Existing approaches to simulating the 3D shape of textile materials in VR are based on three approaches to their properties: geometric (shell modeling based on geometric primitives), physical (modeling textile material as a combination of a huge number of thin force elements with a certain energy based on the finite element method [17–20], finite volume models [21], partial system models [22, 23]), and hybrid. A partial system model is the simplest and most effective way to simulate tissues as a set of vertices of a polygonal network in cases of large displacements and small deformations.

The largest number of studies is devoted to the most important and visually-perceived indicator—the draping of TM [24]. In [25], two estimates of drapery were compared – the drapery coefficient and the number of folds that occur—directly on the Cusick device and indirectly by calculating the extensibility, bending and shear parameters in the Optitex software environment. **Figure 4** shows photographs of real and virtual drapes of different compositions.

It was found that the virtual simulation does not fully correspond to the real drapery due to ignoring changes at the microlevel of fibers. Although the difference in the

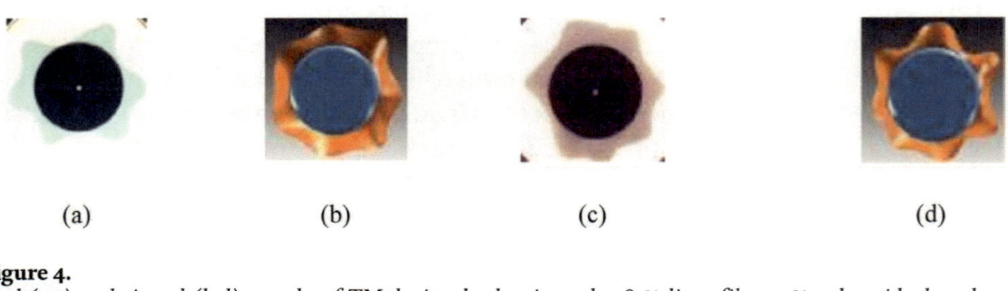

(a) (b) (c) (d)

Figure 4.
Real (a,c) and virtual (b,d) samples of TM during the draping: a,b – 85% linen fiber, 15% polyamide thread, c,d – 98% cotton, 2% elastane [25].

number of folds is only 7.2%, and the drapery coefficient is 6.3%, the depth of the folds and their distribution differ quite a lot, which is visually perceived as unrealistic modeling.

The change in the shape of the surface of a flat part is caused by the manifestation of physical and mechanical properties.

Different measuring systems are used to parameterize TM properties.

The most widely used and scientifically sound measurement system for fabrics is the KES-F (Kawabata's evaluation system for fabrics). Due to its worldwide prevalence and widespread use, a huge database of almost all types of materials has been formed since 1988. An alternative to this system is Fabric Assurance by Simple Testing, which is a rapid measurement system for similar indicators of physic-mechanical properties of TM. The developers of 3D CAD systems anticipated these difficulties and offered their own methods of measuring individual indicators of properties using the simplest complexes. The CLO CAD system works with the KIT tool kit to measure individual indicators. CAD VIDYA (Germany) suggests using non-instrumental express methods to determine a set of indicators. Express methods are quite simple, do not require special equipment, and simulate the features of the process of shaping clothes and the formation of folds.

Each CAD system has its own algorithms for the digital TM model and its application in a virtual twin, which may differ in the final shape of the virtual clothing model. As an example, the appearance of the same jumpsuit generated by Browzwear, Style 3D, and CLO was different. To obtain a virtual jumpsuit, initial information was used to construct the product, fabric (85% polyester, 15% elastane, surface density 112 g/m^2, coefficient of friction 0.2, thickness 0.23 mm). The fabric was tested using different measuring complexes of Browzwear, Style 3D, and CLO. The following parameters were measured: surface density (mass), friction characteristics (friction), thickness (thickness), bending stiffness (bend), extensibility (stretch), linearity of stretching (stretch linearity), shear force (shear) and shear linearity (shear linearity). **Figure 5** shows the measurement results and the appearance of virtual jumpsuits generated in CAD Browzwear, Style 3D, CLO: a - the appearance of draped fabric, b - virtual jumpsuits, d - side contours. The table shows the values of its properties measured using the Browzwear, Style 3D, and CLO measuring complexes.

As can be seen in **Table 4**, all indicators belonging to physic-mechanical properties and testing by different test schemes have difference values of the same property. The variation of values reaches 198%. Despite the apparent similarity of the virtual models (**Figure 5**), it is necessary to state the obvious differences between the virtual counterparts. The horizontal lines of the bottom and the shape of the side curves of the trousers (**Figure 5b**) are not always preserved in the trousers. The shape of the side contour depends on the depth of the folds, and their location, depth, length, and number also vary. The upper parts of the overalls are slightly different in the area of the waist folds. The discrepancies are caused by layering at the locations of the folds.

In general, in order to obtain static virtual apparel, the developed algorithms for obtaining virtual TM twins based on a set of indicators of physical and mechanical properties provide satisfactory results so far in terms of search design.

The feeling of comfort during wear depends on the structural design and the properties of the TM used, which manifest themselves precisely under the influence of constructive solutions. In design, the degree to which a TM implements its indicators (for example, extensibility, drapery, the ability to repeat or change the plastic surface of an avatar, etc.) depends on the designer's experience.

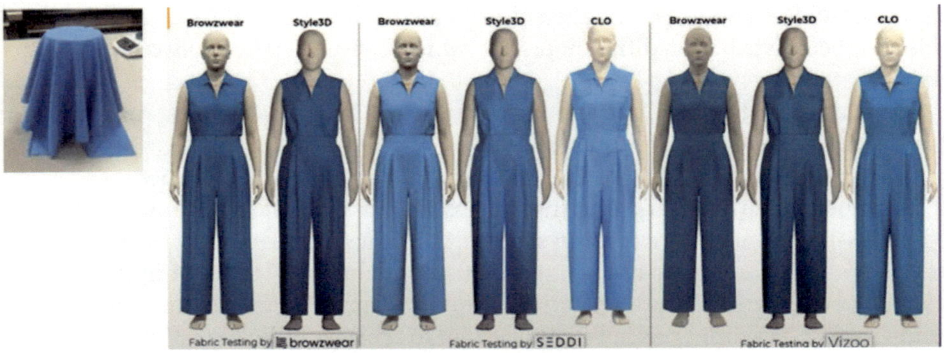

(a) (b)

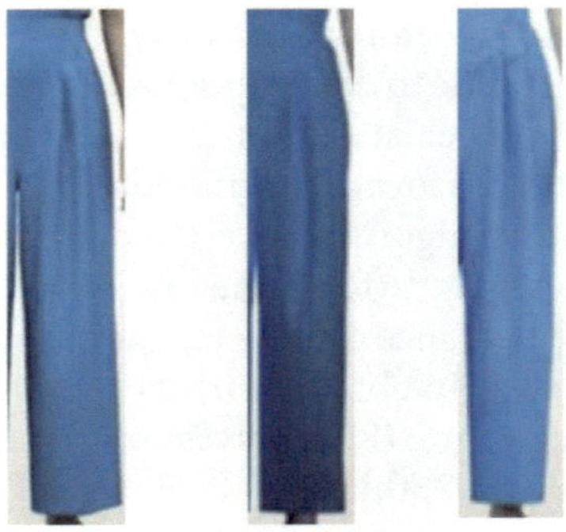

(c)

Figure 5.
The appearance of virtual jumpsuits measurement: a - the appearance of draped fabric, b - virtual jumpsuits generated in CAD Browzwear, Style 3D, CLO, d - side contours.

Index	Index value measured by			Variation, %
	Browzwear	Style3D	CLO	
Wrap stiffness, cN/cm	35,1	37,6	28,7	26
Weft stiffness, cN/cm	43,1	44,5	33,8	26
stretching along wrap, %	214,6	1383,4	173,6	198
stretching along weft, %	327,8	2157,3	303,1	197
shear force, cN/degree	31,2	65,8	28,8	88

Table 4.
Indexes of TM properties measured in different 3D CAD.

The development of AI has allowed for realistic algorithms for solving some tasks without human participation, which previously seemed unattainable. The development of humanistic fashion design sets the task of providing the avatar with the ability to respond to the irritations that clothing can cause [26]. The neuropsychological reaction of a person to external stimuli can have different reasons. For example, the disproportionality of clothing to individual parts of the body, which can be felt when performing movements, tactile contact of the fabric surface with skin receptors, or excessive pressure of clothing on the skin. These reactions mainly occur in areas of clothing that repeat the avatar morphology or force changes in the dynamic postures.

It is clear that these reverse neuropsychological reactions should be taken into account at the early stage in the development of the Metaverse. Such requirements arise precisely in the 4D environment, which involves taking into account the reaction to dynamic changes in the "avatar - clothing" system. For the development of 4D modeling, not solid-state avatars are needed, but soft-bodied avatars that simulate the reactivity of real people to external stimuli.

Upgrading the design level to 4D will face more complex dynamic tissue deformations. The main difference between 4D and 3D design is that there is no formal feedback from a person after exposure to clothing. It is clear that the existing tissue testing methods will not allow you to obtain the full amount of information. To implement a human-friendly design, it will be necessary to measure the properties of TM directly on the human body with which the garment will come into contact. However, such a database has not yet been formed including new measurement methods, criteria for evaluation, formalized relations between the properties of TM and human neuropsychological reactions. Without such data based on qualitatively different technologies for measuring the TM properties, it is impossible to have high-quality and realistic virtual "avatar-clothing" systems.

New directions in TM science due to its application in Metaverse include the study of feedback after deformation or other types of impact of TM on human soft tissues. Modeling the effects of TM in a VR should take into account the physiological characteristics that the avatar should be endowed with:

- simulation a human tissue reactions during contact with TM;
- to experience resistance when performing basic ergonomic movements;
- to experience a feeling of warmth or cold when in contact with a TM;
- react to compression pressure, including the areas where increased pressure is unacceptable (neck, breasts, groin, calf);
- react to excess weight of apparel.

Based on these feedback responses, constructive changes can be made to virtual clothing. Such neuropsychological data should complement the existing databases and provide new information support for 4D design. The direction of the TM impact on the skin should become a new stage in the development of virtual design technologies, and fill it with not only esthetic but also humanistic content.

3. Contemporary clothing in Metaverse

3.1 Algorithm of generation

A digital twin of clothing, also called virtual apparel (VA), is a virtual model designed to accurately reflect its physical properties such as shape, draping, gravity, surface strain, folding, and other features existing in virtual space [16]. A complete DTCA is usually generated through several steps. **Figure 6** shows the basic steps to generate a DTCA in Style3D.

As usual nine steps are should be completed to generate DTCA:

1. draft 2D PB or import generated before from other software;
2. select an standard avatar from the asset library, edit it with specific body dimensions (if it necessary) or import scanatar of real body (**Figure 6a**);
3. arrange 3D PB pieces around avatar (**Figure 6b**);
4. sew PB (**Figure 6c**);
5. edit and simulate necessary craftsmanships (pleat, dart, button, zip, stiching, etc.);
6. edit TM texture and physical properties or import scanned image of material (**Figure 6d**);
7. edit other objects (accessories, scenario, shoes, etc.) (**Figure 6e**);
8. simulate and improve the "avatar - clothing" system;
9. export 3D model, virtual images, videos, etc.).

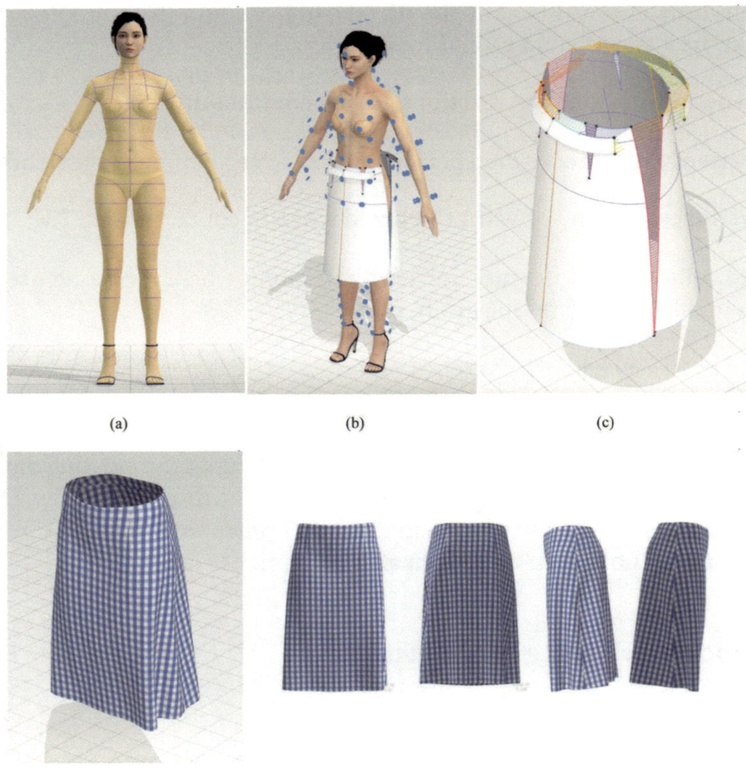

Figure 6.
Basic steps to generate a DTCA in Style3D: (a) avatar selection and editing with body dimensions, (b) arrangement of 3D PB, (c) arrangement of virtual sewing threads, (d) TM texture and physical properties editing, (e) export of the apparel.

3.2 Virtual fashion-show

In Metaverse, the fashion industry and other fields require a virtual space exhibiting brand image and concept to bring more benefits. The establishment of DTCA is beneficial to apparel marketing, as it transforms the traditional retail experience to a new digital level, and improves the consumer's interaction [27]. Unlike the traditional physical show, a virtual fashion show is held by dressed avatars. The visualization can not only show the realism of the garment, but it can also easily create a sense of fashion with the cooperation between the avatar and the garment in terms of scenario.

There are two examples of virtual fashion shows.

Example 1. The main objective is to express the spirit of the Olympic Winter Games. The members of the team are ANTA, Style3D and Baidu. Ice and Fire, Chinese speed, champion, Olympic Winter Games, sports, Jiajia Xi and Kaikai Lin are key words.

Figure 7 shows the windows of Style3D with apparel design in static and dynamic, and **Figure 8** shows the icy Möbius loop in the sky (the start point of the fashion show), the virtual idol Jiajia Xi, Kaikai Lin, and, etc., who wore apparel, walked along the loop, simultaneously played ice and snow sports.

As **Figure 9** shows, the virtual show clearly exhibited the apparel, and expressed the spirit of the Olympic Winter Games.

Example 2. During the pandemic, Balenciaga moved its show to virtual as well. In the VR game "Afterworld: The Age of Tomorrow", Balenciaga released its autumn/winter show in 2021 through Unreal Engine. This game puts the fashion show to the next digital level, creating a diverse, interactive 3D space for apparel exhibiting (**Figure 9**).

3.3 Virtual garment as research object

Scholars use the functions of virtual and other technologies to enhance the clothing in Metaverse, and improve its quality and efficiency. Metaverse allows scientists and practical experimenters to conduct scientific and practical experiments using avatars instead of real volunteers.

This function of VR opens the door to new directions in applied research.

In accordance with the first direction, when DTCA can simulate the TM draping, the stress or strain in real-time by using a visualized heat map, the virtual pressure tool applies to monitor the pressure of apparel on the avatar (especially compression apparel) and make modifications to PB. **Figure 10** shows the pictures that illustrate the steps of the virtual experiment with the wetsuit during the validation of how it fits on the variable avatar postures.

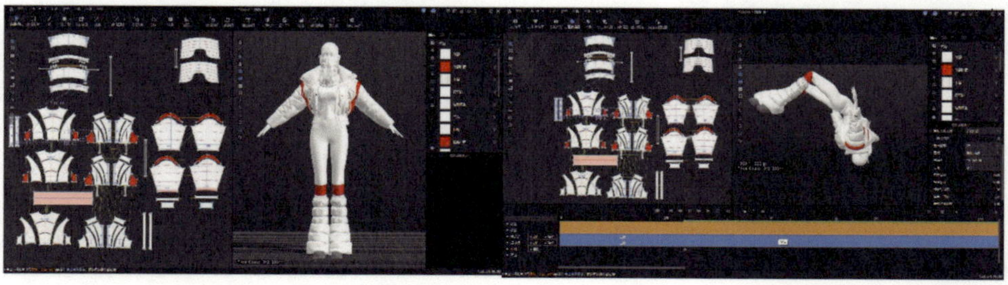

(a) (b)

Figure 7.
DTCA generating in Style3D: (a) static apparel, (b) dynamic apparel [28].

Figure 8.
Virtual fashion show from ANTA [28].

Figure 9.
Balenciaga's virtual fashion show in VR game "Afterworld: The Age of Tomorrow" [29].

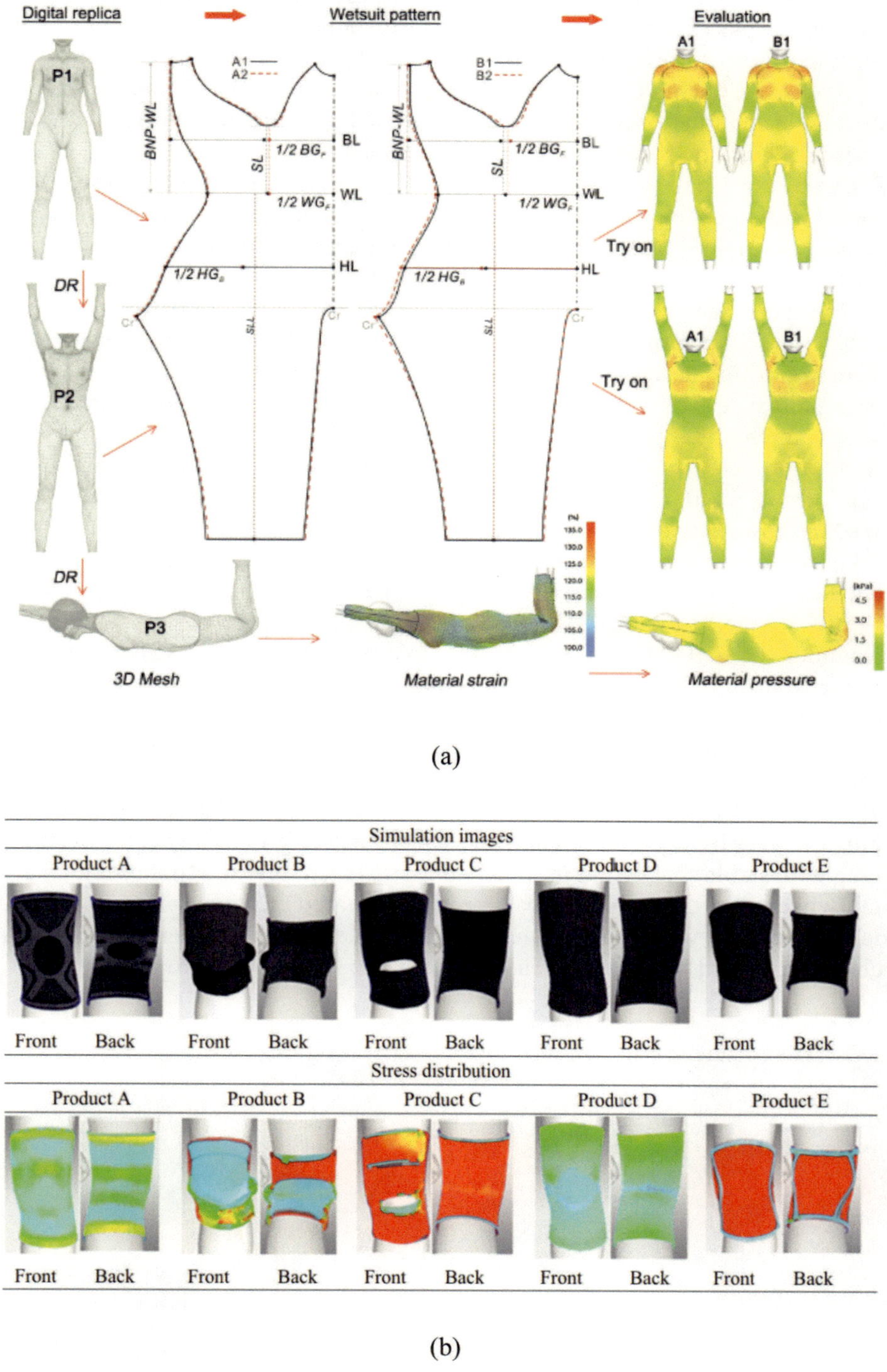

Figure 10.
Clothing pressure and strain simulation in VR: (a) wetsuit pattern try-on and evaluation, (b) virtual pressure distribution on cycling knee brace named products A, B, C, D, E [30, 31].

The pressure distribution is used to determine the pressure and the strain. The map shows the places with the good fit (comfort feeling) and the misfit (discomfort feeling). In this way, the optimization of different types of clothing could be done in VR, for example, the bra PB [32]. The cloth pressure distribution is important for the comfort and function of the knee brace. The virtual pressure distribution is analyzed to choose the best knee brace as **Figure 10b** shows.

The visualization of pressure is not simple. To be certain of the correctness of the measured and indicated values, the huge database on comfort perception should be collected and stored in special modules of 3D simulation software. After solving this problem, we can better simulate virtual clothing.

In accordance with the second direction, the 3D-to-2D pattern flattening method could be used for generating individualized apparel for VC and solving the biggest problem in clothing design how to establish the good combination of ease allowances (an ease allowance is the difference between the human body dimension and the related parameter of apparel) between avatar and DTCA.

First, after increasing the human body dimensions of the original avatar, loosely woven clothing could be directly designed on the surface of modified avatar. **Figure 11a** shows how the waist, hip and arm girths of initial avatars increased to get the PB of the apparel named cheongsam [33]. By this method, the ease allowances to girth which were put in clothing PB are: to upper arm 25,31 – 22,31 = 3 cm, to waist 65,7 – 61,7 = 4 cm, to hip 92,09 - 88,09 = 4 cm.

Second, a method with a 3D space vector and corresponding air gap was used to characterize fitting PB and construct personalized apparel [34]. Different types of hats can also be obtained based on the head standard model [35]. Furthermore, with the 3D scanned apparel model, PB of an unacquainted apparel could be generated by the garment reverse modeling method [36].

Although DTCA is useful, it still has some problems. Special knitted cloth and clothing can very hardly be simulated because the existing VFS can help simulate clothing with stable shapes and in specified motions. To solve the first problem, a digital twin of a weft-knitted kneepad is proposed based on a quadrilateral mesh model (**Figure 12a**) with complex shapes that simulated the knee bending. Second, a simulator for virtual warp knitted fully-formed apparel was also proposed.

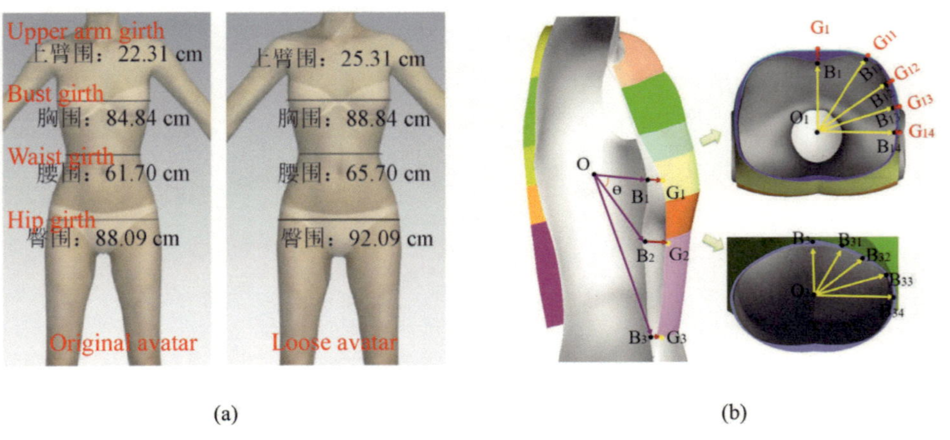

(a) (b)

Figure 11.
Personalized apparel generating by 3D-to-2D flattering method: (a) by increasing the avatar dimensions to design loosely apparel, (b) 3D scapce vectors and corresponding distance eases [33, 34].

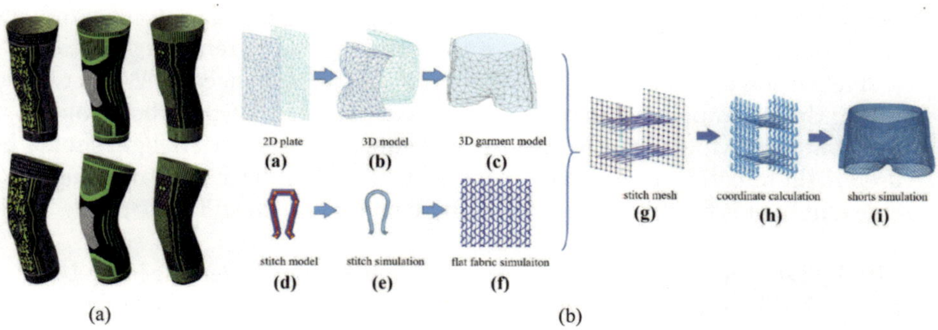

Figure 12.
Methods of virtual knitted apparel simulation: (a) virtual display of weft-knitted kneepads, (b) stages of simulation system for the wrap knitted fully-formed apparel.

3D dynamic clothing has many advantages due its ability to be shaped changeable shaping. DTCA could be displayed when the avatar is in dynamic. To design a dynamic "avatar - clothing" system, the hierarchical model of 3D apparel skeleton can be based on two types of human motion: first, distinguishing the trunk (global) from the limbs (local), and, second, integrating the apparel model with the body circumferential features extracted using Kinect camera.

4. Historical costume in Metaverse

Generating a virtual replica of a historical costume is an actual contemporary multidisciplinary area combining cultural research, science-based methods of reconstruction, and VR. The new approach to cultural heritage application in archaeology allows to get tangible effects in the conservation and enhancement of historical costumes due to the possibilities of computer graphics (CG) and computer-aided design (CAD). Historical objects that are demonstrated in digital forms could be done with the help of multimedia technologies and CG tools and allow the visitor in Metaverse to watch all details of the costume located as outside such as inside. So DTHC in Metaverse has been developing for more accurate, realistic exhibition and communication and better preservation.

Two approaches can be used to obtain virtual replicas of historical costumes.

1. A replica of a real costume was created by creating a digital and virtual twin named the replica. This method is simple to implement and achieves maximum similarity. To implement this approach, a historical costume is needed.

2. Reconstruction a partially preserved or completely lost historical costume. To get digital twin of historical costumes (DTHC), a very extensive database about costume history, texts, images, TM, fashion trends, embroidery craftsmanships, etc. is needed to implement this approach.

For the first approach, the photogrammetry for 2D image capturing is used, especially. A few photos should have the appropriate brightness (each segment is observable, neither too bright nor too dark), resolutions (details are clear), accurate colors (balance, temperature, etc.), which are usually solved through the following instruments:

1. For places where the light brightness is low or color is unbalanced, constant lights with appropriate power, color temperature and high color rendering index (CRI) and television lighting consistency index (TLCI) > 99 are needed. When capturing the integral, light boxes should be used to illuminate the whole object or environment; while capturing the micro detail, a portable macro light should be used to illuminating a tiny part. It should be noted that flash light and long-term constant light is forbidden due to their high power, which will damage the fabric.

2. The digital camera must have an interchangeable lens. The lens needs to be changed. When capturing integral, the lens' focal length depends on the object and environment. A macro lens with a high magnification is recommended for capturing micro detail. A microscope is needed to observe fiber constituents.

3. A color chart with standard printed colors is necessary to calibrate to a precise color balance. If the real costume is within reach, a spectrophotometer is more convenient.

4. Depending on the object and scenario, additional instruments may be needed, e.g., a tripod and a slider.

5. The color balance of photographs calibration can be calibrated using color calibration software such as SpyderCheckr. In image processing software such as Adobe Lightroom and Photoshop, macro photos can be stacked to a clearer one, and detail photos are possible to integrate to a larger size.

A 3D scanner can capture point cloud data from a real object and generate a 3D model, especially useful for investigating its exterior shape. There is also a 3D body scanner available. The compatible software can control the scanning process, visualize and optimize the scanned model, and export to universal files, such as .obj, .fbx. **Figure 13** shows the virtual exhibition with a replica of historical costume. Two real and virtual objects are present together and allow the ability to compare the two.

Figure 13.
Virtual exhibition of replica of historical costume of the XIX century obtaining from real prototypes https://www.spatial.io.

For second approach, the establishment of a database is a key aspect for the digitalization of costumes. This method is similar to the reverse engineering method. To obtain digital counterparts of partly destroyed or lost historical clothing with a complex 3D shape, additional knowledge about coloristic, structural design, and other artistic and constructive solutions of the real body. Additional information about the appearance, structural design, materials and manufacturing technologies, as well as the relationships between internal structural elements can be obtained by studying the preserved artifacts, their fragments, images, and reliable descriptions.

The data should be as accurate as possible for subsequent reconstruction and investigation. Professional instruments and software are necessary due to the variety of data. Modern 3D technologies allow to create the virtual replicas of historical costume using pictures, illustrations, and photos. To obtain a 3D virtual replica of historical costume, three key computer technologies were used after analyzing the 2D images above mentioned:

1. The technology of 3D modeling which is used for avatars, generating a digital copy of historical human bodies which have different dimensions and proportions. It is done using MakeHuman, iClone, DAZ Studio, Clo3D, and Adobe Fuse, SolidWorks, Free CAD, Creo Parametric, Fusion 360, OpenCAD and Brics CAD. By these software, historical avatars generate based on linear body dimensions taken from historical sizing tables.

2. The technology of automated historical pattern drafting based on body dimensions, pattern block indexes, properties of historical TM and the known algorithm.

3. The technology of virtual try-on operates with special virtual fitting software for generating 3D apparel by physical simulation of TM draping. Virtual historical clothing can be simulated by Clo3D, Marvelous Designer, DC Suite, TUKA 3D, Vstitcher, Lotta, Optitex, Assyst Vidya, and LookStailorX. For rendering digital clothing, 3DSMax, Blender, Maya, Rhinoceros, and Cinema 4D can also be used, as well as real-time rendering engines, such as Marmoset Toolbag, Unity and Unreal Engine. Virtual fitting software allows to simulation of clothing only after measuring physicalmechanical properties of the textile material. Because similar indexes of historical materials are unknown, the software should be transformed to evaluate the adequacy between contemporary TM from the digital library and historical prototypes, on one side. On the other hand, to get the realistic look of historical TM, historical methods of costume shaping should be known and taken into account during 3D modeling, both static and dynamic.

With the help of computer graphics and animation, 2D and 3D images of historical artifacts were obtained for the museums and the public (outside galleries and museums) VR and MR, live audiovisual and interactive multimedia performances. New forms allow to distribution of virtual images at high speeds and make them available for viewing by a huge number of people.

A "virtual museum" consisting of digital textiles and historical costumes is being developed due to fusion of CAD tools and innovative products. Virtual replicas of historical clothes are being presented by the Metropolitan Museum of Art, The Kyoto Costume Institute, and GoogleArts and Culture project. In parallel, demonstrate good examples of conservation, enhancement, and adaptation of cultural heritage to the public. All virtual museums use traditional 2D format and a new one "360" where

Figure 14.
Historical costumes obtaining from pictures https://sketchfab.com/.

the viewer can see the replica in rotating around vertical axis. The new format "360" is a more important challenge now. The quality of the replica is dependent on the initial stages of shaping and manufacturing where the style and silhouette are being designed, a desirable size and color are chosen, and textile materials are also used.

The ability to view historical clothing from a variety of perspectives is a great benefit. **Figure 14** shows different historical costumes derived from historical pictures such as Russian folk pictures.

5. Limitations, challenges, and risks

Despite the impressive successes achieved, scientific research and development in different fields of knowledge are necessary for the complete transfer of modern and historical clothing to the Metaverse. Here are the main problems that relate to the individual elements of the virtual design process.

5.1 Human body twins

The difficulty is in granting avatars of human bodies with reactionary abilities peculiar to real humans and manifested by them under the influence of clothing, dynamic movements, and external factors. To design humanoid avatars, a new database is needed, which would include information about neuropsychological reactions caused by exposure to clothing and external conditions, for example, climatic ones.

5.2 Historical costume twins

1. The lack of data on the dimensions and morphology of human bodies in different historical periods. The publication of the first dimensional tables

on human bodies dates back to the second half of the 19th century, when the production of RtW clothing began. Therefore, there are no reliable methods and data for building virtual avatars that could be used to demonstrate historical costumes.

2. The lack of information about historical fabrics to obtain their virtual twins. Due to their high historical value, preserved tissue samples cannot be tested using modern destructive and non-destructive testing methods. In addition, irreversible changes in structural characteristics and coloristic design limit the realism of virtual twins.

5.3 Textile materials twins

1. The lack of methods and means of measuring the properties of woven fabrics and knitted fabrics, which they exhibit not as independent objects, but as components of the "avatar - clothing" system. These indicators differ significantly from similar results obtained after testing samples according to ASTM and ISO standards. The "avatar - clothing" system uses small multi-cycle loads acting in different directions. Gravitational, seams that are jointed of clothing parts (thread, adhesive, welded, mechanical), and ergonomic movements cause complex deformations in materials, for which mathematical models have not yet been developed. The schedule of indicators used in 3D CAD is not able to describe the forced deformations of textile materials qualitatively and quantitatively. Such deformations of textile materials are necessary to shape clothing constructively or technologically.

2. The textile materials used in RtW clothing are often components of multilayer systems. As a result of synergies, it is still difficult to model the behavior of such multi-layer systems in virtual reality;

5.4 Twins of "avatar - clothing" systems

1. Lack of information about the process of clothing shaping as a closed shell around an avatar. The final shape of the garment depends on its design (the size and number of parts made of the materials used, the number and configuration of the internal dividing lines), the methods of making clothing, and the air gaps between an avatar and clothing. Models for predicting the final shape of clothing have not yet been developed, and to obtain them, the formal experience of clothing designers is necessary.

2. The lack of indicators and criteria by which it is possible to verify the identity of virtual clothing to material prototypes having complex three-dimensional shape and decorative and coloristic solutions. The resulting virtual counterparts may have systemic differences from the material prototypes in esthetic, functional, ergonomic, and other aspects. The international Standard ISO 20947-2:2020(E) Performance Evaluation Protocol for Digital Fitting Systems. Part 2: Virtual garment" only some indicators are indicated that are used to evaluate the virtual "avatar - clothing" system - stretching of clothes in certain areas, the air gap between the avatar and clothing, the presence of folds, etc. – without detailing and criteria.

The existing discrepancy between real and virtual design can be eliminated by creating a new database for the quality of virtual twins based on parameterized professional experience.

6. Conclusion

Converting clothing into virtual form is a complex esthetic, technological, and technical task due to the need to identify, describe, parameterize, and find relationships between many factors affecting the appearance and functionality of the "avatar - clothing" system. Almost all the elements of this system are soft-bodied, unstable in the shape, and difficult to parameterize. However, clear progress in the development of virtual clothing for various purposes and the expansion of its field of application indicate the high demand for this area.

Virtual clothing is currently used in several ways:

- separately as historical costume, an object of decorative and applied art or an object for scientific research,
- in "real consumer - virtual apparel" system,
- in "avatar - clothing" system.

Further development of virtual clothing will require further study of the main components: human body, textile materials, and clothing construction.

The avatar is virtual human body that meets the requirements of morphological similarity to an individual or standard body in statics and dynamics, as well as the ability to respond to the shape of clothing and its effect on the skin tissues. The transition to virtual dynamic "avatar - clothing" systems from 3D to 4D will require the development of new methods for testing tissues, deformations of which must be consistent with ergonomic poses, dynamic increments to dimensional features of the body, and the reverse neuropsychological reaction of humans to external stimuli arising between the body and tissue.

The textile materials used to construct the shell around body should exhibit the same properties as their actual prototypes. The existing set of indicators of physical and mechanical properties of textile materials is not sufficient for designing static virtual clothing in the Metaverse. 4D virtual design with the implementation of the humanistic design concept will require complex tests using instrumental methods and sensory analysis to form a new database about interaction in the "avatar - apparel" system and its inclusion in modules for the selection of virtual textile materials.

The clothing sewing patterns, which now exists exclusively in the digital form of flat parts thanks to CAD, should be described from the perspective of predicted transformation into shells with different options: repeating the body shape (without air gaps between the body and apparel), changing the body shape due to compression and relocation of soft tissues, covering the body with different air gaps.

The emergence of real "smart" clothing which is capable of responding to changes in human body functioning will require additional research in multidisciplinary fields before virtual counterparts of such clothing appear.

Obviously, to solve these problems, the development of new software, the creation of extensive libraries of avatars, textiles, and new modules should be organized.

Funding

The work was carried out with the financial support of the Russian Science Foundation, grant No. №24-29-00268 'Digital twins of costumes from the XVIII-XIX centuries: a new format for the Russian cultural heritage'.

Author details

Victor Kuzmichev[1*] and Jiaqi Yan[2]

1 Ivanovo State Polyttechic University, Russia

2 Zhongyuan University of Technology, Zhengzhou, China

*Address all correspondence to: wkd37@list.ru

References

[1] Kuzmichev V, Yan J. The application of digital twins in the field of fashion. In: LvZ FE, editor. Digital Twins: Basics a4

[2] Chaoku. The girl who lives out her true self as a 'virtual character' is also the 'behind-the-scenes' producer of Wang Jiaer and Bridge's music videos [Internet]. 2020. Available from: https://www.163.com/dy/article/FMT2VJ1C05188NJM.html [Accessed: May 30, 2024]

[3] Flightclub.cn. The "National Domination"has a new version! Netizens: It's a combination of Chinese and Western elements! [Internet]. 2023. Available from: https://www.flightclub.cn/news/a/sneaker/2023/0403/74922.html [Accessed: May 30, 2024]

[4] The International Organization for Standardization, Switzerland. ISO 20947-1:2021 (2021) Performance evaluation protocol for digital fitting systems - part 1: accuracy of virtual human body representation. 46 pages

[5] Alvanon. Alvanon Standard China [Internet]. 2022. Available from: https://alvanon.com/wp-content/uploads/2022/11/AF-SPECS_ASD_CN_AthleticMen_v22.0.pdf [Accessed: May 30, 2024]

[6] Xia M, Lu H, Xu X, Zhang L. Quantitative analysis of the relationship between the male body shape and block pattern based on the three-dimensional human model. Textile Research Journal. 2024;**94**(3-4):323-340. DOI: 10.1177/00405175231204375

[7] Feng W, Li XR, Li X, Li Y, Wen J, Li H, et al. The construction of a three-dimensional human body based on semantic-driven parameters to improve virtual fitting. Textile Research Journal. 2024;**94**(3-4):451-462. DOI: 10.1177/00405175231207

[8] Li X, Li G, Li T, Lv J, Mitrouchev P. Design of a multi-sensor information acquisition system for mannequin reconstruction and human body size measurement under clothes. Textile Research Journal. 2022;**92**(19-20):3750-3765. DOI: 10.1177/00405175221093663

[9] Chen J, Wang X, Luo W, Mei C, Wei J, Zhong Y. VR-oriented personalized head and face texture generation technology of dressed human body. Journal of Textile Research. 2023;**44**(9):188-196. DOI: 10.13475/j.fzxb.20220706301

[10] The International Organization for Standardization, Switzerland. ISO20947-2:2020(E). Performance evaluation protocol for digital fitting systems. Part 2: Virtual garment. 27 pages

[11] Jevšnik S, Geršak J. Modelling the fused panel for a numerical simulation of drape. Fibres and Textiles in Eastern Europe. 2004;**1**:47-52. DOI: 10.1023/B:FICH.0000025545.60090.7c

[12] Chen B, Govindaraj M. A physically based model of fabric drape using flexible shell theory. Textile Research Journal. 1995;**6**:324-330. DOI: 10.1177/004051759506500603

[13] Collier JR, Collier BJ, O'Toole G, Sargand SM. Drape prediction by means of finite-element analysis. Journal of the Textile Institute. 1991;**1**:96-107. DOI: 10.1080/00405009108658741

[14] Ascough J, Bez HE, Bricis AM. A simple beam element, large displacement model for the finite element simulation of cloth drape. Journal of

the Textile Institute. 1996;**1**:152-165. DOI: 10.1080/00405009608659063

[15] Hu J, Chen S. Numerical drape behavior of circular fabric sheets over circular pedestals. Textile Research Journal. 2000;**7**:593-603. DOI: 10.1177/004051750007000706

[16] Breen DE, House DH, Wozny MJ. A particle-based model for simulating the draping behavior of woven cloth. Textile Research Journal. 1994;**11**:663-685. DOI: 10.1177/004051759406401106

[17] Provot X. Deformation constraints in a mass-spring model to describe rigid cloth behavior. Graphics Interface. 1995:147-154

[18] Ji F, Li R, Qiu Y. Three-dimensional garment simulation based on a mass-spring system. Textile Research Journal. 2006;**76**(1):12-17. DOI: 10.1177/0040517506057169

[19] Jevsnik S, Pilar T, Drujic D, Rudolf A, Celcar D, Stjepanovič Z. The Study of Fabric Drape Behavior in the Virtual Environment. Istanbul, Turkey: The International Istanbul Textile Congress; 2013. pp. 1-6

[20] Guo MN, Kuzmichev VE. Pressure and comfort perception in the system "female body–dress". Autex Research Journal. 2013;**13**(3):71-78. DOI: 10.2478/v10304-012-0032-6

[21] Wang X, YuX. Current situation and development in applying metaverse virtual space in field of fashion. Journal of Textile Research. 2024;**45**(04):238-245. DOI: 10.13475/j.fzxb.20230300202

[22] DIGITALING. Anta Virtual Fashion Show: Yu Long Metaverse, full of Olympic elements [Internet]. 2023. Available from: https://www.digitaling.com/projects/264004.html [Accessed: May 31, 2024]

[23] Unreal Engine. What Balenciaga's Afterworld: The Age of Tomorrow tells us about the future of fashion [Internet]. March 5, 2021. 3 videos, 7 figures. 2021. Available from: https://www.unrealengine.com/en-US/spotlights/what-balenciaga-s-afterworld-the-age-of-tomorrow-tells-us-about-the-future-of-fashion [Accessed: May 31, 2024]

[24] Wu X, Kuzmichev V. A design of wetsuit based on 3D body scanning and virtual technologies. International Journal of Clothing Science and Technology. 2020;**33**(4):477-494. DOI: 10.1108/IJCST-02-2020-0021

[25] Kim HY, Oh KW. Cycling knee brace design analysis using 3D virtual clothing program to assess clothing pressure distribution and variance. Fashion and Textiles. 2023;**10**(36). DOI: 10.1186/s40691-023-00354-8

[26] Son W, Zhang P. Pressure comfort optimization design of intelligence bra based on 3D simulation. Journal of Clothing Research. 2023;**8**(4):315-322

[27] Ji Y, Wang L, Liu K. Custom design of cheongsam based on digital 3-D human model. Journal of Textile Research. 2021;**42**(1):133-137. DOI: 10.13475/j.fzxb.20200505706

[28] Zhang Y, Ma L, Guo Z, Li T, Zou F. Personalized garment pattern generation based on space vector and distance ease. International Journal of Clothing Science and Technology. 2023;**35**(5):715-737. DOI: 10.1108/IJCST-10-2022-0152

[29] Jun J, Ryoo Y, Choi K, Park S. Development of prototype hat patterns for elderly women based on three-dimensional modeling. Fashion and Textiles. 2021;**8**(26). DOI: 10.1186/s40691-021-00258-5

[30] Zhou L, Fan P, Jin Y, Zhang L, Li X. Digital design method of clothing reverse

modeling. Journal of Textile Research. 2023;**44**(12):138-144. DOI: 10.13475/j.fzxb.20221001901

[31] Cong H, Shen Y, Zhang J. Research on the virtual display of a weft-knitted seamless kneepad based on the free-form deformation model. Textile Research Journal. 2022;**92**(19-20):3545-3553. DOI: 10.1177/00405175221081444

[32] Liu H, Jiang G, Dong Z. Three-dimensional simulation based on mesh modelling for warp-knitted fully-formed garments. International Journal of Clothing Science and Technology. 2024;**36**(1):117-131. DOI: 10.1108/IJCST-09-2021-0122

[33] Choi KH. 3D dynamic fashion design development using digital technology and its potential in online platforms. Fashion and Textiles. 2022;**9**(9). DOI: 10.1186/s40691-021-00286-1

[34] Li B, Wang P, Liu Y. 3-D virtual try-on technique based on dynamic feature of body posture. Journal of Textile Research. 2021;**42**(9):144-149. DOI: 10.13475/j.fzxb.20201200406

[35] Grigorieva ZR, Budeeva ON, Solodushenkova TS, Khammatova EA, Khanbekova ND. Addition of the anthropometric database for three-dimensional design of clothing. Izvestiya Vysshikh Uchebnykh Zavedenii, Seriya Teknologiya Tekstil'noi Promyshlennosti. 2023;**6**(408):182-187. DOI: 10.47367/0021-3497_2023_6_182

[36] Moskvin AYU, Moskvina MA, Kuzmichev VE. Block pattern generation of the scanned historical garments. Izvestiya Vysshikh Uchebnykh Zavedenii, Seriya Teknologiya Tekstil'noi Promyshlennosti. 2022;**4**(400):147-152. DOI: 10.47367/0021-3497_2022_4_147

Chapter 7

Digital Partnerships: Understanding Delegation and Interaction with Virtual Agents

Ningyuan Sun and Jean Botev

Abstract

With recent advances in artificial intelligence and the metaverse, virtual agents have become increasingly autonomous and accessible. Due to their growing technological capabilities, interaction with virtual agents gradually evolves from a traditional user-tool relationship to one resembling interpersonal delegation, where users entrust virtual agents to perform specific tasks independently on their behalf. Delegating to virtual agents is beneficial in numerous ways, especially regarding convenience and efficiency. Still, it poses problems and challenges that may drastically harm users in critical situations. This chapter explores the trust and delegation relationships between users and virtual agents, introducing a trust-based conceptual model to abstract and differentiate users' delegation decisions based on three major dimensions covering the impact of rationality, affection, and technology. Practical guidance for virtual agent designs and potential applications of the model for metaverse development are also presented, followed by an outlook and an overview of future research opportunities.

Keywords: delegation, interaction, trust, virtual agents, metaverse

1. Introduction

Over the last few decades, significant progress has been made in the technologies that underpin virtual environments. For example, computing devices have become exponentially more powerful and capable of highly realistic real-time image rendering. Newer telecommunications technologies like 5G can transmit data at a much greater scale and speed, enabling shared experiences with more users and lower latency. Immersive media devices are also evolving rapidly, allowing users to experience virtual environments more naturally and immersively than is possible with traditional display technologies. With these technological advances, building a metaverse is becoming increasingly realistic and has become the subject of intense debate [1].

In contrast to virtual environments that isolate users from physical reality, the current metaverse vision comprises a collection of 3D digital worlds closely connected to the real world [2]. It aims to merge the virtual and the real in a blended space so that interpersonal activities (e.g., meetings, teaching, socializing) can be facilitated and complemented by digital elements.

While interactions between users are a significant focus, other interactions with digital entities (e.g., with non-player characters in video games) are also essential to the metaverse experience. These entities are typically controlled by scripts and are often referred to as *software agents* due to their autonomy. Traditionally, interaction with a software agent occurs via a panel-like or 3D user interface following the WIMP[1] paradigm, which represents and operates an information system with abstract widgets such as icons and buttons. Nevertheless, there are increasing efforts to integrate human communication channels—including gestures, facial expressions, natural language, and more—to make the interaction feel natural and personable [3, 4]. In research, these human-like agents in digital environments are more specifically called *virtual agents*.

The vision of a metaverse as an embodied virtual environment where users are represented with avatars is one of the main driving forces behind the burgeoning research and development of virtual agents. Using avatars can enhance physical and social presence, promoting an immersive and sociable environment [5, 6]. Consequently, software agents are also increasingly represented by avatars and, using artificial intelligence (AI) technologies, can already perform complex tasks with minimal human supervision. For example, large language models (LLMs) allow users to describe a task without specifying how it can be accomplished. This type of interaction is similar to interpersonal delegation, where a *principal* (i.e., the person delegating) authorizes an agent to act independently on the principal's behalf. As a result, the need for fine-grained control is decreasing, while natural human communication is becoming more critical.

In the metaverse, delegation-like interactions with virtual agents that embody a virtual character, communicate using natural language, and perform tasks set by the user are likely to predominate. Delegating tasks to virtual agents in such a manner benefits users in several ways, particularly in terms of efficiency and convenience. Users can easily transfer their tasks to virtual agents without having to tender strategies and initiatives. On the other hand, delegation inherently involves risks as users must transfer part or all of their authority to virtual agents, making themselves vulnerable to the agents' actions. These risks can be particularly pronounced in a metaverse scenario, where virtual agents may influence users' delegation decisions with their advanced communication abilities [7, 8]. Therefore, it is essential to investigate this delegation relationship and identify its underlying factors, especially for critical tasks with potentially far-reaching, real-world implications, to facilitate user-agent interaction and resolve potential issues.

This chapter explores the trust and delegation relationships between users and virtual agents. Following a discussion of delegation and agency relationships, a trust-based conceptual model is introduced to explain users' trust in and delegation to virtual agents. Taking a macroscopic perspective, the model abstracts and differentiates three major dimensions covering the impact of rationality, affection, and technology. Practical guidance for virtual agent designs is further derived from the model, and potential applications of the model for metaverse development are presented with an outlook and overview of related research opportunities.

[1] WIMP stands for "windows, icons, menus, and pointer".

2. Delegation

Delegation is one of human societies' most important and common interpersonal relationships. The operation of most organizations requires effective management, i.e., delegation from managers to subordinates, and successful collaboration, i.e., delegation among specialized members or departments within an organization. With its significance and prevalence, delegation has been extensively studied in many disciplines, particularly economics, politics, and management [9]. Recent years have also seen the emergence of a new research line on delegation to intelligent artifacts, such as robots and software agents [10].

2.1 Interpersonal delegation

Delegation is a dyadic relationship between a principal and an agent, where the principal lets the agent carry out specific tasks on the principal's behalf while remaining responsible or accountable for the task outcomes [11, 12]. Delegation can provide principals with several benefits, for example, allowing them to access and utilize agents' expertise and knowledge [13] or increase efficiency by shifting some of their workloads to agents [14]. Delegation can also be used strategically as a commitment device to express principals' determination in a negotiation [15]. Conversely, principals must bear the risk of transferring part or all of their authority to agents during delegation. Such a risk can be even higher if there is a lack of effective measures to monitor and regulate agents' actions [16].

Among the research on delegation, *agency theory* has been one of the most cited and fundamental contributions [16–18]. It originates from early studies on risk-sharing problems within an organization whose members hold different attitudes toward risk [19]. Later, these studies evolved into a more inclusive theory, i.e., agency theory, mainly addressing the agency relationship between two rational entities. The theory posits that delegation is susceptible to the so-called *agency problems*, which often arise in two situations: (a) when it is difficult for principals to verify what agents are actually doing and (b) when principals and agents have conflicting goals or different attitudes toward risks [16]. These problems are detrimental to delegation, as exemplified by the so-called *moral hazard*, a situation where agents do not act as agreed or even furtively impair principals' interests [17]. To mitigate the influences of these problems, agency theory proposes to formulate some pre-defined protocols—i.e., a *contract*—to regulate the interaction between the principal and the agent during delegation [16, 18]. There are mainly two types of contracts. With *behavior-oriented* contracts, agents receive a fixed amount of money or equivalent upon finishing the tasks delegated to them, regardless of the task outcomes. *Outcome-oriented* contracts give agents minimal remuneration for finishing the tasks, but they can take a share of the task outcomes (e.g., bonus, commission, stocks). The two types of contracts fit different situations depending on several factors, including agent observability [20, 21], task programmability [22, 23], the measurability of task outcomes [24], and more. For example, in programmable tasks, principals are more likely to employ behavior-oriented contracts because agents' performance in such tasks is relatively easy to observe and assess [16].

Much of the literature on delegation is related to agency theory, viewing the principal-agent relationship mainly as an economic issue [25–27]. Nevertheless, many researchers assume a psychological stance and focus on principals' delegation decision-making process. For example, eight factors were found underlying a manager's decisions on delegating a task to subordinates, including the manager's workload, the task's importance, and subordinates' age, gender, trustworthiness, performance, job capability, and job tenure [11]. This set of factors was later validated in broader contexts and also expanded to include subordinates' experience in managing, the goal congruence between managers and subordinates, and whether there is a favorable exchange relationship [14, 28]. In some cases, decisions on delegation are dominated by subjective causes. For example, people may delegate a task to others to avoid feeling responsible or blamed for negative task outcomes [29, 30]. A manager may refuse to delegate to appear "busy" [31]. Overall, these psychology-oriented studies suggest that delegation is a challenging and prone-to-failure task for principals. Managers of all levels, from leaders of small groups to CEOs of successful corporations, are not free from making sub-optimal or wrong decisions on delegation [31]. People generally prefer making decisions themselves over delegating them to others, even if retaining control would lose potential benefits and incur additional costs [32].

2.2 Delegation to software agents

Although the term "delegation" has been predominantly used and studied in interpersonal contexts, recently it is increasingly assumed by computer scientists to describe the relationship between human users and software agents.

The interaction between human users and software agents is mainly characterized by the latter being designed to support and streamline human tasks. As discussed in **Section 1**, this relationship evolves with increasingly intuitive interfaces and advanced computational capabilities. Software agents leverage AI, natural language processing, and machine learning to interpret and respond to user inputs naturally and efficiently. They aim to improve productivity and user experience by automating routine tasks, providing personalized recommendations, and facilitating decision-making processes. As these technologies advance, the boundary between human and machine interaction and collaboration becomes increasingly seamless, fostering an environment where users can focus on more complex endeavors instead of devising lower-level strategies and initiatives.

Most of the research on software agents today originates from the well-established literature on human-automation interactions, which mainly takes the perspectives of use [33, 34] and reliance [35, 36]. As software agents become increasingly autonomous and capable, a different perspective based on the notion of delegation recently received more attention, as reflected in the quote below.

> *"[...] the delegation lens will yield more relevant and nuanced insights regarding human agent and agentic IS[2] artifact relationships, and this lens will be increasingly needed as the agentic capabilities of IS artifacts increase." [10]*

The pioneering works on delegation to software agents can be dated back to the 1990s, during which there were initial concerns about the "dramatic change" of software user interface from tool-oriented to delegation-oriented ones [12]. As a result of this rapid change, problems common to interpersonal delegation might similarly occur during interaction with software agents, which imposed new challenges on user interface designs. To overcome these drawbacks, five major dimensions must be

[2] IS = information systems.

considered when designing delegation-oriented user interfaces, including trust, communication, performance control, user demographics, and cost-benefit analysis [12].

There was also an early theoretical work that formalized delegatory relationships within a multi-agent system [37]. Despite its focus on delegation between software agents, the theory still lends us a unique perspective to explaining users' delegation decisions. Differing from other approaches, the theory defines delegation as a state of the principal, where "an agent A needs or likes an action of another agent B and includes it in its own plan" [37]. This definition moderates the aspect of responsibility and instead views delegation more of the principal's expectation of the agent. With this definition, delegation can be further divided into three subtypes (cf. **Table 1**) according to the following two criteria: whether there is an agreement between a principal and an agent and whether the principal actively induces certain behaviors in the agent.

Following these early studies, research on delegation to software agents was limited only until recent years, during which this topic received more attention due to the development of AI. A frequently discussed topic is whether people prefer human agents or software agents. The evidence is mixed; some studies found that software agents are preferred [38–40], whereas others showed the opposite [41]. Many factors can influence this preference. For example, people may prefer letting software agents carry out tasks involving sensitive data (e.g., credit card information) due to their user-centered design [42, 43] and limited intentional capacity [43, 44], whereas human agents may exploit the sensitive data for their own interests. On the other hand, tasks involving moral decisions (e.g., life-and-death decisions in law, military, or medicine) are less likely delegated to software agents given their lack of empathy [45]. The term *delegability* was recently conceptualized to describe people's general preference for delegating a task to AI [46]. In a survey investigating the delegability of 100 different tasks, it was found that the ones with the highest and lowest levels of delegability were "moving & packing merchandise in a warehouse for shipping to customers" and "picking out and buying a birthday present for an acquaintance", respectively [46].

Another often-mentioned topic is the factors governing users' decisions on delegation to software agents. Research shows that some factors have similar influences on delegation to human and software agents. To give a few examples, both interpersonal and human-software delegation were found to be positively correlated with perceived controllability [47], perceived attachment [48], and agents' trustworthiness [46, 47]. Among them, perceived controllability seems to be particularly crucial; people are more likely to delegate a decision to an algorithm when they are allowed to modify the decision made by the algorithm, even if the modification is severely restricted [49]. On the other hand, certain factors may exert different impacts on delegation depending on whether the agent is a human or a software application. For instance,

Delegation type	Agreement exists?	Behavior inducing?
Weak delegation	No	No
Mild delegation	No	Yes
Strict delegation	Yes	Yes or No

Table 1.
The delegation classification in [37].

high-level task accountability can encourage delegation to software agents but inhibit delegation to human agents [47].

Several studies took an economic perspective and focused on the user-agent dyad [40, 50–52]. An interesting implication from these studies is that software agents may be more proficient at delegation than humans are. In certain tasks, a hybrid team of a human user and a software agent can perform best if the software agent assumes the leading role and delegates tasks to the human user [40]. In contrast, the team may perform less when the human user is the leader or when any party has full control [40].

3. A trust-based model of delegation to virtual agents

Trust is a critical aspect underlying most interpersonal relationships, whether between individuals or within an organization. Owing to its significance and omnipresence, trust has been the subject of extensive study in many disciplines, including economics, psychology, and sociology. While the majority of these studies focus on interpersonal trust, a large body of research on the trust relationship between users and intelligent artifacts such as robots, automation, and software agents has emerged in recent decades. Numerous factors were identified and demonstrated to impact users' trust in these artifacts, constituting a vast and complicated parameter space.

Delegation to virtual agents is potentially governed by a similar parameter space, which, unlike that of trust, remains largely unexplored due to limited research. Nevertheless, given the connection between trust and delegation [11, 28, 46, 47, 53], factors underlying trust in virtual agents may have similar influences on delegation to virtual agents, either directly or through the mediation of trust. To approach and explore these factors, we introduce a trust-based conceptual model of delegation to virtual agents. The model considers various factors and explains how they collectively shape users' trust in and delegation to virtual agents.

3.1 Definitions of trust

The definition of trust has been a contentious topic and varies across disciplines. Some researchers approach it from a sociopsychological perspective, considering trust as a major social relation among individuals [54]. Others take a more psychological stance and view it mainly as the product of affective states [55, 56]. There are also theoretical models quantifying trust, primarily in economics and computer science [57].

> *"The definition of trust [...] is the willingness of a party to be vulnerable to the actions of another party based on the expectation that the other will perform a particular action important to the trustor, irrespective of the ability to monitor or control that other party." [58]*

This definition regards trust as an individual's willingness to be vulnerable to others' actions. This basic idea was later broadly accepted in trust research [59, 60]. By the beginning of the millennium, the publication from which this definition originates had already been cited "far more frequently than others on the topic of trust" [61]. Today, it remains the most influential one among different definitions of trust.

DOI: http://dx.doi.org/10.5772/intechopen.1006301

> *"Trust: confidence that [one] will find what is desired rather than what is feared." [62]*

This definition argues that trust is rooted in the cost-benefit analysis of future events. A rational individual always desires and thus pursues benefits, but fears and avoids costs. Trust arises when an individual "is confronted with an ambiguous path, a path that can lead to an event perceived to be beneficial or to an event perceived to be harmful" [63]. When trusting, an individual believes that taking this path will be beneficial.

> *"Interpersonal trust is defined here as an expectancy held by an individual or a group that the word, promise, verbal or written statement of another individual or group can be relied upon." [64]*

From a sociological perspective, trust can be seen as an expectancy that others will do what they state or promise. Social interactions with others (like parents, teachers, and peers) provide an individual with rich feedback to validate whether their expectancy is accurate. With accumulating feedback, an individual develops a *generalized expectancy* about the extent to which other people can be relied upon. Some individuals may have been surrounded by honest persons and believe that people are trustworthy in general. Others may have experienced much betrayal, which makes them less trusting. This generalized expectancy changes slowly in the long term and becomes a personal trait [64].

> *"Trust can be defined as the attitude that an agent will help achieve an individual's goals in a situation characterized by uncertainty and vulnerability. [...] an agent can be automation or another person that actively interacts with the environment on behalf of the person." [61]*

The notion of *trust in automation* has been gaining relevance in trust research as automated systems are extensively used today. There are several definitions of trust in automation. For example, in the one quoted above, the trustee is considered an agent that "can be automation or another person". The use of the term "agent" suggests that the trustee's agency, rather than their identity, contributes to the trustor's perception of uncertainty and vulnerability.

3.2 Trust in Virtual Agents

As discussed above, trust has been defined in diverse ways, encompassing concepts such as willingness, attitude, confidence, and expectancy. The different definitions share a common view that trust is a mental construct, which can be modeled as an information-processing procedure [65]. As **Figure 1** illustrates, the processor functions like a black box, perceiving information from the external world as input and generating mental constructs as output. Based on this model, trust in a virtual agent is essentially the product of users' perception and processing of information related to their interaction with the agent.

The processor determines how perceived information is processed into trust. Each processor represents an individual user and may respond to perceived information in a unique way. Consequently, the same information may result in different levels of trust depending on the processor, which makes it challenging to predict trust in virtual agents at an individual level. Nevertheless, there are still some patterns in the

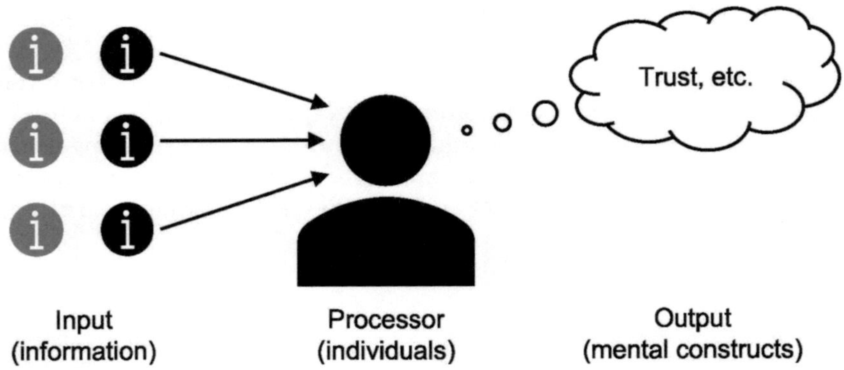

Figure 1.
Trust in virtual agents as information processing. The gray and black information icons represent information overlooked and perceived by the processor, respectively.

trusting attitudes among demographically different groups. For instance, females tend to put a higher level of trust in virtual agents than males [66]. Older people consider a virtual agent more trustworthy than young people when the agent uses non-verbal behavior to communicate emotions [67].

On the other hand, the same processor may produce different levels of trust if perceived information differs. The literature has documented various pieces of information that, when perceived by users, can impact their trust in virtual agents. These can be generally classified into two categories—*analytical information* and *affective information*—based on a commonly used dual division of trust into cognitive and affective aspects [68, 69]. Analytical information (e.g., the probability of whether an agent can achieve a task) forms the basis for users to make rational assumptions about the trustworthiness of a virtual agent. These assumptions give users "good reasons" to trust or distrust another [68] and are widely regarded as a fundamental component of trust [58, 70, 71]. Affective information influences trust in virtual agents mainly through psychological and social channels related to emotions, feelings, or stereotypes, etiquette, etc. For example, the Uncanny Valley effect can impair a virtual agent's trustworthiness by inducing a sense of eeriness [72].

The two categories (i.e., analytical and affective information) are not mutually exclusive. Certain information can influence trust in both rational and affective ways. For instance, task urgency is not only an important factor to be considered in rational thinking but also a stressor that may bias users' trust [73].

The list below provides several examples of analytical and affective information. Many of them are drawn from research on trust in virtual agents, and the remaining ones come from studies on trust in automated systems or software agents, to which virtual agents also belong. To facilitate the discussion, within the list, we use the term "agentic system(s)" or simply "system(s)" to generally refer to an artificial entity with some degree of autonomy for carrying out users' tasks. Such an entity can be an automated system, a software agent, or a virtual agent.

3.2.1 Analytical information examples

- *Reliability.* The reliability of an agentic system is an influential factor in its trustworthiness [34, 61, 71]. Users tend to trust reliable systems, whereas signals indicating low reliability, such as errors or task failures, are generally detrimental to their trustworthiness [74, 75]. Notably, users are particularly attentive to mistakes and errors due to the stereotype that machines can perform tasks perfectly [76].

- *Predictability.* Predictability describes the extent to which an agentic system's behavior, whether reliable or not, is predictable to its users. Predictability is considered a fundamental factor of both interpersonal trust [58] and trust in software agents [77].

- *Benevolence.* In certain critical scenarios, agentic systems may appear more trustworthy than human agents owing to their user-centered design. For example, people are more likely to reveal their credit card information to a software agent than to a human agent [43]. Similarly, in massive multiplayer online games, players often prefer to trade valuable virtual items through a non-player character escrow rather than a third player [78].

- *Transparency.* An agentic system is considered more trustworthy if its algorithms are transparent [79, 80]. Transparency is particularly relevant nowadays as algorithms have grown increasingly complex.

3.2.2 Affective information examples

- *Anthropomorphism.* Agentic systems are more likely to be rated as trustworthy when they exhibit anthropomorphic features [81, 82]. For example, virtual agents with human-like visual representations are perceived as more trustworthy than those embodied in non-human characters [7, 83]. The same applies to the auditory channel: users tend to put a higher level of trust in agents dubbed with a natural human voice than a low-quality synthesized voice [84].

- *Similarity.* Individuals tend to hold favorable opinions of those who share similarities with them [85] and, consequently, are more likely to trust those similar to others [86, 87]. This similarity effect exists not only interpersonally but also between users and agentic systems. A user is more likely to trust a virtual agent if its face resembles the user's face [88] or if it mimics the user's body movements [89].

- *Politeness.* When communicating with users, agentic systems that conform to social etiquette can appear more trustworthy than systems disregarding it. Users are more likely to trust an automated system that communicates in a relatively non-interruptive manner, for example, postponing the notification of non-critical messages when users are focusing on important tasks [90].

- *Attractiveness.* Humans intrinsically tend to label physically attractive individuals with more favorable characteristics, such as being more trustworthy [91], compared to average individuals. Similarly, virtual agents with human-like visual representation are also considered more trustworthy if their face looks attractive [92].

From a macroscopic perspective, there are mainly three dimensions governing virtual agents' trustworthiness in this information-processing model, including an *analytical dimension*, an *affective dimension*, and a *technological dimension*. The analytical dimension impacts trust in virtual agents by being directly involved in rational thinking, while the affective dimension biases user trust through psychological and social channels. During interactions with virtual agents, users act as an information processor that continuously perceives and evaluates information from the interaction. The perceived information, in turn, shapes users' trust in virtual agents via the analytical and affective dimensions, as **Figure 2** illustrates. Some information exerts its influences mainly through a single dimension, whereas others can have a significant impact through both dimensions.

The technological dimension accounts for the indirect influence of technologies underlying virtual agents. The perception of a virtual agent may vary depending on the media device used (e.g., desktops vs. head-mounted displays), which in turn may lead to different levels of trust according to the model. Furthermore, technologies underlying virtual agents are highly relevant to data security. Trust in a virtual agent may decrease if the agent runs on an insecure infrastructure threatening personal data and privacy. This can be crucial when experiencing the Metaverse on immersive media devices whose embedded sensors are usually more invasive than those in laptops or smartphones [93].

3.3 From trust to delegation

Trust and delegation are intrinsically related concepts. Theoretically, delegation entails two essential components of trust defined in [58], including *uncertainty* (agents' actions and the ensuing outcomes are neither entirely predictable nor completely unknown) and *vulnerability* (users are accountable or responsible for

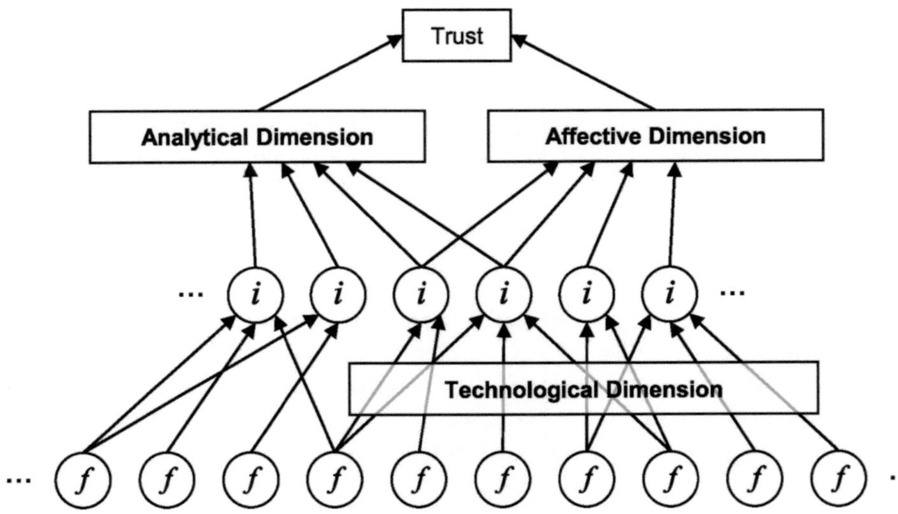

Figure 2.
A conceptual model of trust in virtual agents. The circled f in the figure bottom represents facts about interaction with virtual agents. These facts are perceived by users and become information (illustrated as circled i). A piece of information may originate from several facts; for example, an agent's capability of financial investment may result from an appraisal of its trading histories in different markets. The bulk of information (represented as the four circled i on the right) is perceived through media devices and thus subject to the technological dimension. The remaining information (represented as the two circled i on the left) is perceived via other channels, such as conversations with other people about the agent's reputation. Perceived information, in turn, influences trust in virtual agents through the analytical and affective dimensions.

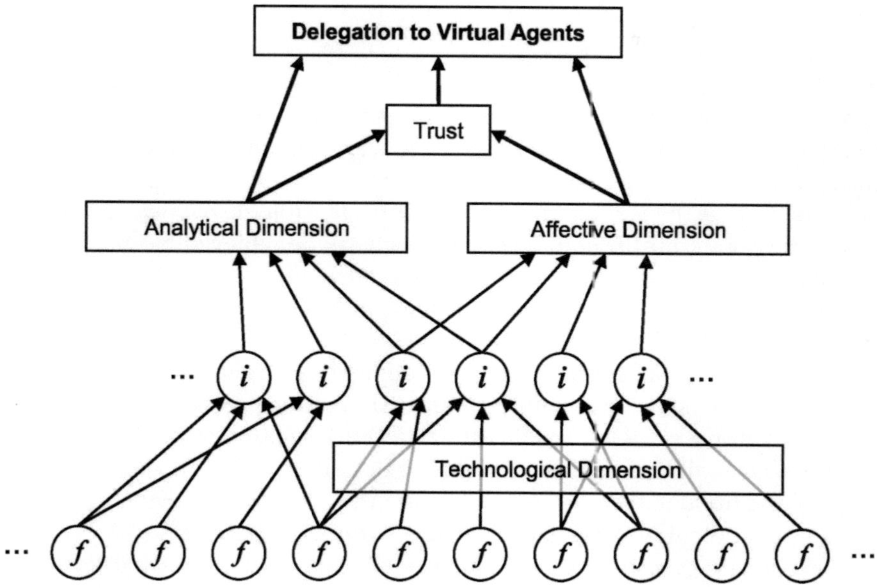

Figure 3.
The conceptual model extended from trust to delegation.

task outcomes). There is also empirical evidence substantiating the connection. For example, trust was found to be correlated with the level of *decentralization*, i.e., the extent to which top managers of an organization empower subordinates to make decisions as opposed to micro-managing. Research shows that the more trust there is within an organization, the more decentralized the organization is, and the more delegation therein [94]. As noted in [95], "a high-trust society can organize its workplace on a more flexible and group-oriented basis, with more responsibility delegated to lower levels of the organization. Low-trust societies, by contrast, must fence in and isolate their workers with a series of bureaucratic rules". Similar results can also be found in psychological studies, where trust in subordinates constitutes a vital factor behind managers' decisions on delegation [11, 28]. In the context of human-computer interaction, trust also plays an important role in delegation to artificial agents [46]. For instance, trust was found to be correlated with students' willingness to let a software agent arrange travels for their job interviews [47].

With the evidence mentioned above, the conceptual model can be further extended as **Figure 3** illustrates, where the three dimensions also influence delegation to virtual agents directly or through the mediation of trust. The extended model provides a theoretical foundation to systematically view and explore factors potentially governing delegation to virtual agents.

4. Discussion

The conceptual model offers a theoretical foundation explaining how different factors collectively shape users' decisions regarding delegation to virtual agents. Based on this, further practical insights can be derived to facilitate the design of virtual agents for delegation and explore future metaverse-related research directions.

4.1 Design guidance

The model provides a systematic approach to designing virtual agents for delegation. As previously discussed, the three dimensions decompose a delegation decision into relatively individual aspects of rationality, affection, and technology. Each dimension includes a set of factors that can be modulated through agent design. For example, to increase the impact of the affective dimension, developers may consider increasing the agents' anthropomorphism, which can be achieved by changing their visual representation to more human-like characters. When designing virtual agents for delegation, developers can focus on the most influential dimensions and adjust the factors associated with these dimensions.

The importance of each dimension varies depending on the nature of the delegated tasks. For instance, the analytical dimension is imperative in performance-critical tasks. Our previous studies investigated the delegation of financial investment and showed that analytical information plays a decisive role [8, 53]. Affective aspects like rapport and human likeness are somewhat influential in this context [7, 96], whereas the technological dimension only has a limited impact [97].

These results suggest that, in performance-critical scenarios, virtual agents are still primarily seen as tools rather than social actors. Delegation to virtual agents therefore remains predominantly a matter of cost-benefit analysis, differing from interpersonal delegation where the social connection between principals and agents also weighs [31]. Thus, developers may only need to focus on performance-related aspects when designing virtual agents for critical tasks. A limited number of affective cues (e.g., facial expression, gesture) can make the interaction more natural and personable. As exemplified by LLMs such as ChatGPT, their apparent near-human performance makes many users willing—sometimes unquestioningly—to delegate critical tasks (e.g., thesis writing, exam essays, medical consultation) to them despite their textual interfaces.

On a different note, it is good practice to consider trust when designing virtual agents for delegation. As illustrated in **Figure 3**, trust constitutes a major factor of delegation, and studies show that they are positively correlated [11, 28, 46, 47, 53]. A lack of trust in virtual agents may likely lead to users' reluctance to delegate. Thus, developers should avoid trust-impairing designs and consider incorporating an adequate number of trust-building elements in virtual agents. There is a substantial body of research on trust in intelligent artifacts [80], which provides more specific guidelines that developers may refer to for agent designs.

4.2 Challenges and open issues

Users are more susceptible to manipulation in an agency relationship with virtual agents than in the traditional user-tool relationship with software programs. Developers may use exploitative features or algorithms in virtual agents to entice users to behave in certain ways for the sake of profit. For example, a virtual agent for financial investments may embody a trustworthy human character and use rapport-building body language to gain users' trust and collect capital. This problem is exacerbated by the fact that when users delegate, they give up some or all of their authority, making them vulnerable to virtual agents and the developers behind them. In addition, virtual agents are increasingly controlled by LLMs whose decisions are less predictable and controllable than those of non-AI programs. It remains debatable whether these models have a sufficient level of empathy and integrity when communicating with users to remain neutral and not influence users to delegate unethically.

Legislation plays a central role in mitigating the above-mentioned ethical concerns. As users increasingly interact with virtual agents in the metaverse and delegate critical tasks with real-world consequences, appropriate regulations should be implemented to penalize manipulation. On the other hand, the regulations could create a legal infrastructure to promote responsibility and risk sharing between virtual agent users and developers. This not only encourages developers to improve the quality of their services but also prevents unethical behavior by aligning the interests of both parties.

Navigating the metaverse and managing engagement with virtual agents is also a major cross-cultural challenge, as different cultural norms and values can clash in interactions. Specific forms of representation, different social etiquette, language barriers, and different levels of digital literacy all impact trust and delegation and can hinder inclusion if they are not taken into account.

4.3 Future research

With virtual agents becoming more capable and autonomous, interactions with them increasingly resemble interpersonal delegation. One of today's most debated topics is identifying influential factors in users' delegation decisions. Future studies can continue this line of research by exploring new factors or re-evaluating known factors in different contexts. The results will provide further insights into users' decision-making process, thereby expanding the theoretical foundation to address the above-mentioned challenges (cf. **Section 4.2**) and facilitating user-agent interactions in a metaverse context. For example, it might be interesting to investigate the delegation of relatively performance-uncritical tasks. Influential factors in critical tasks, such as performance and capability, may degrade to insignificant ones, whereas the impact of the affective and technological dimensions may become more relevant.

From a sociological perspective, the metaverse as a concept is gradually evolving from an inter-user platform to a hybrid digital society of humans and AI, where delegation occurs arbitrarily among a massive number of users and virtual agents. The underlying dynamics at this macroscopic level are complicated and largely unexplored, but merit further investigation for this hybrid society's overall efficiency and welfare. Thus, researchers may consider using multi-agent and multi-task scenarios for future studies to confirm the findings obtained from minimal settings (e.g., one user delegates a single task to a virtual agent). The results will lend us more sociological and economic perspectives on the future of virtual agents and the metaverse, in addition to the psychological stance that many studies today have assumed.

5. Conclusion

As technology advances rapidly, the digital sphere, including the metaverse, will become increasingly populated with AI-powered, intelligent virtual agents. With their enhanced autonomy and capability, these agents are more and more assuming the role of delegate in addition to their traditional role as mere tools. This agency relationship has already found wide acceptance in recent years due to the emergence and adoption of generative AI applications and LLMs like ChatGPT. However, the relevant research can hardly keep pace with technological developments and is still limited today.

Thus, this chapter introduced a trust-based conceptual model to explain how different factors collectively influence and shape users' decisions on delegation to virtual agents. The model distinguishes three dimensions, each related to a set of factors that uniquely impact trust and delegation decisions. Practical implications for virtual agent designs and potential applications of the model for metaverse development were discussed, together with future research opportunities.

Acknowledgements

This research was funded by the Luxembourg National Research Fund (FNR) under Grant 12635165.

Author details

Ningyuan Sun and Jean Botev*
University of Luxembourg, Esch-sur-Alzette, Luxembourg

*Address all correspondence to: jean.botev@uni.lu

References

[1] Ning H, Wang H, Lin Y, Wang W, Dhelim S, Farha F, et al. A survey on the metaverse: The state-of-the-art, technologies, applications, and challenges. IEEE Internet of Things Journal. 2023;**10**(16):14671-14688

[2] Weinberger M. What is metaverse? – A definition based on qualitative meta-synthesis. Future Internet. 2022;**14**(11):310

[3] Lugrin B, Pelachaud C, Traum D, editors. The Handbook on Socially Interactive Agents: 20 Years of Research on Embodied Conversational Agents, Intelligent Virtual Agents, and Social Robotics Volume 1: Methods, Behavior, Cognition. 1st ed. Vol. 1. New York, NY, United States: Association for Computing Machinery; 2021

[4] Lugrin B, Pelachaud C, Traum D, editors. The Handbook on Socially Interactive Agents: 20 Years of Research on Embodied Conversational Agents, Intelligent Virtual Agents, and Social Robotics Volume 2: Interactivity, Platforms, Application. 1st ed. Vol. 2. New York, NY, United States: Association for Computing Machinery; 2022

[5] McDonnell R, Mutlu B. Appearance. In: The Handbook on Socially Interactive Agents: 20 Years of Research on Embodied Conversational Agents, Intelligent Virtual Agents, and Social Robotics: Methods, Behavior, Cognition. 1st ed. Vol. 1. New York, NY, United States: Association for Computing Machinery; 2021. pp. 105-146

[6] Kim J. Advertising in the metaverse: Research agenda. Journal of Interactive Advertising. 2021;**21**(3):141-144

[7] Sun N, Botev J. Virtual agent representation for critical transactions. In: Proceedings of the 13th International Workshop on Immersive Mixed and Virtual Environment Systems (MMVE). New York, NY, United States: Association for Computing Machinery; 2021. pp. 25-29

[8] Sun N, Botev J. Why do we delegate to intelligent virtual agents? Influencing factors on delegation decisions. In: Proceedings of the Ninth International Conference on Human-Agent Interaction (HAI). New York, NY, United States: Association for Computing Machinery; 2021. pp. 386-390

[9] Lupia A. Delegation of power: Agency theory. In: International Encyclopedia of the Social and Behavioral Sciences. San Mateo, California, United States: Pergamon; 2001. pp. 3375-3377

[10] Baird A, Maruping LM. The next generation of research on IS use: A theoretical framework of delegation to and from agentic IS artifacts. MIS Quarterly. 2021;**45**(1):315-341

[11] Leana CR. Power relinquishment versus power sharing: Theoretical clarification and empirical comparison of delegation and participation. Journal of Applied Psychology. 1987;**72**(2):228-233

[12] Milewski AE, Lewis SH. Delegating to software agents. International Journal of Human-Computer Studies. 1997;**46**(4):485-500

[13] Jensen MC. Agency costs of free cash flow, corporate finance, and takeovers. The American Economic Review. 1986;**76**(2):323-329

[14] Yukl G, Fu PP. Determinants of delegation and consultation by managers.

Journal of Organizational Behavior. 1999;**20**(2):219-232

[15] Sengul M, Gimeno J, Dial J. Strategic delegation: A review, theoretical integration, and research agenda. Journal of Management. 2012;**38**(1):375-414

[16] Eisenhardt KM. Agency theory: An assessment and review. Academy of Management Review. 1989;**14**(1):57-74

[17] Shapiro SP. Agency theory. Annual Review of Sociology. 2005;**31**:263-284

[18] Jensen MC, Meckling WH. Theory of the firm: Managerial behavior, agency costs and ownership structure. Journal of Financial Economics. 1976;**3**(4):305-360

[19] Wilson R. The theory of syndicates. Econometrica. 1968;**36**(1):119-132

[20] Fama EF. Agency problems and the theory of the firm. Journal of Political Economy. 1980;**88**(2):288-307

[21] Fama EF, Jensen MC. Separation of ownership and control. The Journal of Law and Economics. 1983;**26**(2):301-325

[22] Eisenhardt KM. Control: Organizational and economic approaches. Management Science. 1985;**31**(2):134-149

[23] Eisenhardt KM. Agency- and institutional-theory explanations: The case of retail sales compensation. The Academy of Management Journal. 1988;**31**(3):488-511

[24] Anderson E. The salesperson as outside agent or employee: A transaction cost analysis. Marketing Science. 1985;**4**(3):234-254

[25] Ross SA. The economic theory of agency: The Principal's problem. The American Economic Review. 1973;**63**(2):134-139

[26] Grossman SJ, Hart OD. An analysis of the principal-agent problem. In: Dionne G, Harrington SE, editors. Foundations of Insurance Economics: Readings in Economics and Finance. Netherlands: Springer; 1992. pp. 302-340

[27] Alonso R, Matouschek N. Relational delegation. The RAND Journal of Economics. 2007;**38**(4):1070-1089

[28] Aggarwal P, Mazumdar T. Decision delegation: A conceptualization and empirical investigation. Psychology & Marketing. 2008;**25**(1):71-93

[29] Steffel M, Williams EF, Perrmann-Graham J. Passing the buck: Delegating choices to others to avoid responsibility and blame. Organizational Behavior and Human Decision Processes. 2016;**135**:32-44

[30] Steffel M, Williams EF. Delegating decisions: Recruiting others to make choices we might regret. Journal of Consumer Research. 2018;**44**(5):1015-1032

[31] Jenks JM, Kelly JM. Don't Do, Delegate! London, United Kingdom: Franklin Watts; 1985

[32] Bobadilla-Suarez S, Sunstein CR, Sharot T. The intrinsic value of choice: The propensity to under-delegate in the face of potential gains and losses. Journal of Risk and Uncertainty. 2017;**54**(3):187-202

[33] Venkatesh V, Morris MG, Davis GB, Davis FD. User acceptance of information technology: Toward a unified view. MIS Quarterly. 2003;**27**(3):425-478

[34] Parasuraman R, Riley V. Humans and automation: Use, misuse, disuse, abuse. Human Factors. 1997;**39**(2):230-253

[35] Dixon SR, Wickens CD. Automation reliability in unmanned aerial vehicle control: A reliance-compliance model of automation dependence in high workload. Human Factors. 2006;**48**(3):474-486

[36] Riley V. Operator reliance on automation: Theory and data. In: Parasuraman R, Mouloua M, editors. Automation and Human Performance: Theory and Applications. Boca Raton, Florida, United States: Taylor & Francis, CPC Press; 1996. pp. 19-35

[37] Castelfranchi C, Falcone R. Towards a theory of delegation for agent-based systems. Robotics and Autonomous Systems. 1998;**24**(3-4):141-157

[38] Candrian C, Scherer A. Rise of the machines: Delegating decisions to autonomous AI. Computers in Human Behavior. 2022;**134**:107308

[39] Logg JM, Minson JA, Moore DA. Algorithm appreciation: People prefer algorithmic to human judgment. Organizational Behavior and Human Decision Processes. 2019;**151**:90-103

[40] Fügener A, Grahl J, Gupta A, Ketter W. Cognitive challenges in human-artificial intelligence collaboration: Investigating the path toward productive delegation. Information Systems Research. 2022;**33**(2):678-696

[41] Dietvorst BJ, Simmons JP, Massey C. Algorithm aversion: People erroneously avoid algorithms after seeing them err. Journal of Experimental Psychology: General. 2015;**144**(1):114-126

[42] Fogg BJ. A behavior model for persuasive design. In: Proceedings of the Fourth International Conference on Persuasive Technology (PERSUASIVE). New York, NY, United States: Association for Computing Machinery; 2009. pp. 1-7

[43] Sundar SS, Kim J. Machine heuristic: When we trust computers more than humans with our personal information. In: Proceedings of the 37th CHI Conference on Human Factors in Computing Systems. New York, NY, United States: Association for Computing Machinery; 2019

[44] Harbers M, Peeters MMM, Neerincx MA. Perceived autonomy of robots: Effects of appearance and context. In: Proceedings of the 2015 International Conference on Robot Ethics (ICRE). Cham, Switzerland: Springer, Cham; 2017. pp. 19-33

[45] Bigman YE, Gray K. People are averse to machines making moral decisions. Cognition. 2018;**181**:21-34

[46] Lubars B, Tan C. Ask not what AI can do, but what AI should do: Towards a framework of task delegability. In: Proceedings of the 33rd International Conference on Neural Information Processing Systems (NeurIPS). Red Hook, NY, United States: Curran Associates Inc.; 2019. pp. 57-67

[47] Stout N, Dennis AR, Wells TM. The Buck stops there: The impact of perceived accountability and control on the intention to delegate to software agents. AIS Transactions on Human-Computer Interaction. 2014;**6**(1):1-15

[48] Leyer M, Aysolmaz B, Iren D. Acceptance of AI for delegating emotional intelligence: Results from an experiment. In: Proceedings of the 54th Hawaii International Conference on System Sciences (HICSS). Honolulu, Hawaii, United States: ScholarSpace; 2021. pp. 6307-6316

[49] Dietvorst BJ, Simmons JP, Massey C. Overcoming algorithm aversion: People will use imperfect algorithms if they can (even slightly)

modify them. Management Science. 2018;**64**(3):1155-1170

[50] Fernández, Domingos E, Terrucha I, Suchon R, Grujić J, Burguillo JC, Santos FC, et al. Delegation to artificial agents fosters prosocial behaviors in the collective risk dilemma. Scientific Reports. 2022;**12**(1):8492. Available from: https://www.nature.com/articles/s41598-022-11518-9

[51] Fügener A, Grahl J, Gupta A, Ketter W, Taudien A. Exploring user heterogeneity in human delegation behavior towards AI. In: Proceedings of the 42nd International Conference on Information Systems (ICIS). Atlanta, Georgia, United States: Association for Information Systems; 2021

[52] Hukal P, Berente N, Germonprez M, Schecter A. Bots coordinating work in open source software projects. Computer. 2019;**52**(9):52-60

[53] Sun N, Botev J, Khaluf Y, Simoens P. Theory of mind and delegation to robotic virtual agents. In: Proceedings of the 31st IEEE International Conference on Robot and Human Interactive Communication (RO-MAN). New York, NY, United States: IEEE; 2022. pp. 454-460

[54] Luhmann N. Trust and Power. Hoboken, New Jersey, United States: John Wiley & Sons; 1979

[55] Dunn JR, Schweitzer ME. Feeling and believing: The influence of emotion on trust. Journal of Personality and Social Psychology. 2005;**88**(5):736-748

[56] Myers CD, Tingley D. The influence of emotion on trust. Political Analysis. 2016;**24**(4):492-500

[57] Marsh SP. Formalising Trust as a Computational Concept [dissertation]. University of Stirling; 1994

[58] Mayer RC, Davis JH, Schoorman FD. An integrative model of organizational trust. The Academy of Management Review. 1995;**20**(3):709-734

[59] Friedman B, Khan PH Jr, Howe DC. Trust Online. Communications of the ACM. 2000;**43**(12):34-40

[60] Cook KS, Yamagishi T, Cheshire C, Cooper R, Matsuda M, Mashima R. Trust building via risk taking: A cross-societal experiment. Social Psychology Quarterly. 2005;**68**(2):121-142

[61] Lee JD, See KA. Trust in automation: Designing for appropriate reliance. Human Factors. 2004;**46**(1):50-80

[62] Deutsch M. The Resolution of Conflict: Constructive and Destructive Processes. New Haven, Connecticut, United States: Yale University Press; 1973

[63] Deutsch M. Cooperation and trust: Some theoretical notes. In: Jones MR, editor. Nebraska Symposium on Motivation. Lincoln, Nebraska, United States: Universiy of Nebraska Press; 1962. pp. 275-320

[64] Rotter JB. A new scale for the measurement of interpersonal trust. Journal of Personality. 1967;**35**(4):651-665

[65] LaViola JJ Jr, Kruijff E, McMahan RP, Bowman DA, Poupyrev I. 3D User Interfaces: Theory and Practice. 2nd ed. Boston, United States: Addison-Wesley Professional; 2017

[66] Khalid HM, Shiung LW, Sheng VB, Helander MG. Trust of virtual agent in multi actor interactions. Journal of Robotics, Networking and Artificial Life. 2018;**4**(4):295-298

[67] Hosseinpanah A, Krämer NC, Straßmann C. Empathy for everyone? The effect of age when evaluating a

virtual agent. In: Proceedings of the Sixth International Conference on Human-Agent Interaction (HAI). New York, NY, United States: Association for Computing Machinery; 2018. pp. 184-190

[68] Morrow JL Jr, Hansen MH, Pearson AW. The cognitive and affective antecedents of general trust within cooperative organizations. Journal of Managerial Issues. 2004;**16**:48-64

[69] Punyatoya P. Effects of cognitive and affective trust on online customer behavior. Marketing Intelligence & Planning. 2019;**37**(1):80-96

[70] Rempel JK, Holmes JG, Zanna MP. Trust in close relationships. Journal of Personality and Social Psychology. 1985;**49**(1):95-112

[71] Lee J, Moray N. Trust, control strategies and allocation of function in human-machine systems. Ergonomics. 1992;**35**(10):1243-1270

[72] Song SW, Shin M. Uncanny valley effects on Chatbot trust, purchase intention, and adoption intention in the context of E-commerce: The moderating role of avatar familiarity. International Journal of Human-Computer Interaction. 2022;**40**:441-456

[73] Potts SR, McCuddy WT, Jayan D, Porcelli AJ. To trust, or not to trust? Individual differences in physiological reactivity predict trust under acute stress. Psychoneuroendocrinology. 2019;**100**:75-84

[74] de Visser EJ, Parasuraman R. Adaptive aiding of human-robot teaming: Effects of imperfect automation on performance, trust, and workload. Journal of Cognitive Engineering and Decision Making. 2011;**5**(2):209-231

[75] Manzey D, Reichenbach J, Onnasch L. Human performance consequences of automated decision aids: The impact of degree of automation and system experience. Journal of Cognitive Engineering and Decision Making. 2012;**6**(1):57-87

[76] Dzindolet MT, Pierce LG, Beck HP, Dawe LA. The perceived utility of human and automated aids in a visual detection task. Human Factors. 2002;**44**(1):79-94

[77] Daronnat S, Azzopardi L, Halvey M, Dubiel M. Impact of agent reliability and predictability on trust in real time human-agent collaboration. In: Proceedings of the Eighth International Conference on Human-Agent Interaction (HAI). New York, NY, United States: Association for Computing Machinery; 2020. pp. 131-139

[78] Lehdonvirta V, Castronova E. Virtual Economies: Design and Analysis. Cambridge, Massachusetts, United States: MIT Press; 2014

[79] Glikson E, Woolley AW. Human trust in artificial intelligence: Review of empirical research. Academy of Management Annals. 2020;**14**(2):627-660

[80] Hoff KA, Bashir M. Trust in automation: Integrating empirical evidence on factors that influence trust. Human Factors. 2015;**57**(3):407-434

[81] Waytz A, Heafner J, Epley N. The mind in the machine: Anthropomorphism increases trust in an autonomous vehicle. Journal of Experimental Social Psychology. 2014;**52**:113-117

[82] Natarajan M, Gombolay M. Effects of anthropomorphism and accountability on trust in human robot interaction. In: Proceedings of the 15th ACM/IEEE International Conference on Human-Robot Interaction (HRI). New York, NY,

United States: Association for Computing Machinery; 2020. pp. 33-42

[83] Matsui T, Koike A. Who is to blame? The appearance of virtual agents and the attribution of perceived responsibility. Sensors. 2021;**21**(8):2646. Available from: https://www.mdpi.com/1424-8220/21/8/2646

[84] Chiou EK, Schroeder NL, Craig SD. How we trust, perceive, and learn from virtual humans: The influence of voice quality. Computers & Education. 2020;**146**:103756

[85] Montoya RM, Horton RS, Kirchner J. Is actual similarity necessary for attraction? A meta-analysis of actual and perceived similarity. Journal of Social and Personal Relationships. 2008;**25**(6):889-922

[86] DeBruine LM. Facial resemblance enhances trust. Proceedings of the Royal Society B: Biological Sciences. 2002;**269**(1498):1307-1312

[87] Verosky SC, Todorov A. Differential neural responses to faces physically similar to the self as a function of their valence. NeuroImage. 2010;**49**(2):1690-1698

[88] Verberne FMF, Ham JRC, Midden CJH. Familiar faces: Trust in facially similar agents. In: Proceedings of the 14th International Conference on Autonomous Agents and Multiagent Systems (AAMAS). Richland, South Carolina, United States: International Foundation for Autonomous Agents and Multiagent Systems; 2014

[89] Launay J, Dean RT, Bailes F. Synchronization can influence trust following virtual interaction. Experimental Psychology. 2013;**60**(1):53-63

[90] Parasuraman R, Miller CA. Trust and etiquette in high-criticality automated systems. Communications of the ACM. 2004;**47**(4):51-55

[91] Patzer GL. Source credibility as a function of communicator physical attractiveness. Journal of Business Research. 1983;**11**(2):229-241

[92] Yuksel BF, Collisson P, Czerwinski M. Brains or beauty: How to engender trust in user-agent interactions. ACM Transactions on Internet Technology. 2017;**17**(1):1-20

[93] Adams D, Bah A, Barwulor C, Musaby N, Pitkin K, Redmiles EM. Ethics emerging: The story of privacy and security perceptions in virtual reality. In: Proceedings of the 14th Symposium on Usable Privacy and Security (SOUPS). Berkeley, California, United States: USENIX Association; 2018. pp. 427-442

[94] Gur N, Bjørnskov C. Trust and delegation: Theory and evidence. Journal of Comparative Economics. 2017;**45**(3):644-657

[95] Fukuyama F. Trust: The Social Virtues and the Creation of Prosperity. New York, NY, United States: Simon and Schuster; 1996

[96] Sun N, Botev J, Simoens P. The effect of rapport on delegation to virtual agents. In: Proceedings of the 23rd International Conference on Intelligent Virtual Agents (IVA). New York, NY, United States: Association for Computing Machinery; 2023

[97] Sun N, Botev J. Technological immersion and delegation to virtual agents. Multimodal Technologies and Interaction. 2023;**7**(11):106

Chapter 8

Distance Learning Using Machine Learning in the Future of Digital Interaction

Ibtehal Nafea

Abstract

The field of metaverse technology has been relatively growing overall, and the concept of boundaries is now not only from the real world to virtual reality, but now there is an education field that is now one of the driving forces here that is transforming society. The traditional educational models cede to advanced scenarios like e-learning supported by machine-learning systems. This is where educational institutions like Taibah University in Saudi Arabia emerge as leaders in this paradigm change. Taibah University traditionally redefined the study process, which is now digitized, and the geographic borders are being discarded using machine learning in distance learning.

Keywords: machine learning, distance learning, Taibah University, Saudi Arabia, digital interaction

1. Introduction

The digital transformation has proved to be precisely what it is—a real game-changer, abolishing geographical limitations, and allowing learners to receive education on demand and on the go. Machine learning (ML) is the core element of such a transition, enabling digital systems to personalize and increase the effectiveness of distance education programs. This chapter zooms in on machine learning, which is the primary driver in the displacement of traditional instruction mode of education. However, a detailed study is presented on applying the technology for the software course in the context of Taibah University [1]. One of the factors drawn from the case study shows how the machine learning algorithm is applied to create active learning communities, responsive interactions, and a constantly evolving school, thus ushering education into a new age in a world of increased sophistication.

1.1 Machine learning for personalized learning

Machine learning algorithms are the key players in the digital educational quantum leap. Various learning styles, interests, and preferences might diagnose individual student excellence. The process is usually followed by algorithms that deliver materials that are logically less than or more than the intended learning [2]. This personalized approach, not solely aimed at facilitating the learning process through an improved understanding of the material, simultaneously triggers a more profound level of immersion. For example, a study by [3] on the use of PIM at Taibah University observed an average enhancement of 15% among the students who used FIN as compared to those who used conventional methods. Additionally, the number of engagement rates, which are the logins in the platform and content engagement, increased by 20% among the students using the PIM.

Taibah University has integrated a PIM that applies artificial neural networks to deliver content and learning materials according to the student's ability and learning rate. Such a platform can also involve using assessment data to make recommendations on the most suitable resources, give feedback, and set the materials' difficulty level [3]. For example, students who perform poorly on some mathematical problems will be given more such problems or explanatory videos, while students who show proficiency will be given more complex issues. Particularly, the SGFP algorithm provided a 10% enhancement to the course completion rates with a 15% decrease in the dropout rates as compared to conventional teaching-learning methodologies.

It has also been effective in raising and encouraging students' performance since every student is different. Research has shown that students who utilize the learning management systems receive higher grades than their counterparts taught in the conventional method; besides, they show more motivation and have fewer dropout incidences. For instance, Smirani et al. [4] noted that the experiment of the SGFP algorithm in 10 sections of 176 students enrolled in the academic year 2020–2021 enabled the success of 174 students and the failure of only two; hence, 98.86% of students got through. Also, the SGFP approach provided reasonable results when applied in addition to the extra students in different Saudi universities. A recent study by Urdaneta et al. [5] established that the use of recommendation systems introduced at Taibah University improved students' satisfaction with the course materials by 25% and their overall performance by 12%.

Taibah University has adopted a learning model that includes innovative technologies like recommendation systems, clustering, and reinforcement learning to deliver learning materials and pace the learning process according to the students' characteristics. Recommendation systems use all the data available for students, like past performances, assignments, and how they interact. They provide them with resources to learn from, like videos, articles, or practice problems [5]. Recommendation systems categorize students by similarity in learning approaches, abilities, and difficulties; thus, they can provide content and learning assistance to particular groups of students [6]. Reinforcement learning enables the system to make further adjustments, given the developments of specific students, by encouraging or punishing student actions and creating the best learning path. Decision trees are used to categorize students according to their characteristics, including academic performance, learning preferences, and activity levels. Neural networks, on the other hand, can take into account a large number of parameters linked to the student and the learning environment and suggest potential learning paths to achieve specific academic results. Reinforcement learning algorithms help in the delivery of instructional content by either incentivizing or penalizing the actions of students.

In the same way, machine learning develops dynamic adaptive learning pathways that keep the pace of teaching and the level of challenge adapted to the actual feedback in real time. This activity then makes the program adaptive to the student's

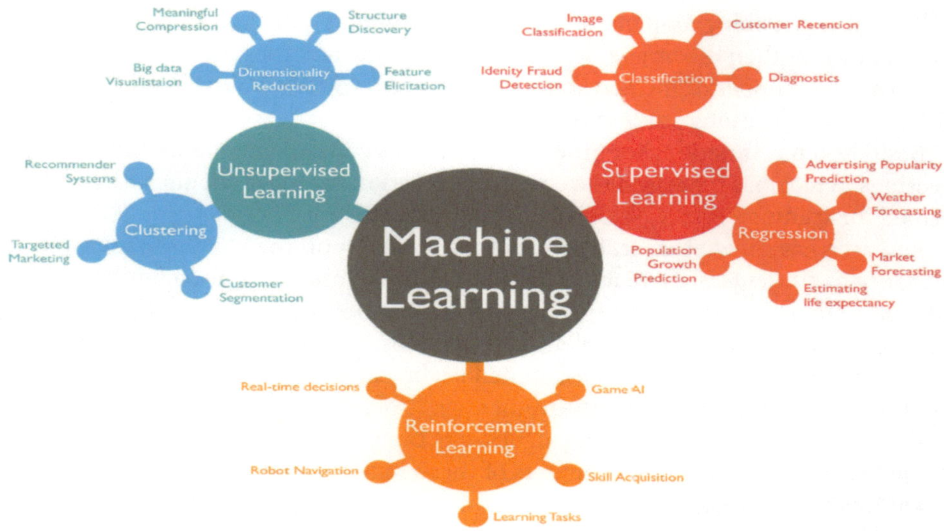

Figure 1.
Machine learning mechanism.

progress. Hence, those learnings are always challenging but still at the right level, promoting continuous improvement and mastery of the subject matter.

Apart from advanced algorithms, which facilitate individualized content delivery, intelligent machines can handle the function of predictive analytics, which allows teachers to foresee student outcomes and act beforehand whenever required. By recognizing the traits and characteristics of the students in danger or where they are most likely to falter, teachers can stage matching interventions to prevent a crisis and help them deal with a situation adequately [2]. Such measures reduce unnecessary learning obstacles and maintain a culturally inclusive, friendly learning environment where every student is given a chance to achieve (see **Figure 1**).

i. Example: An engineering student, for instance, could be pointed toward advanced coding tutoring, while a design enthusiast may be shown material about UI/UX concepts.

ii. Adaptive learning pathways: Machine learning supports dynamic self-figuring learning that allows teachers to set up the pace of teaching and challenge at the current level as the feedback is gathered in real time.

1.2 Enhanced collaboration and peer learning

Machine learning can be considered an essential component of a student's learning that nurtures distance or online learning collaboration. Machine learning is one of the analytical methods through which social interaction data is processed, and online study groups and peer-to-peer mentoring are organized, thus creating a dynamic learning society [2]. The university, which is a pioneer in applying machine learning in its education specifically, utilizes the benefits of machine learning to promote collaborative elements that overreach geographical boundaries and improve the student's quality of learning.

Taibah University's existing automated machine learning system helps students' group according to their preferences, learning mode, and efficiency. It is also possible to determine possible group members based on students' data and ensure that all of them can strengthen the others' weaknesses. After the incorporation of this particular platform, the number of formed study groups rose by 30%, while the satisfaction with group work among students grew by 25%.

Besides, it has functions for group work, such as editing documents and having meetings, which has increased the level of interaction among students in the groups formed for study.

Research has shown that students teaching their counterparts can enhance the performance of students in their academic activities. Johansson has also identified that students who make use of study groups are likely to perform better in other aspects, such as critical thinking and problem-solving skills. For example, Arco-Tirado et al. [7] found that in one of the studies, students who participated in peer tutoring programs received an average improvement of 10% in their grades.

Furthermore, machine learning algorithms can potentially be designed to be able to learn examples of how members of these communities work together. These algorithms are quite good at determining the best communication rate, as well as the optimal level of engagement, in order to complete the tasks at hand and identify the patterns of cooperation in the team [8]. This learning opportunity enables the teachers at Taibah University to offer specific solutions and resources to each listener with a focus on improving the community's cohesiveness and learning.

In addition, machine learning algorithms can quicken the process of monitoring group interactions for hassle-free supervision of educators when conflicts or problems arise. The educational assistants, through providing supported services and guidance, can guide students in overcoming challenges, thereby enhancing the performance of the collaborative settings.

- Example: Machine learning algorithms can detect students with similar academic interests and capabilities and, subsequently, help them foster group studies or peer tutoring sessions.

- Smart recommendation systems: Using technologies such as chat rooms or mentors assigned to the student makes up for the lack of belonging and companionship they might encounter within the educational setting.

Real-time analytics for continuous improvement.

In real-time, analytics give teachers decision-making power just by pointing out educational content and teaching methods that will be more effective. Taibah University applies the analyses carried out by machine learning to improve its software engineering course, maintaining the course's applicability and effectiveness in the face of any changing demands and industry requirements. Machine learning algorithms are the critical technology applied in data analysis of students' performance to create trends and discover patterns [9]. The educators at Taibah University can cultivate positive learning environments by making the most of these analytics and adjusting the panel of learning and teaching strategies accordingly to help in the student preferences and results. Inevitably, we use an insightful and rigorous data-gathering process, enabling us to react rapidly to and anticipate the changing demands of the students and maintain a stimulating and intriguing learning setting.

These involve real-time analysis of student participation, achievement, and satisfaction that educators use to evaluate teaching efficiency and optimize results. For instance, using live data regarding students' attendance and performance, Taibah

DOI: http://dx.doi.org/10.5772/intechopen.1006664

University recognized that learners have difficulties understanding a specific programming concept [10]. As a result, the university created other online learning aids like tutorials and practice exercises to enhance the students learning achievement. This intervention resulted in a 20% increase in the student's performance regarding the problematic assessment concept.

Besides, active analytics gives teachers immediate feedback on student growth and commitment level, bringing the opportunity for early intervention when it is needed. By pinpointing difficulties where students are stumbling or detached from learning, educators have the opportunity to cater instruction appropriately, which will not only encourage learning but also create a welcoming and inclusive learning environment.

i. Example: With real-time analytics, teachers can tell which subject's students most often struggle with and modify the methods to maximize students' knowledge of given concepts.

ii. Teaching quality evaluation: The feedback obtained via analytics endorses the topicality and the subject's impact.

2. How ML supports distance learning

2.1 Distance learning using machine learning: Workflow chart

The ML system perpetually feeds on data, trains its models, and uses these trained models to address individual learning needs. The cycle is repeated continuously to guarantee that the content and suggestions promoted by the systems are constantly aligned with students' characteristics with the help of ML for digital learning platforms. This brings educators on board to oversee the events and ensure human interaction supplements the mechanical systems employed in the educational environment. **Figure 2** below illustrates the overall system engineering design for the ML-based system to facilitate digital learning through data preparation, model training, and content recommendation steps. Here is a detailed explanation of each component and the overall workflow:

Raw data collection (Step 1): Users (students and educators) generate raw data through interactions with the learning platform. This data includes user behavior, performance metrics, content engagement, quiz scores, etc., and is sent to the data store. All collected data is stored in this centralized repository for further processing [11].

Data transformation (Step 2): Data in the data store is subject to a data transformation process in which the data is transformed or converted from raw format to structured format, which can be used for analytics and modeling. This might include data cleaning, normalization, feature extraction, and selection, which are part of preprocessing. The collected data stream then flows into the data transformation and forwards the data to the model training in the presented pipeline [refer to Ref 12]. In data preprocessing, missing data treatment can be done with imputation and normalization for feature scaling, while categorical variables can be transformed using one hot encoding [13]. The preprocessing step can also reduce dimensionality by using techniques like PCA or t-SNE for feature dimensionality reduction.

Model training (Step 3): The collected data is subjected to several transformations and handed over to the algorithms for pattern/forecasting analysis. This part of the

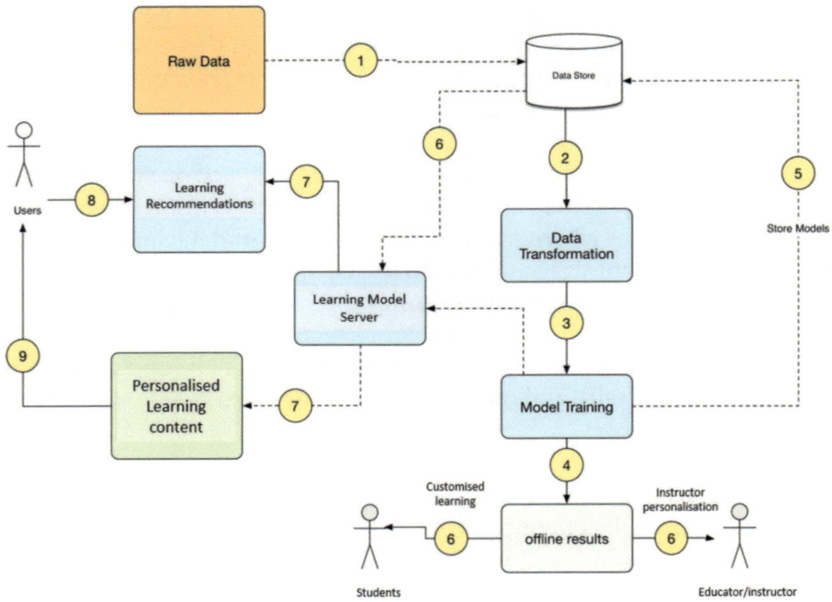

Figure 2.
ML to support distance learning workflow chart.

training phase is vital in developing accurate models for predicting performance and evaluating students' requirements. The partially or fully trained models are saved to the data store (Step 5) and downloaded to the learning model server for real-time applications. The choice of an algorithm may vary depending on the task and the data: Decision Trees, Random Forests, Support Vector Machines, or Neural Networks can be used for the model's training.

Offline results and feedback (Steps 4 and 6): Offline results relate to the processed and predicted data by the trained models. These results are applied in two main modes: first, they establish the value of learning for students since, depending on the model's output, they get a personalized instructional plan. Second, educators receive information about the progress of each student and the opportunities to provide individual approaches to learning. This step guarantees a double advantage for both the student and educator sides, using the insights from ML.

Learning model server (Step 7): The learning model server is the central function where the developed models are hosted for actual applications. It analyzes the received information and suggests learning strategies based on how the models predict outcomes [12]. On the other hand, the server communicates with the personalized learning content module to provide students with relevant learning content.

Learning recommendations (Step 8): Recommendations are generated using the data generated by the learning model server with the help of individual profiles. These recommendations may include exercises that are remarkable for the student, suggestions to read more, or even suggestions to review some parts of the course. Also, it affords feedback that lets the learner know if he is improving or when he is regressing to the norm.

Personalized learning content (Step 9): The last impact is the generation of personalized learning content as the output to the users (students). This is because such content is unique in that it is specifically developed to match the level of the particular student as opposed to the conventional mode of learning, which is the same for all students. The interaction is recurrent and helps the system advance and adjust to the student's success plan by becoming a part of an exciting and persistent learning process.

2.2 Application of ML in distance learning

Distance learning is one area where ML has had a significant impact in enhancing aspects of personalization, administrative tasks, and analytics, but it has not been without significant challenges. Based on the evaluation of the outcomes of ML in this respect, one gets a somewhat mixed picture of how efficient this technology is in enhancing learning performance and tackling inequality in learning environments.

First, it can develop a unique lesson plan with content and speed according to students' capabilities [14]. Therefore, adaptive learning systems use reinforcement learning and Bayesian knowledge tracing algorithms to provide the students with a learning environment that adapts to the student's performance and interactivity. For example, ML in adaptive learning systems monitors the student's interaction with the studied material and highlights their "blind spots"; based on this information, the system will customize the content presented to the student. This can involve better engagement and learning in general, as the students will receive instructions customized to their learning paths (**Figure 3**).

Second, ML assists educators in streamlining repetitive tasks, including grading and providing feedback [15], which will lessen the educators' burden and enable them to devote greater attention to interacting with students. One of the most essential forms of computerized grading is the ability to determine the scores of students essays, short answers, and multiple-choice questions using natural language processing (NLP) and machine learning. Students' responses to the assessment questions can be analyzed based on the sentiment they convey and the texts' classification. Automated essay scoring by AI and real-time feedback mechanisms are

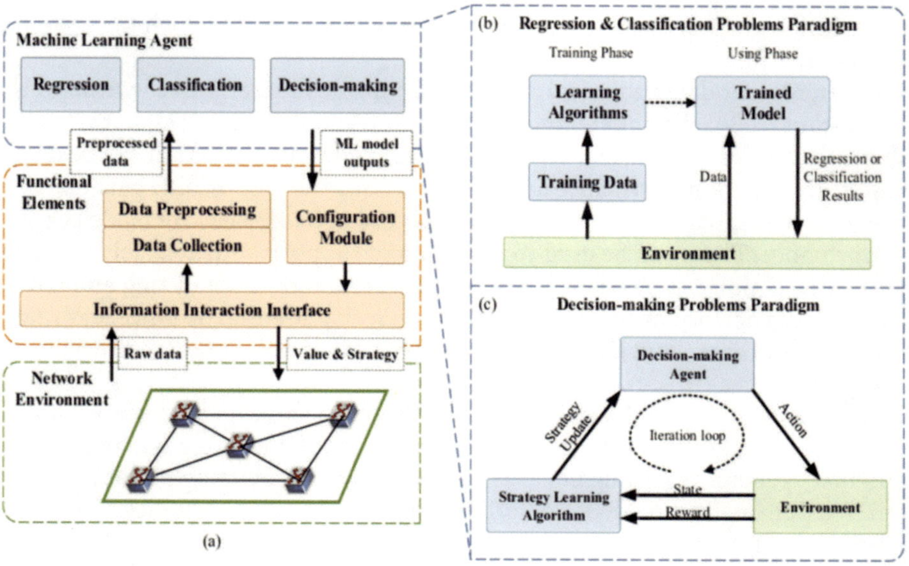

Figure 3.
How machine learning can engage with students learning patterns for a differentiated experience.

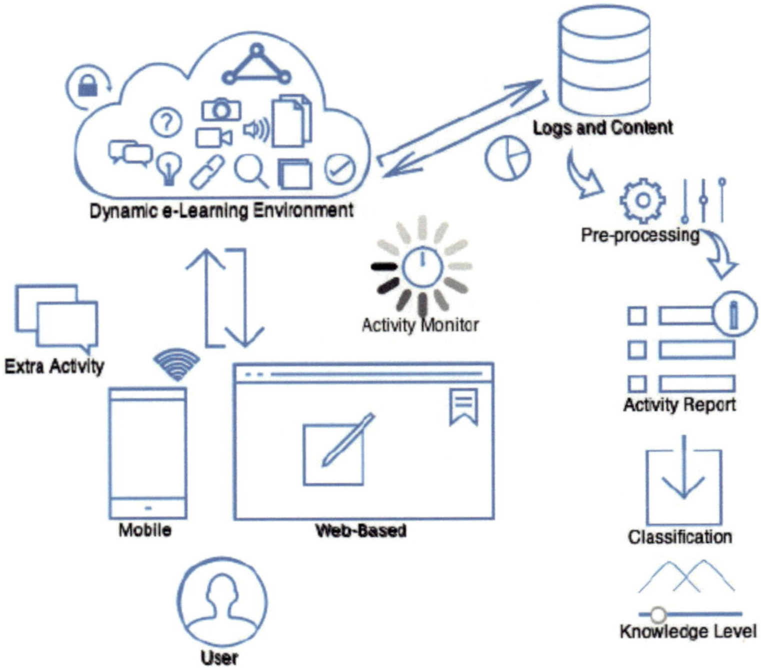

Figure 4.
System architecture of instructor ML in distance learning [16].

examples of how AI/ML can help optimize the assessment process to give students instant feedback. Although this helps increase efficiency, it also gives rise to issues of accuracy and fairness of machine-graded tests. **Figure 4** below shows an example of a system architecture that achieves such a goal [16]. In this case, the teacher or instructor is the user whose grading activities in a dynamic e-learning environment are constantly monitored. The system stores the logs and content from the user's activity, which are processed to obtain an activity report, from which the system can automate repetitive tasks.

Further, ML has data analytical abilities that enable the teacher or instructor to obtain instant feedback about learner performance and behavior [17]. In this case, predictive analytics can flag learners likely to lag, and remedial action can be taken promptly. In student performance analysis, some ML features include clustering and decision trees, where students' data is analyzed and forecasts are made based on performance. These can be used to identify and support students likely to lag so that remedial action can be taken. These are great pointers for analyzing and molding educational performance. Additionally, integrating ML into distance learning platforms will enhance and fill the gaps in current education systems, especially in impoverished areas.

In conclusion, it is possible to say that the ML perspective on distance learning brings a lot of improvements to the system. Still, its potential usage also requires careful management regarding benefits and drawbacks. Protecting privacy, ensuring ML-driven personalization does not lead to bias, ensuring the reliability of automated assessments, addressing the privacy of student data, and addressing the digital divide will be critical to ML for learning's success. Researchers, officials, and developers need to work together to design and implement inclusive and integrated approaches that capitalize on the potential of ML without neglecting other fundamental, necessary, and positive aspects of learning.

2.3 Advantages of ML compared to other approaches

ML has specific benefits in distance learning compared to such techniques as videoconferencing, distance open-schedule courses, and distance fixed-time classes. A careful examination of these critical strengths explains how ML technology can improve learning experiences and achieve results that cannot be achieved through other approaches.

2.3.1 ML vs. videoconferencing

In terms of personalization, ML is a better option than videoconferencing. Videoconferencing platforms allow for interactions between instructors and students in real time, which is essential for learning as it helps to keep students engaged and increase immediacy. However, they cannot meet the dynamic demand for content adjustment according to student performance. ML-driven systems can continuously analyze student interactions to adapt and offer more individualized feedback and instruction [18]. This could result in better learning as it fills knowledge gaps and tunes the learning level to attain proficiency. It could be challenging to acquire in static video sessions that all learners engage in.

2.3.2 ML vs. open-schedule online course

Concerning open-schedule online courses, ML is comprised of a directed and less organized environment for learning regarding time. Open-schedule courses can be completed any time the students want, which is favorable for combining the course with other responsibilities. However, without guided support, students might not stay motivated and consistent. ML can fill the abovementioned, taking responsibility for student progress and providing necessary assistance based on learning behavior: reminders, encouragements, additional resources, etc. [19]. It thus combines the use of open-schedule courses with the requisite guided support so that students can stay on track—something that would otherwise be difficult to achieve via the use of open-schedule classes alone.

2.3.3 ML vs. fixed-time online learning

Fixed-time online learning is characterized by partially imitating the traditional classroom setting, with students being required to visit a specific site (student portals) at predetermined times. A similar regularity and deference to authority are encouraged. But it seldom goes hand in hand with the dynamism and change ML brings to distance learning. Fixed-time models are mainly implemented so all students are taught simultaneously and with the same instruction. ML, on the other hand, can make a student content dependent, thus making the student content dependent, that is, content depending on the rate at which a student can learn or the mode of learning [20]. This characteristic is beneficial in diverse classrooms where learners' backgrounds and learning skills differ.

Moreover, ML's analysis is more sophisticated than that of other methods. Many video conferencing and fixed-time platforms do not provide much data on student attentiveness or achievement—sometimes, hardly anything beyond attendance and rudimentary participation records. On the other hand, ML systems can process a vast amount of information that includes response times, trends in quiz answers, and interaction with various types of content, to name a few [21]. These analytics can detect struggling students before they fall behind, help forecast future outcomes, and recommend individual needs. Such detailed information is time-consuming and not easily accessible using videoconferencing or static website portals, often providing insufficient analytical capability in ML systems.

3. Case study: Taibah University's software engineering course

3.1 Taibah University's software engineering course

A critical application of machine learning-driven collaboration tools at Taibah University is the creation of intelligent recommendation systems that students and lecturers use. Exploring group dynamics and individual learning habits, these systems connect students across the university to fellow students with similar interests and skills, thanks to which they can discover study groups and peer tutors who will be helpful in their learning [9]. Tools that connect students or assigned mentors respond to the need for belonging and comradeship within the educational setting, leading to increased engagement and student motivation. Through the use of such advanced technologies, the university has created an online site that is flexible to meet students' varying needs in faraway places and mainly addresses the issue of geographical limitation in facilitating a conducive learning setting for accomplishing goals in the electronic era.

As it is the basis of the software engineering course at Taibah University, the commitment will stay constant—personalized learning pathways tailored to individual students. With the introduction of machine learning algorithms into the curriculum, the university has developed a teaching system that adjusts to the individual student's specific learning modes, tastes, and curiosity [22]. The algorithms can perceive and comprehend the richness of data derived from the digital learning ecosystems and produce patterns and underlying meanings that prompt the creation of personalized learning settings. Thus, the process becomes more meaningful, and the learning experience becomes more comprehensible.

Taibah University's classrooms are designed to push students to interact with total concentration, brought through machine learning technologies. Therefore, machine learning algorithms establish informal study circles and help one another become a mutually enriching and knowledge-sharing experience among students. These joint ventures not only help students find profound reasons in coursework but also enable students to develop teamwork and communication skills that are top priorities in the new global scenario.

Further, through the delivery of the software engineering course in the distance learning program at Taibah University, the goal to bring constant growth and innovation through distance learning education is evident. Using live analytics and teaching quality evaluation tools, the university determines the places in the curriculum and teaching strategies that need improvement, thus ensuring the continuous relevance and effectiveness of the university's educational program [23]. Machine learning algorithms analyze student performance data and use them to uncover recurrent trends and patterns. This helps instructors implement new instructional designs and pedagogies that dynamically adapt to the evolving needs and tastes of students.

Driven by value and innovation, Taibah University will always stay on top of the distance learning league by offering new and fresh insights that make students study sessions dynamic and memorable, equipping them with the necessary knowledge for a successful digital life and the future [11]. Through machine learning technologies and integration into its software engineering course, the university demonstrates how these futuristic technologies can help transform the education sector and develop a learning culture beyond life and scholarly competence.

3.2 Lessons and experiences

In reflection on the case study of the Taibah University software engineering course, several lessons and experiences are of great importance. These aspects show the upsides and downsides of implementing modern teaching and learning methods and technologies in higher education. One of the most valuable lessons learned was the need for curriculum design to be adaptable. According to Miller et al. [24], the software engineering field changes daily, and offering the same topics and content for a long time is not practical and actual anymore. Taibah University realized this and developed a dynamic curriculum framework that supports periodic reviews and revisions of the curriculum. This approach made students study all that was most timely and important for their prospective job and life.

Another crucial matter was the integration of theory and practice. The university identified project-based learning as a key pedagogical approach with students working on real-world software development projects [25]. This helped students use the theoretical knowledge in practice and develop the most desirable soft skills, including working in a group and collaborating with clients and partners. In tasks representing realistic working conditions, the students were even more prepared for the labor market and had increased confidence in their problem-solving skills.

The extensive employment of learning technologies and the incorporation of ML and AI served as a game-changer in the course. Taibah University adopted ML algorithms to enhance the "flipping the classroom" approach to academic learning by matching students to appropriate content and feedback. This catered to the differences between students, where some learn best when taught individually while others in a group setting. Different students learn at different rates, and hence, it was able to help every student achieve their best potential. In addition, using AI-based analytics ensured that instructors received comprehensive data on student performance and attendance, which helped them identify those who should be identified at risk to prevent dropouts [26].

In conclusion, Taibah University's software engineering course case study presents an opportunity for students and practitioners to gain insight into the opportunities and threats of technology and teaching developments in higher learning institutions to educate customers better. The recommendations deriving from this case also emphasize the values of flexibility, experiential learning, individualized instruction, and quality improvement. These are areas that, if addressed, will improve the employability of graduates from institutions of education in line with the needs of the modern workforce.

3.3 Addressing challenges and ensuring accessibility

Although machine learning is utilized to bridge the gap between distance education and education in the same place, it also brings about some drawbacks in accessibility and inclusivity [27]. Taibah University acknowledges that there is a need for equal opportunities for learners and therefore considers this requirement to be of paramount importance and employs measures to ensure accessibility as a way of achieving this goal, such as multilingual support at the level of the students and interface design that is custom-made for diverse learning styles. Ethical concerns, including data privacy and security, have become the pivot point in how machine learning influences universities.

i. Example: Taibah University brings equitability by providing multilingual services and a user interface for different learning styles.

ii. Ethical concerns: Data privacy or security is demanded, with no exception in building machine learning technology-based education programs.

The other issue was the resistance to change among students and faculty members. The prevailing teaching patterns had to be discarded and replaced with technology-centered ones—the more profound changes in mindsets and practices. This was rectified at Taibah University by providing sufficient training to faculty members concerning the new tools as well as the methodology for the use of the tools. Moreover, the university offered orientations and workshops to involve students in the change, highlight the new system's advantages, and tackle concerns.

4. Challenges and limitations

4.1 Challenges

Incorporating ML for distance learning generates a variety of concerns that may influence the potency and uptake of ML. These challenges include technical, ethical, and logistical issues, with the most impact arising from privacy concerns.

4.1.1 Data privacy and security

The first constraint in using ML in distance learning is safeguarding the students' information and data. ML systems are expensive because they require considerable data to train algorithms [28]. Such data sometimes contains personal details, school records, and behavioral patterns. Controlling the security of this data against breaches and unauthorized access is essential since any compromise of this data would mean massive privacy invasions and a loss of trust among the users. Furthermore, data privacy laws like GDPR or FERPA impose strict data governance obligations that cannot be fulfilled without comprehensive data governance frameworks and practices.

4.1.2 Data quality and bias

The effectiveness of ML algorithms is strongly related to the training data used. Data of poor quality (incomplete, inaccurate, or outdated) may result in unreliable models, which may generate unintended results [29]. Moreover, the use of biased data may lead to the further entrenchment of existing unequal patterns in education. For instance, the dataset used to train ML models may include samples from minority groups, so the algorithm does not work well for them. This implies that the issues of diversity and representativeness are challenging to address regarding the training corpora and are rather ongoing and maintained.

4.1.3 Technical infrastructure

However, technical support is another need that must be met to implement ML in distance learning. This is because the data generated and the mathematical computations performed are extensive and complex [30]. Also, a stable internet connection is required to interact with students and teachers utilizing robust and efficient modern ML solutions. The study done by Goolsby and Perepletchikova (2014) noted that such infrastructural resources are lacking in different parts of the world, including the Third World, which may hamper the use of ML technologies in learning activities.

4.1.4 Ethical considerations

There are several ethical issues related to the application of ML in distance learning. In this case, some ethical issues that educators and administrators may have to consider include ensuring that the developed ML systems are used ethically and that the decisions made by these systems are explainable [31]. It also raises the danger of developing dependence on such systems, which, in return, may degrade the human interface. However, it is central to promoting students' critical thinking and socio-emotional growth.

4.2 Limitations

4.2.1 Lack of human touch

A significant limitation of ML in distance learning is that the model ignores the human element in its learning process [32]. Education is the acquisition of knowledge, the provision of information, and the building of character and social contacts. Human educators possess essential qualities, such as the ability to relate to and motivate students, which ML systems cannot and cannot emulate. This deprives the students of critical human interactions that keep them engaged and help them cultivate soft skills like sympathy, cooperation, and speaking.

4.2.2 Interpretability and transparency

Another limitation is that many ML models lack transparency or interpretability and are intense learning models [33]. Such models may not be easily explained or interpreted to show the decisions made and how. This inability to rationalize or explain results makes it unsuitable for the educational system, where users require a great deal of confidence in the system's ability to make the right decisions on their behalf. According to Linardatos et al. [33], transparency is essential because it can be challenging to know what to correct when there is no explicit indication of a possible problem with the system.

4.2.3 Scalability issues

Although ML systems can be adapted to process large amounts of data and numerous users, such scaling has some practical limits [34]. With every expansion in the number of users, there is a need for more computational power, data storage, and bandwidth requirements, all of which can negatively impact performance and costs. Among the challenges associated with mastering the concept is the ability to personalize learning for a large and diverse audience of students.

5. Conclusion

In conclusion, machine learning has radically transformed distance learning, and, as a result, universities such as Taibah can allow students living anywhere on the planet to get the best education on the Internet. This is because machine learning offers personalized learning experiences, engages learners, and applies real-time analytics, bolstering distance education success. Nevertheless, the challenges in developing machine learning for education are evident; however, its potential to create a new learning experience is challenging to overlook, subsequently shaping the future of internet communication. Thus, recognizing the challenges in distance education is crucial to appreciating the vast advantages of using ML in the process. Challenges like data privacy, bias, and the requirement for strong technical support will always be there. However, one has to emphasize the significance of the human factor's presence in the educational process. Moving forward, there are great possibilities for enhancing the educational system with the help of ML. New patterns like AI-based tutorial facilities and the individualized learning environment have the potential to increase students' outcomes even more. However, ethical issues must be the focus when these technologies advance and this will require further research. On the future work, more studies should be carried out on establishing sound and fair ML models, data protection, and closing the digital gap to optimize the benefits of this disruptive technology.

Author details

Ibtehal Nafea
Computer Science and Engineering College, Taibah University, Saudi Arabia

*Address all correspondence to: inafea@taibahu.edu.sa

References

[1] Osmanoğlu UÖ, Atak ON, Çağlar K, Kayhan H, Talat CAN. Sentiment analysis for distance education course materials: A machine learning approach. Journal of Educational Technology and Online Learning. 2020;**3**(1):31-48

[2] Sarker IH. Machine learning: Algorithms, real-world applications and research directions. SN Computer Science. 2021;**2**(3):160

[3] Albreiki B, Zaki N, Alashwal H. A systematic literature review of student' performance prediction using machine learning techniques. Education Sciences. 2021;**11**(9):552. DOI: 10.3390/educsci11090552

[4] Smirani LK, Yamani HA, Menzli LJ, Boulahia JA. Using ensemble learning algorithms to predict student failure and enabling customized educational paths. Scientific Programming. 2022;**2022**:e3805235. DOI: 10.1155/2022/3805235

[5] Urdaneta-Ponte MC, Mendez-Zorrilla A, Oleagordia-Ruiz I. Recommendation systems for education: Systematic review. Electronics. 2021;**10**(14):1611. DOI: 10.3390/electronics10141611

[6] Flamia Azevedo B, Rocha AMAC, Fernandes FP, Pacheco MF, Pereira AI. Evaluating student behaviour on the MathE platform - Clustering algorithms approaches. In: Simos DE, Rasskazova VA, Archetti F, Kotsireas IS, Pardalos PM, editors. Learning and Intelligent Optimization. LION 2022. Lecture Notes in Computer Science. Vol. 13621. Cham: Springer; 2022. DOI: 10.1007/978-3-031-24866-5_24

[7] Arco-Tirado JL, Fernández-Martín FD, Hervás-Torres M. Evidence-based peer-tutoring program to improve students' performance at the university. Studies in Higher Education. 2019;**45**(11):1-13. DOI: 10.1080/03075079.2019.1597038

[8] Mahesh B. Machine learning algorithms-A review. International Journal of Science and Research (IJSR). [Internet]. 2020;**9**(1):381-386

[9] Villegas-Ch W, Román-Cañizares M, Palacios-Pacheco X. Improvement of an online education model with the integration of machine learning and data analysis in an LMS. Applied Sciences. 2020;**10**(15):5371

[10] Alotaibi SMF. Big data analysis role in advancing the various activities of digital libraries: Taibah University case study-Saudi Arabia. International Journal of Computer Science & Network Security. 2021;**21**(8):297-307

[11] Khanal SS et al. A systematic review: Machine learning based recommendation systems for e-learning. Education and Information Technologies. 2019;**25**(4):2635-2664. DOI: 10.1007/s10639-019-10063-9

[12] Hardegen C et al. Predicting network flow characteristics using deep learning and real-world network traffic. IEEE Transactions on Network and Service Management. 2020;**17**(4):2662-2676. DOI: 10.1109/tnsm.2020.3025131

[13] Werner L. What is data preparation for machine learning? In: Klippa. 2023. Available from: https://www.klippa.com/en/blog/information/what-is-data-preparation/

[14] Er-radi H et al. Machine learning in adaptive online learning for enhanced

learner engagement. In: Khaldi M, editor. Technological Tools for Innovative Teaching. IGI Global; 2024. pp. 43-63. DOI: 10.4018/979-8-3693-3132-3.ch003

[15] Zhai X. Practices and theories: How can machine learning assist in innovative assessment practices in science education. Journal of Science Education and Technology. 2021;**30**(2):139-149. DOI: 10.1007/s10956-021-09901-8

[16] Ghatasheh N. Knowledge level assessment in e-learning systems using machine learning and user activity analysis. International Journal of Advanced Computer Science and Applications. 2015;**6**(4):1-8. DOI: 10.14569/ijacsa.2015.060415

[17] Mumtaz F et al. Quality of interaction-based predictive model for support of online learning in pandemic situations. Knowledge and Information Systems. 2023;**66**(3):1777-1805. DOI: 10.1007/s10115-023-01995-3

[18] Gligorea I et al. Adaptive learning using artificial intelligence in e-learning: A literature review. Education Sciences. 2023;**13**(12):1216. DOI: 10.3390/educsci13121216

[19] Abhay R, Abi A, Othayoth PK, Kureethara JV, Puliyanmakkal JK. Artificial intelligence-monitored procedure for personal ethical standard development framework in the E-learning environment. In: Chaurasia MA, Juang CF, editors. Emerging IT/ICT and AI Technologies Affecting Society. Lecture Notes in Networks and Systems. Vol. 478. Singapore: Springer; 2023. DOI: 10.1007/978-981-19-2940-3_20

[20] Ismail N, Yusof UK. A systematic literature review: Recent techniques of predicting stem stream students. Computers and Education: Artificial Intelligence. 2023;**5**:100141. DOI: 10.1016/j.caeai.2023.100141

[21] Huyen C. Designing Machine Learning Systems. Beijing: O'Reilly; 2022

[22] Alshabandar R, Hussain A, Keight R, Khan W. Students performance prediction in online courses using machine learning algorithms. In: 2020 International Joint Conference on Neural Networks (IJCNN), Glasgow, UK. 2020. pp. 1-7. DOI: 10.1109/IJCNN48605.2020.9207196

[23] Saranya T, Sridevi S, Deisy C, Chung TD, Khan MA. Performance analysis of machine learning algorithms in intrusion detection system: A review. Procedia Computer Science. 2020;**171**:1251-1260

[24] Miller C et al. "How was your weekend?" software development teams working from home during COVID-19. In: 2021 IEEE/ACM 43rd International Conference on Software Engineering (ICSE). 2021. pp. 624-636. DOI: 10.1109/icse43902.2021.00064

[25] Pan G et al. An exploration into key roles in making project-based learning happen. Journal of International Education in Business. 2020;**14**(1):109-129. DOI: 10.1108/jieb-02-2020-0018

[26] Reethika A, Priya PK. Using AI-powered predictive analytics tools to identify students falling behind or dropping out. In: Innovation in the University 4.0 System Based on Smart Technologies. Chapman and Hall/CRC; 2024. pp. 101-115. DOI: 10.1201/9781003425809

[27] Ang KL-M, Ge FL, Seng KP. Big educational data & analytics: Survey, architecture, and challenges. IEEE Access. 2020;**8**:116392-116414. DOI: 10.1109/access.2020.2994561

[28] Adadi A. A survey on data-efficient algorithms in big data era. Journal of Big Data. 2021;**8**(1):24. DOI: 10.1186/s40537-021-00419-9

[29] Munappy AR et al. Data management for production quality deep learning models: Challenges and solutions. Journal of Systems and Software. 2022;**191**:111359. DOI: 10.1016/j.jss.2022.111359

[30] Qureshi MS et al. A comparative analysis of resource allocation schemes for real-time services in high-performance computing systems. International Journal of Distributed Sensor Networks. 2020;**16**(8):155014772093275. DOI: 10.1177/1550147720932750

[31] Bogina V et al. Educating software and AI stakeholders about algorithmic fairness, accountability, transparency and ethics. International Journal of Artificial Intelligence in Education. 2021;**32**(3):808-833. DOI: 10.1007/s40593-021-00248-0

[32] Sanusi IT, Oyelere SS, Omidiora JO. Exploring teachers' preconceptions of teaching machine learning in high school: A preliminary insight from Africa. Computers and Education Open. 2022;**3**:100072. DOI: 10.1016/j.caeo.2021.100072

[33] Linardatos P, Papastefanopoulos V, Kotsiantis S. Explainable AI: A review of machine learning interpretability methods. Entropy. 2020;**23**(1):18. DOI: 10.3390/e23010018

[34] Liu Y et al. Blockchain and machine learning for communications and networking systems. IEEE Communications Surveys & Tutorials. 2020;**22**(2):1392-1431. DOI: 10.1109/comst.2020.2975911